Auditing Your Human Resources Department

AUDITING YOUR HUMAN RESOURCES DEPARTMENT

A Step-by-Step Guide

John H. McConnell

AMACOM
American Management Association
New York • Atlanta • Boston • Chicago • Kansas City • San Francisco • Washington, D. C.
Brussels • Mexico City • Tokyo • Toronto

Special discounts on bulk quantities of AMACOM books are available to corporations, professional associations, and other organizations. For details, contact Special Sales Department, AMACOM, a division of American Management Association, 1601 Broadway, New York, NY 10019.
Tel.: 212-903-8316. Fax: 212-903-8083.
Web site: www.amacombooks.org

This publication is designed to provide accurate and authoritative information in regard to the subject matter covered. It is sold with the understanding that the publisher is not engaged in rendering legal, accounting, or other professional service. If legal advice or other expert assistance is required, the services of a competent professional person should be sought.

Library of Congress Cataloging-in-Publication Data

McConnell, John H.
    Auditing your human resources department: a step-by-step guide / John H. McConnell.
        p.   cm.
    Rev. ed. of: How to audit the human resources department. c1986.
    Includes index.
    ISBN 0-8144-7467-5
    1. Personnel departments—Auditing.   2. Personnel management—Auditing.   I.
McConnell, John H. How to audit the human resources department.   II. Title.

HF5549.M33954   2000
658.3—dc21

00-036232

Printing number

10 9 8 7 6 5 4 3 2 1

CONTENTS

ABOUT THIS BOOK

The American Management Association is dedicated to the development of professional managers. For more than seventy-five years, it has been providing services and products to improve management skills and knowledge.

In 1977, as a result of the growing sophistication of the human resources function and continual requests for assistance in evaluating it, AMACOM developed a manual called *How to Audit the Personnel Department*. A highly successful publication, it was used by professional managers to evaluate the human resources function within their organizations. It also was used by college professors as an introduction to human resources, by seminar leaders for sessions with similar titles, and by consultants for their initial meetings with clients. During the following nine years, the then-named personnel function increasingly was seen as a vital contributor to an organization's success. Reflecting this development, the name of the function changed. It became human resources. Those using the original book requested an updated version. In 1986 a second edition with the title changed to *How to Audit the Human Resources Department* was developed and published. That publication received even more use than the original.

In 1999, it was recognized that the function had undergone still further change, and again requests were received for additional updates.

The result is a completely new book. However, the basic concept of providing a method for managers to evaluate the effectiveness of their human resources function without outside assistance has been maintained. The use of a wide variety of professionals as the Advisory Board was continued to ensure compatibility with all types and sizes of organizations.

This book recognizes the latest developments in the field. It is a valuable evaluation and learning tool that can be used on an ongoing basis for analyzing and improving the human resources department.

THE ADVISORY BOARD

An Advisory Board of human resources professionals was employed to assist in creating an audit that could be adjusted to the needs of a wide variety of organizations. Advisory Board members represented organizations ranging from as few as two hundred employees to those with several thousand employees. Members were from every area of the United States and Europe. They were experienced in financial services, manufacturing, retail, sales, government, technology, and service organizations. Their education varied from high school graduates to PhDs, and their experience in human resources from ten to forty years.

The Advisory Board for this edition consisted of twenty members. They performed four tasks: reviewing and defining the audit categories; developing questions, responses, and category evaluations; ensuring relevancy and validity of the final audit; and contributing rationale for the evaluations. The same tasks were not requested of all members. Each made an individual contribution—ranging from reviewing and weighting the audit categories to completing all four tasks. This variety of input has resulted in an audit that covers the complete human resources function and provides a method for adjusting the results to the specific needs of an organization.

R. BRAYTON BOWEN is a senior consultant and president of The Howland Group, a human resources and change management consulting firm. He previously served as senior officer for a number of companies including Federated Department Stores and Capital Holding Corporations. He holds a BA and an MA from Brown University. He is a contributing instructional writer to Seton Hall's Virtual University on Systemwide Leadership, is host and coproducer of a PBS documentary on anger in the workplace, and has several published articles in *Industry Week* and AMA's *Management Review*. He is a member of the Institute of Management Consultants.

RALPH J. BROWN is a management consultant specializing in human resources systems. His former positions have included director of employee relations for Philip Morris USA; director of management information systems for Flintkote, Inc.; and director of personnel and administration for Wolverine Tube Division of Allied Signal. He holds a BA from Wayne State University and is a frequent speaker and seminar leader.

GEORGE W. DAVIS is senior vice president and director of corporate human resources for Lincoln National Corporation. Prior to joining his current company, he held numerous human resources positions with Eastman Kodak including director of personnel for the European region, director of personnel relations for manufacturing and distribution, director of personnel relations for the Photographic Products Group, director of corporate HR strategy, and director of corporate executive resources. He has a BS from Boston College and has completed the Advanced Management Program at the Harvard University Business School. He is a member of the Northeast Indiana Private Industry Council, cochaired the Fort Wayne Chamber of Commerce's Workforce Development Council, chaired the School-To-Work Transition Committee of the National Alliance of Business, and served on the board of directors of the Women's Career Center. He was appointed by the governor of Indiana to the Indiana Commission on Vocational and Technical Education and is currently chair of the American Management Association's Human Resources Council.

BRIAN DUFFY is a founder, president, and CEO of Alliance United.com, a business-to-business electronic commerce company specializing in the property and casualty insurance industry. His former positions have been executive vice president of Fireman's Fund Insurance Companies, senior vice president for Colonial Penn Group, and operations and industrial relations manager with Procter and Gamble. He is a graduate of the University of Pennsylvania and the Wharton Graduate School. He has conducted numerous training seminars and provided extensive industrial relations consulting.

PAUL FALCONE is director of employment and development with Paramount Pictures. He previously was director of labor relations for The City of Hope National Medical Center, and prior to that was engaged in executive search activities. He is a graduate of the University of California at Los Angeles with a BA and an MA. He is a contributing editor to *HRMagazine* and a UCLA Extension faculty member and has authored three books for AMACOM: *101 Sample Write-Ups for Documenting Employee Performance Problems: A Guide to Progressive Discipline and Termination, 96 Great Interview Questions to Ask before You Hire*, and *The Complete Job-Finding Guide for Secretaries and Administrative Support Staff.*

LESLYE FULLER is educational program analyst for the chancellor for education and professional development in the Department of Defense, where she is developing academic quality standards for the department's civilian educational institutions and professional development programs. Past assignments have included distance learning and Web-based and satellite-delivered courses for the Office of the Under Secretary of Defense, comptroller at the Defense Business Management University, team leader on Vice President Gore's National Partnership for Reinventing Government, and head of career management Division of the Department of the Navy Acquisition Intern Program. She has a BA from Florida State University, and an MA from the University of Central Florida. She is a frequent speaker at national conferences on the application of technology to education and training.

RUSSELL A. GLICKSMAN currently is president and CEO of The Beam Group, an executive search and management consulting firm. Prior to cofounding the Beam Group, he was executive vice president of operations for Colonial Penn Group, and before that, senior vice president of human resources. Mr. Glicksman is a graduate of Gettysburg College with a BA in psychology. He is a member of the Human Resources Council for the Life Office Management Association (LOMA) and is a frequent speaker at human resources association conventions.

STEVE JENKINS is business manager for Michigan State Fair and Exposition Center in Detroit. In addition to revenue and budget oversight responsibilities, he is accountable for all operational and human resources policies and procedures. Prior to his current position, he owned and operated a human resources consulting firm, "Alternatives for Success," and held several human resources and labor relations positions in state government. He is a graduate of Spring Arbor College, and has a masters of management degree from Central Michigan University. He is an adjunct professor at Lansing Community College, past president of Industrial Relations Research Association, and past president of Lansing Area Joint Labor/ Management Committee.

ROY J. KAHN is a management consultant specializing in organizational and management development and administrative services. Previously he was vice president of human resources for Washington Gas Company; a principal in the personnel services division of F.R. Schwab and Associates, Inc.; vice president–personnel for John Wanamaker Department Stores; and corporate manager–personnel for Hertz Corporation. He received a BS in Industrial Relations from Rider College and has authored several articles for *Management World*.

KATHRYN Z. McMASTER currently is vice president of human resources for Nobel Learning Communities, the largest for-profit operator of private schools, in addition to charter school educational materials and international educational materials. Prior to her current assignment she was vice president of human resources for Colonial Penn/GE Financial Services. She has a BA from Temple University and is a certified benefits specialist and compensation professional. She is a member of the Penjerdel Employee Benefits Association, Philadelphia Human Resources Planning Group and its Membership and Outreach Committees, and the Society for Human Resource Management, and conducts a series of interviewing skills workshops.

BARBARA McNAMARA is vice president employment and employee relations with WellPoint Health Networks, a health care company. Her experience includes eighteen years in human resources with financial services and health care. In her current assignment, she serves as the project leader for all acquisition integrations. She is a graduate of Michigan State University with both a BA and a BS. She holds a certification in human resources from UCLA. She is a speaker for AMA on "Retention Programs That Work."

CHRISTINE M. MORRIS currently is manager of human resources information services for ARVIDA, a real estate development firm. Prior to her current position she was director of human resources for Singer Asset Finance Company,

LLC; director of human resources for Life Care Retirement Communities; vice president director of administration for International Trade Systems, Inc.; and personnel administrator for the City of Boca Raton, Florida. She is a graduate of Barry University and is certified in human resources management information systems.

ROBERT A. NOWACZYK currently is vice president and director of administration for OppenheimerFunds. Prior to joining his current company, he was vice president of human resources for Vanguard Group and held several human resources positions with a major financial services and insurance company. He has a BS from the University of Delaware and an MBA from Widener University. He is past chairman of the Society for Human Resource Management's Employment Practices Committee and past president and founding member of the Greater Valley Forge Human Resources Association.

ARTHUR E. PEARSON currently is president of Management Development Services, Inc. His firm specializes in providing human resources services and products. Prior to his current position, he was director of planning and organizational development for M. Lowenstein & Company and director of the Evening Education Program for the American Management Association. He has held several positions with Western Electric Company, Graybar Electric, and General Motors. He is a graduate of the College of Wooster and the author of several articles on corporate aid to education.

ARTHUR ROCHESTER is managing director of Rochester Associates in London, England. His firm offers human resources development services and programs for management, marketing, and sales professionals. He formerly was a partner in Rochester and Scott, marketing director of Xerox Learning Systems, and managing director of Management Centre Europe. He is a frequent speaker at international human resources conventions and has authored a series of books on management education and numerous professional journal articles.

ROBERT RYAN is chief, headquarters education branch of the Internal Revenue Service. Prior to his current assignment, he was director of the Naval Career Management Site, a principal adviser to the secretary of the navy, and a senior official of the Naval Postgraduate School. He holds a BS from the University of Dayton, an MEd from Wright State University, and an EdD from Auburn University. He has received a Distinguished Civilian Special Act Award, is a past adjunct faculty member at Prince George's Community College and Pensacola Junior College, and conducts numerous workshops and seminars on career development.

FERDINAND J. SETARO is managing director of TLE Consultants. The firm specializes in organizational development and improvement services. Formerly he was an educational officer for Vanguard Group, director of organizational and management development for Colonial Penn Group, director of human resources for CPG Data Group, and director of supervisory development for the American Management Association. He has a BA from Columbia University and is a graduate of the Advanced Program in Organizational Development. He is past president and chairman of the board of directors for the Association of Internal Management Consultants and is a prolific author and seminar leader.

ELIZABETH N. TREHER is cofounder of The Learning Key. The firm provides consulting and coaching to enhance and facilitate individual and organizational performance. Prior to establishing the firm, she held project leader positions in government, academia, and industry, including management of Squibb's Center for Science Education and the design and implementation of a corporate college. She is a graduate of Washington University and also holds an MA and a PhD from the same school. She has more than sixty publications and patents, is past president of the Association of Psychological Type, and was an invited member of the first United States delegation to China on human resources training and development.

CHRISTINE M. WELLS is vice president of corporate education for OppenheimerFunds. Prior to her current assignment, she held positions with the same firm in compensation and benefits, employee relations, recruiting, and training. Before joining OppenheimerFunds, she held human resources positions with Citicorp, Wells Fargo, and First Chicago. She is a graduate of the University of Illinois with a BS. She is a member of the Investment Companies Institute and the New York Stock Exchange Continuing Education Committee.

PAUL YAKULIS is vice president, human resources, for Shared Medical Systems. Prior positions are senior vice president of human resources for National Liberty Insurance, vice president with Banker's Trust Company, and various human resources assignments with Rockwell International Company. He has an AB from Princeton University and is a certificated professional in human resources. He is a member of the Society for Human Resource Management, The Philadelphia Human Resources Planning Group, and the Radnor Township School District Board of School Directors.

THE HUMAN RESOURCES FUNCTION

Human resources can be described as the organizational function accountable for obtaining and maintaining qualified employees. In today's complex environment, fulfilling that mission is a major contributor to an organization's success.

In the past few decades organizations have changed. Technology has become an increasingly complex and vital part of operations. The skills and knowledge required of employees has rapidly expanded, and, accordingly, so have the jobs. As an author recently wrote, "There are a great number of jobs today that were not in existence ten years ago, so how could people have even planned or prepared for them?"

In the past few years, with a strong and growing economy, unemployment has been reduced to its lowest level in decades. More people have jobs than ever before. Obtaining and maintaining qualified employees is an increasing challenge.

In addition to changing technology and low unemployment, there are new trends in work. Today, there are more service jobs than production jobs. Lifetime employment with a single organization is far less likely than in the past. Flexible hours and working at home are now possible and increasingly are offered by organizations of all sizes and types. There also have been changes to conditions of employment. Twenty years ago some form of employer contribution pension plan was fairly common. Today it is a rarity. Instead, employee contribution plans such as 401ks (some with employer contributions) are the rule. Health insurance costs have risen faster than inflation, with health maintenance organizations now providing much of the coverage. Cafeteria benefits, time-off banks of days, and deferred compensation plans now are typical conditions of employment.

All these changes have created new human resources challenges and opportunities. People have always been referred to as one of an Organization's major assets. Twenty years ago business books mentioned *men, materials,* and *machines* as major assets. Today, *employees, supplies,* and *equipment* have replaced men, materials, and machines, and a fourth asset has been added—*information.*

Another factor affecting the profession is the trend to outsource many traditional human resources activities. A major financial firm has outsourced all of its employee training. A manufacturing company has outsourced the administration of both its benefit and compensation programs. These companies and many others have maintained senior human resources professionals to provide advice and counsel in the area, but are having external companies do the actual work.

These trends show no indication of declining. If anything, the future holds even more changes. The personal computer and the Internet are having an expanding impact on traditional employment. Futurists believe we are moving to seven-day, twenty-four-hour operations in most organizations.

What does all this actually mean for the human resources professional and the human resources function? Human resources, once viewed as an administrative function, is now a vital contributor to an organization's success. Human resources has to address the rapidly changing conditions affecting the type of employees required and their changing needs, so the function requires flexible and knowledgeable practitioners. As the presidents of major companies are saying, "It is important that the head of our human resources department be both a professional in that field and a competent business person."

The combination of human resources professionalism and business orientation, the trend toward more mergers and acquisitions, and the recognized importance of employees have resulted in new activities for the human resources function. For example, human resources representatives are now important members of merger and acquisition teams and the initial management group dealing with acquired organizations.

It is in recognition of these developments and the crucial nature of employees as an organizational resource that this audit was developed.

HOW TO USE THIS BOOK

This audit of the human resources department is a four-step process: information gathering, evaluation, analysis, and action planning. Each step begins with specific instructions. In the first step, Information Gathering, you will answer a series of questions regarding human resources in your organization. These questions have been divided into 16 categories and a summary area. This step includes a procedure for adjusting these categories to reflect the unique requirements and structure of your organization.

The second step, Evaluation, provides a "scoring" system for your answers to the questions in Step One. The scoring system is based on the input from our twenty Advisory Board members. It is meant to reflect what they believe to be the best situation for the human resources function; it is not a scoring system designed for any one company, industry, or geographic area. As with the first step, there are instructions for adjusting it to meet your specific situation.

Step Three, Analysis, provides a way to compare your evaluations in each category and for the overall function. The result is the identification of your department's strengths, areas that are operating as one would expect in a typical human resources function, and areas that need to be reviewed for possible improvement. In addition, Step Three provides specific directions for obtaining more detailed information, and includes procedures to customize this audit to your unique situation.

Step Four, Action Planning, is designed to provide a structure for you to convert the analysis into specific actions that can be taken to capitalize on your department's strengths and make needed corrections.

The first step, Information Gathering, is the initial step necessary to determine the effectiveness of your human resources department. It is similar to a consultant's first visit, in which the consultant wants to obtain an overall evaluation in order to identify areas that appear to require improvement. The consultant meets and questions an individual or individuals with knowledge of the function. In this case you will be performing both the role of the knowledgeable person and the role of evaluator. Essentially you are serving as your own consultant.

THE CATEGORIES

Human resources performs a wide variety of activities. For this audit sixteen categories of activities have been utilized. Although the category names have been retained, actual tasks have changed significantly.

The Advisory Board, therefore, revised the definitions to reflect the human resources function as it currently exists. However, your particular human resources department may not be accountable for all these areas. You will be asked to customize them for your specific situation.

Some human resources departments may be accountable for areas not included in these sixteen categories, for example, payroll. Advisory Board members felt that areas such as payroll are not actually human resources activities, so they are not included here as categories. In the analysis section of this book you can put such situations into perspective.

But first, let's deal with a couple of definitions. The term "Organization" (with a capital "O") is used in the audit to refer to the overall company, division, corporation, or other entity of which human resources is a part. Other definitions with which you need to be familiar deal with management (those who plan, organize, implement, and control an Organization):

Managers or Management—a group of managers within a specific department, function, or the entire Organization.

Senior Executive—the top management position within the Organization.

Senior Manager—the top manager within a specific department, function, or the entire Organization.

Manager—anyone in a managerial position.

Supervisor—a manager who directly supervises people doing the work of an area.

Finally, the word "department" is used to formally identify functions within the Organization.

Now, let's begin by adjusting the categories to meet your situation. The sixteen human resources categories used in this audit and their definitions appear below and on the next page. The following are the initial steps to take:

1. Read all category titles and their definitions. Do not use the category title alone. You may discover the definitions are somewhat different than you

might use, but to make this audit work you need to stay with the definitions provided.

2. Place an "X" on the short line preceding any category that is not the responsibility of your human resources department.

3. Indicate how important each category is to the operation of your human resources department by assigning a number to each. The number can be from 0 to 1,000, but you only have 1,000 points in total to assign. A more important category for your department should be given a higher number than a category of less importance. Do not assign numbers to categories that are not a part of your human resources department.

4. When you have assigned an X or a number to every category, total the numbers to ensure they equal 1,000.

_____ Department Mission—The overall objective or purpose of the human resources department within the Organization and its relationship to the Organization's overall mission.

_____ Department Organization—The department's internal relationships; relationships with other functions, departments, and employees of the Organization; and the structuring of resources within the department.

_____ Department Employees—The selection, training, motivation, development, and retention of a qualified human resources team.

_X_ Labor Relations—The human resources role in the relationship between the Organization and any bargaining unit of an employee-organized labor group, including labor-organizing campaigns.

_____ Recruitment and Selection—Obtaining and evaluating qualified candidates from internal and external sources for positions throughout the Organization.

_____ Education, Training, and Development—Providing performance skills training and career development to employees, utilizing both internal and external resources, including providing expertise in assessing education, training, and development needs and identification of high-potential employees.

_____ Employee Relations—The formal policies and procedures governing all conditions of employment, including specific human resources activities not otherwise categorized.

_____ Benefits—The noncash compensation provided to employees of the Organization including, but not limited to, such components as insurances, retirement saving plans, and paid time off, and the systems, support services, and communications to successfully deliver the benefits.

_____ Compensation—All cash payments to employees and also the systems by which positions are evaluated, salary and wage ranges and bands are determined, and adjustments are made, including commissions, lump sum payments, incentive payments, and bonuses.

_____ Human Resources Planning—The collection and analysis of data providing long-term (strategic) and short-term (tactical) plans and forecasts to meet the department's and Organization's missions, including such activities as succession planning, leadership development, and recruiting schedules.

_____ Organization Development—Improving communication and understanding in the Organization in order to produce effective, functioning management and employee teams; establishing or changing to a desired culture; responding to changing conditions; and analyzing and influencing Organization personnel, systems, structures, policies, and rewards to ensure synergy and maximize internal consistency.

_____ Diversity and Equal Employment Opportunity—Developing and implementing workforce programs to maximize employment of productive people with different characteristics, qualifications, and talents while recognizing the legal requirements and social responsibilities of equal treatment for all employees and the actions necessary to ensure those requirements are met.

_____ Safety and Environment—The training, communication, and leadership required to provide a safe working environment; to provide an appropriate level of employee involvement and responsibility for implementing safe practices, using safety equipment, and complying with Organization safety rules and practices; and to ensure that federal, state, and local safety and environmental requirements are met.

_____ Security—Maintaining and protecting the Organization's employees, assets, and human resources documents, information, and facilities.

_____ Equipment and Facilities—Providing the necessary equipment and facilities to fulfill the human resources mission and provide optimum service to the Organization.

_____ Documentation and Information Systems—Preparing, storing, and maintaining employee records and information, including computerized human resources information systems, and meeting federal, state, and local requirements.

You will return to these category weightings later. It is important that you accomplish this task prior to answering the information-gathering questions in Step One.

ACKNOWLEDGMENTS

I am deeply indebted to the many people and organizations assisting in the research for this book. Their input from a variety of backgrounds has produced a practical device for managers who wish to evaluate the human resources function without external assistance. Those individuals and organizations deserve to be acknowledged.

Particular thanks is due Russell A. Glicksman, president of The Beam Group in Philadelphia, Pennsylvania. Mr. Glicksman collaborated on two earlier editions of this book (1977 and 1986), as well as the present volume. His contributions resulted in the basic format, which has remained consistent throughout all editions. He provided advice and assistance for each edition. In effect, he served as a technical expert for the entire project.

In addition, a group of knowledgeable professionals in human resources management have individually and collectively contributed to the book's development. They are members of an Advisory Board on how to audit the human resources department and are identified on pages xi–xv. They also deserve acknowledgment and thanks.

Finally, a word of appreciation is due Ruth Long for her assistance in preparing the final manuscript for this book.

—John H. McConnell

AUDITING YOUR HUMAN RESOURCES DEPARTMENT

STEP ONE—
INFORMATION GATHERING

Beginning on the following page are the questions for each of the sixteen categories of human resources and summary information. If you cannot answer a question, do not guess. Instead, take the time to discover the answer. Writing "Don't Know" for an answer prohibits a later accurate evaluation.

Some of the questions require you to select an answer from those provided. Some require brief written answers. Many questions include an "Other" selection. "Other" is to be used when the correct answer is other than one of those provided. It is not meant to be used for an answer you do not know or as "Not applicable." Do not answer in categories that do not apply to your human resources function. You should answer each question in a category before moving on to the next category, and you should attempt to answer all questions in a single category at one time. The time required to answer the questions in all sixteen categories will vary but is probably somewhere between six and eight hours. Each category requires between thirty and sixty minutes. For this first step, ignore the short lines in front of the questions. They will be used in Step Two.

Keep in mind that this is not a test of your knowledge. It is a collection of factual information for evaluation of the department. Such an evaluation will only be as accurate and useful as your information is accurate, so answer as things are and not as you wish they were.

DEPARTMENT MISSION—INFORMATION GATHERING

The overall objective or purpose of the human resources department within the Organization and its relationship to the Organization's overall mission.

    If this category is not one for which your human resources department is accountable, go directly to the next category beginning on page 9.

_____ 1. Does your Organization have an identified functional unit accountable for human resources activities?

        _____ Yes   _____ No

_____ 2. Has that functional unit been defined as a specific department or division?

        _____ Yes   _____ No

_____ 3. Does that functional unit (department) have a clear mission?

        _____ Yes   _____ No

_____ 4. Has a human resources department mission been published?

        _____ Yes   _____ No

_____ 5. Has a human resources mission been communicated to all human resources department employees?

        _____ Yes   _____ No

_____ 6. Has a human resources department mission been communicated to all other departments within the Organization?

        _____ Yes   _____ No

_____ 7. Who prepares, reviews, and approves revisions to the human resources mission? (Check all that apply.)

3

Prepares   *Reviews*   *Approves*

_____   _____   _____   Senior executive of the Organization and/or person to whom senior human resources manager reports

_____   _____   _____   Organization's board of directors

_____   _____   _____   Senior human resources manager

_____   _____   _____   Human resources department managers

_____   _____   _____   Human resources nonmanagement employees

_____   _____   _____   Senior managers in other than human resources

_____   _____   _____   Other

_____   8. How often is the human resources department's mission reviewed? (Check just one.)

     _____ Once a year

     _____ Every one to three years

     _____ Every three to five years

     _____ More than every five years

     _____ Never

_____   9. Has the human resources department's mission been coordinated with the mission of the Organization?

     _____ Yes   _____ No

_____ 10. Is the human resources department's mission in agreement with the Organization's mission?

_____ Yes _____ No

_____ 11. How often is the human resources department mission considered in making human resources decisions? (Check just one.)

_____ Never

_____ Sometimes

_____ Usually

_____ Always

_____ 12. How often do human resources situations occur within the Organization that appear to differ or conflict with the human resources department's mission? (Check just one.)

_____ Never

_____ Rarely

_____ Sometimes

_____ Often

_____ Always

_____ 13. Does the human resources department mission clearly describe the department's purpose within the Organization?

_____ Yes _____ No

_____ 14. Does the human resources department have a strategic plan (three years or more)?

_____ Yes _____ No

_____   15. If your answer to the previous question was yes, is the strategic plan in writing?

      _____ Yes   _____ No

_____   16. If your answer to the previous question was yes, has that plan been communicated to all human resources department employees?

      _____ Yes   _____ No

_____   17. If your answer to Question 14 was yes, has that plan been communicated to all other departments within the Organization?

      _____ Yes   _____ No

_____   18. If your answer to Question 14 was yes, how often is the human resources department's performance to strategic plan formally reviewed? (Check just one.)

      _____ Every six months

      _____ Once a year

      _____ Every one to three years

      _____ Every three to five years

      _____ More than every five years

      _____ Never

_____   19. If your answer to Question 14 was yes, who prepares, reviews, and approves the human resources strategic plan? (Check all that apply.)

Prepares Reviews Approves

_____ _____ _____ Senior executive of the Organization and/or person to whom senior human resources manager reports

_____ _____ _____ Organization's board of directors

_____ _____ _____ Senior human resources manager

_____ _____ _____ Human resources department managers

_____ _____ _____ Human resources nonmanagement employees

_____ _____ _____ Senior managers in other than human resources

_____ _____ _____ Other

_____ 20. If your answer to Question 14 was yes, has the human resources department's strategic plan been coordinated with the Organization's strategic plan?

_____ Yes _____ No

_____ 21. If your answer to the previous question was yes, is the human resources department's strategic plan in agreement with the Organization's strategic plan?

_____ Yes _____ No

_____ 22. If your answer to Question 14 was yes, has the human resources department's strategic plan been coordinated with the department's mission statement?

_____ Yes _____ No

_____ 23. If your answer to the previous question was yes, is the human resources department's strategic plan in agreement with the department's mission statement?

_____ Yes _____ No

_____ 24. On a scale of one to nine (one being low, five being typical, and nine being high), how do you think the human resources department has performed in this category? _____

_____ 25. On a scale of one to nine (one being low, five being typical, and nine being high), how do you think employees of the human resources department feel the human resources department has performed in this category? _____

_____ 26. On a scale of one to nine (one being low, five being typical, and nine being high), how do you think the clients of the human resources department within the Organization feel the human resources department has performed in this category? _____

Department Organization—Information Gathering

The department's internal relationships; relationships with other functions, departments, and employees of the Organization; and the structuring of resources within the department.

If this category is not one for which your human resources department is accountable, go directly to the next category beginning on page 21.

_____ 1. Have the human resources department's key result areas (the main activities human resources is to accomplish) been identified?

_____ Yes _____ No

_____ 2. How many of these key result areas have been specifically assigned to positions within the human resources department? (Check just one.)

_____ None

_____ Some

_____ About half

_____ Most

_____ All

_____ 3. Are any human resources key result areas assigned to positions or people not in the human resources department?

_____ Yes _____ No

_____ 4. If your answer to the previous question was yes, do you know what those key result areas are and to whom they are assigned?

_____ Yes _____ No _____ Not applicable

9

_____ 5. If your answer to the previous question was yes, do you know the reasons these key result areas are assigned to other than positions in the human resources department?

       _____ Yes   _____ No   _____ Not applicable

_____ 6. If your answer to the previous question was yes, is the reason these key result areas are assigned to other than positions in the human resources department in agreement with the human resources department's mission and the unique needs of your Organization?

       _____ Yes   _____ No   _____ Not applicable

_____ 7. Has consideration been given to outsourcing any human resources activities?

       _____ Yes   _____ No

_____ 8. Is there one position in the human resources department accountable for the management of the entire human resources function?

       _____ Yes   _____ No

_____ 9. On what organizational level is the senior management position of the human resources department? (Check just one.)

       _____ Same as senior management positions in other departments

       _____ Lower than senior management positions in other departments

       _____ Higher than senior management positions in other departments

       _____ Nonmanagement levels in our Organization

_____ 10. To what position does the senior human resources management position report? (Check just one.)

_____ A senior operating management position

_____ A senior staff management position

_____ The senior executive position in the Organization

_____ Other

_____ 11. Is there a human resources department organizational structure; that is, have all positions in the department and their reporting relationships been identified?

_____ Yes _____ No

_____ 12. Is the department's organizational structure in writing, such as
an Organization chart?

_____ Yes _____ No

_____ 13. Has the human resources Organization been communicated to
all employees of the human resources department?

_____ Yes _____ No

_____ 14. Has the human resources Organization been communicated to
the balance of the Organization?

_____ Yes _____ No

_____ 15. Is the human resources department organizational structure
based on identified key result areas or on the abilities of the
employees in the department at the time the structure was designed? (Check all that apply.)

_____ Key result areas _____ Employees' abilities

_____ Other

_____ 16. Does each human resources department position have a mission or an overall objective?

_____ Yes _____ No

————————   17. Does each human resources department position have a written description?

—————— Yes   —————— No

————————   18. If you have position descriptions, do they have defined responsibilities or tasks, authorities, and competencies or requirements? (Check all that apply.)

—————— Position title

—————— Department

—————— Reporting relationships

—————— Responsibilities or tasks

—————— Authorities

—————— Competencies or requirements

————————   19. Does every human resources department position report to a single position?

—————— Yes   —————— No

————————   20. Has decision-making authority been delegated to the lowest possible levels within the human resources department?

—————— Yes   —————— No

————————   21. If you have written position descriptions, does each human resources department employee have a copy of her position description?

—————— Yes   —————— No

————————   22. If you have written position descriptions, how often are they reviewed? (Check just one.)

—————— Once a year

—————— Every one to three years

_____ Every three to five years

_____ More than every five years

_____ Never

_____ 23. If you have written position descriptions, who prepares and approves human resources department position descriptions? (Check all that apply.)

Prepares *Approves*

_____ _____ Senior human resources manager

_____ _____ Person in the position

_____ _____ Supervisor of person in the position

_____ _____ Manager of supervisor of person in the position

_____ _____ Senior manager to whom senior human resources manager reports

_____ _____ Position or compensation evaluation committee

_____ _____ Other

_____ 24. If you have written position descriptions, what is the primary function of human resources department position descriptions?

_____

_____ 25. Have two or more human resources department positions (not people) been assigned the same responsibilities?

_____ Yes _____ No

_____ 26. If your answer to the previous question was yes, do you know the reason these responsibilities are assigned to more than one position?

_____ Yes _____ No

—————— 27. If your answer to the previous question was yes, is the reason those responsibilities are assigned to more than one position in agreement with the human resources department mission and the unique needs of your Organization?

—————— Yes —————— No

—————— 28. Do people within the Organization know whom to contact regarding specific human resources activities?

—————— Yes —————— No

—————— 29. Have standards of performance or objectives been established for each human resources department position?

—————— Yes —————— No

—————— 30. Are standards of performance or objectives in writing?

—————— Yes —————— No

—————— 31. If your answer to the previous question was yes, does each human resources department employee have a copy of her standards of performance or objectives?

—————— Yes —————— No

—————— 32. If you have standards of performance or objectives for human resources department employees, who prepares, reviews, and approves position standards or objectives? (Check all that apply.)

Prepares   *Reviews*   *Approves*

—————— —————— ——————   Senior human resources manager

—————— —————— ——————   Person in the position

—————— —————— ——————   Supervisor of person in the position

—————— —————— ——————   Manager of supervisor of person in the position

———— ———— ————   Senior manager to whom
senior human resources
manager reports

———— ———— ————   Position or compensation
evaluation committee

———— ———— ————   Other

————   33. If you have standards of performance or objectives for human resources department employees, what are the functions of department standards of performance or objectives? (Check all that apply.)

———— Achieving department performance objectives

———— Salary adjustment

———— Hiring

———— Bonus consideration

———— Employee development

———— Promotion or assignment

———— Planning

———— Other

————   34. How often is a human resources employee's performance formally reviewed? (Check all that apply.)

———— Never

———— Monthly

———— Once a quarter

———— Every six months

_____ Once a year

_____ Other

_____   35. Who prepares, conducts, and approves a human resources department employee's performance reviews? (Check all that apply.)

Prepares   *Conducts*   *Approves*

_____ _____ _____ Employee's supervisor

_____ _____ _____ Manager of employee's supervisor

_____ _____ _____ Senior human resources manager

_____ _____ _____ Employee

_____ _____ _____ Other

_____   36. Is an employee shown his formal performance evaluation?

_____ Yes _____ No

_____   37. Do employees sign their final formal performance evaluations?

_____ Yes _____ No

_____   38. Who maintains a copy of an employee's performance evaluations? (Check all that apply.)

_____ Employee's supervisor

_____ Manager of employee's supervisor

_____ Senior human resources manager

_____ Employee

_____ Employee's file in human resources department

_____ Other

_____ 39. Does the human resources department have a tactical plan (one year or less)?

_____ Yes _____ No

_____ 40. If your answer to the previous question was yes, is the plan in writing?

_____ Yes _____ No

_____ 41. If your answer to the previous question was yes, has that plan been communicated to all human resources department employees?

_____ Yes _____ No

_____ 42. If your answer to Question 40 was yes, has that plan been communicated to all other departments within the Organization?

_____ Yes _____ No

_____ 43. If your answer to Question 39 was yes, how often is the human resources department performance to tactical planning formally reviewed? (Check all that apply.)

_____ Never

_____ Every month

_____ Every quarter

_____ Once a year

_____ Other

_____ 44. If your answer to Question 39 was yes, who prepares, reviews, and approves the human resources department tactical plan? (Check all that apply.)

Prepares   Reviews   Approves

_____   _____   _____   Senior executive of the Organization and/or person
to whom senior human re-
sources manager reports

_____   _____   _____   Organization's board of directors

_____   _____   _____   Senior human resources
manager

_____   _____   _____   Human resources department managers

_____   _____   _____   Human resources nonmanagement employees

_____   _____   _____   Senior managers in other
than human resources

_____   _____   _____   Other

_____ 45. If your answer to Question 39 was yes, has the human resources
tactical plan been coordinated with the Organization's tactical
plan?

_____ Yes   _____ No

_____ 46. If your answer to the previous question was yes, is the human
resources department's tactical plan in agreement with the Organization's tactical plan?

_____ Yes   _____ No

_____ 47. If your answer to Question 39 was yes, has the human resources
tactical plan been coordinated with the department's strategic
plan?

_____ Yes   _____ No

_____ 48. If your answer to the previous question was yes, is the human resources department's tactical plan in agreement with the department's strategic plan?

_____ Yes _____ No

_____ 49. Does the human resources department have an annual budget based on an annual or tactical plan?

_____ Yes _____ No

_____ 50. Does the human resources department budget indicate planned expenses by key result area, position, or other functional assignment?

_____ Yes _____ No

_____ 51. Who prepares, reviews, and approves the human resources department annual budget? (Check all that apply.)

Prepares	_Reviews_	_Approves_	
_____	_____	_____	Senior executive of the Organization and/or person to whom senior human resources manager reports
_____	_____	_____	Organization's board of directors
_____	_____	_____	Senior human resources manager
_____	_____	_____	Human resources department managers
_____	_____	_____	Human resources nonmanagement employees
_____	_____	_____	Senior managers in other than human resources

—————   —————   —————   Someone from a financial
                                        function of the Organiza-
                                        tion

—————   —————   —————   Other

—————   52. How often are performance to budget reports received by the
                             human resources department? (Check just one.)

    ————— Never

    ————— Every month

    ————— Every quarter

    ————— Once a year

    ————— Other

—————   53. Are human resources managers accountable for budget items
                             required to analyze results and variances?

    ————— Yes   ————— No

—————   54. On a scale of one to nine (one being low, five being typical,
                             and nine being high), how do you think the human resources
                             department has performed in this category? —————

—————   55. On a scale of one to nine (one being low, five being typical, and
                             nine being high), how do you think employees of the human
                             resources department feel the human resources department
                             has performed in this category? —————

—————   56. On a scale of one to nine (one being low, five being typical, and
                             nine being high), how do you think the clients of the human
                             resources department within the Organization feel the human
                             resources department has performed in this category? —————

DEPARTMENT EMPLOYEES— INFORMATION GATHERING

The selection, training, motivation, development, and retention of a qualified human resources team.

If this category is not one for which your human resources department is accountable, go directly to the next category beginning on page 29.

_____ 1. Is the human resources department staffed in accordance with its formal published Organization?

_____ Yes _____ No

_____ 2. What percentage of human resources department employees have been in their current positions? (Answer all.)

_____ Less than six months

_____ Between six months and one year

_____ Between one and five years

_____ More than five years

_____ 3. What percentage of department employees are technically qualified for their positions?

_____ 4. Who establishes and approves the required qualifications for a human resources department position? (Check all that apply.)

Establishes *Approves*

_____ _____ Supervisor of the position

_____ _____ Manager of supervisor of person in the position

_____ _____ Senior manager to whom top human resources manager reports

21

————— —————   Compensation evaluation com-
                mittee

————— —————   Other

—————   5. What percentage of human resources department positions are currently filled? —————

—————   6. If there are currently department positions not filled, what is the longest times these positions have remained unfilled?

————— Nonmanagement   ————— Management

—————   7. Who authorizes hiring of a new employee for a budgeted human resources department position? (Check just one.)

————— Supervisor of the position

————— Manager of position's supervisor

————— Senior manager in the human resources department

————— Senior manager to whom senior human resources manager reports

————— Other

—————   8. Who authorizes the hiring of a new employee for a newly created human resources department position, one that was not previously budgeted? (Check just one.)

————— Supervisor of the position

————— Manager of position's supervisor

————— Senior manager in the human resources department

————— Senior manager to whom senior human resources manager reports

————— Other

_____ 9. Who interviews candidates for a human resources department position? (Check all that apply.)

_____ Supervisor of the open position

_____ Manager of position's supervisor

_____ Senior human resources manager

_____ Other human resources managers

_____ Senior manager to whom top human resources manager reports

_____ Human resources department employees in similar positions

_____ Managers of client departments

_____ Other

_____ 10. Is there a formal human resources department orientation program?

_____ Yes _____ No

_____ 11. Is compensation for human resources department employees competitive for similar positions in your industry?

_____ Yes _____ No

_____ 12. Is compensation for human resources department employees competitive for similar positions in the geographic area?

_____ Yes _____ No

_____ 13. What is the annual employee turnover rate for the human resources department?

_____ Internal _____ External

_____ 14. What is the average number of days nonmanagement employees in the human resources department are absent each year? _____

_____ 15. Is involvement in professional associations and conferences encouraged for human resources department employees?

           _____ Yes   _____ No

_____ 16. Does the Organization pay for professional association dues and conference registrations for human resources department employees?

         Association dues   _____ Yes   _____ No

         Conference registrations   _____ Yes   _____ No

_____ 17. Are professional journals and magazines purchased for human resources department employees?

           _____ Yes   _____ No

_____ 18. Are professional journals and magazines routed through to all human resources department employees?

           _____ Yes   _____ No

_____ 19. Is there a library (storage or files of professional books, journals, magazines, and articles) of human resources books and journals?

           _____ Yes   _____ No

_____ 20. Are in-house seminars in human resources subjects offered to department employees?

           _____ Yes   _____ No

_____ 21. Are human resources department employees offered rotational assignments in other functional areas of the Organization?

           _____ Yes   _____ No

_____ 22. Are employees from other areas of the Organization offered temporary rotational assignment in the human resources department?

           _____ Yes   _____ No

_____ 23. What percentage of human resources department employees have specific individual development objectives? _____

_____ 24. Are human resources department employees' performance reviews separated from salary reviews?

_____ Yes _____ No

_____ 25. If your answer to the previous question was yes, by how much time are they separated? _____

_____ 26. Does the human resources department have an employee replacement plan document?

_____ Yes _____ No

_____ 27. If your answer to the previous question was yes, what percentage of assignments and promotions follow the plan? _____

_____ 28. If your answer to Question 26 was yes, how often is it reviewed and updated? (Check no more than two.)

_____ Never

_____ Every six months

_____ Once a year

_____ Every one to three years

_____ More than every three years

_____ Whenever someone leaves the department

_____ Other

_____ 29. If your answer to Question 26 was yes, is the plan solely a department activity or is it coordinated with an Organizationwide plan? (Check just one.)

_____ Department only _____ Organizationwide

_____ Both

_____ 30. Are exit interviews held with all departing human resources department employees?

_____ Yes _____ No

_____ 31. If your answer to the previous question was yes, who generally conducts exit interviews and reviews exit interview information? (Check just one in the Conducts column, but all that apply in the Reviews column.)

Conducts   *Reviews*

_____ _____ Supervisor of employee

_____ _____ Manager of employee's supervisor

_____ _____ Other human resources department personnel

_____ _____ Senior human resources manager

_____ _____ Other

_____ 32. If a human resources department employee is not performing to standard, what actions are taken? (Check all that apply.)

_____ Performance review conducted

_____ Employee issued an oral warning

_____ Employee issued a written warning

_____ Employee discharged

_____ Employee given disciplinary time off

_____ Employee transferred to another job

_____ 33. Are new human resources department employees initially on probationary periods?

_____ Yes _____ No

_____ 34. Does the human resources department have specific rules, guidelines, and regulations regarding department employee behavior?

_____ Yes _____ No

_____ 35. If your answer was yes to the previous question, are those rules in writing?

_____ Yes _____ No

_____ 36. If your answer to the previous question was yes, is each human resources department employee given a copy of those rules, guidelines, and regulations?

_____ Yes _____ No

_____ 37. If there are human resources department rules, guidelines, and regulations, are they applied equally to all department employees?

_____ Yes _____ No

_____ 38. Are human resources department employees encouraged to obtain professional certification in subjects for which certification is available?

_____ Yes _____ No

_____ 39. On a scale of one to nine (one being low, five being typical, and nine being high), how do you think the human resources department has performed in this category? _____

_____ 40. On a scale of one to nine (one being low, five being typical, and nine being high), how do you think employees of the human resources department feel the human resources department has performed in this category? _____

_____ 41. On a scale of one to nine (one being low, five being typical, and nine being high), how do you think the clients of the human resources department within the Organization feel the human resources department has performed in this category? _____

LABOR RELATIONS—INFORMATION GATHERING

The human resources role in the relationship between the Organization and any bargaining unit of an employee-organized labor group, including labor-organizing campaigns.

If this category is not one for which your human resources department is accountable, go directly to the next category beginning on page 39.

_____   1. Who has the primary authority for establishing the Organization's labor relations policy? (Check just one.)

       _____ External labor attorney

       _____ Internal labor attorney

       _____ Senior human resources manager

       _____ The Organization's senior labor relations manager, if not the senior human resources manager

       _____ Senior manager in other than human resources

       _____ Senior executive of the Organization

       _____ A team, group, or committee of the Organization

       _____ No one

       _____ Other

_____   2. Does the Organization have continuous access to internal and/ or external labor relations legal counsel? (Check just one.)

       _____ External legal counsel   _____ Internal legal counsel

       _____ Both   _____ Neither

_____ 3. Is the legal counsel utilized for labor relations a specialist in labor relations?

            _____ Yes _____ No

_____ 4. Who is primarily accountable for labor relations decisions? (Check just one.)

            _____ External labor attorney

            _____ Internal labor attorney

            _____ Senior human resources manager

            _____ The Organization's senior labor relations manager, if not the senior human resources manager

            _____ Senior manager in other than human resources

            _____ Senior executive of the Organization

            _____ A team, group, or committee

            _____ No one

            _____ Other

_____ 5. Have managers within the Organization been informed of what to do in case of a union organization attempt?

            _____ Yes _____ No _____ Not applicable

_____ 6. Do the managers within the Organization receive regular updates on union organization methods?

            _____ Yes _____ No _____ Not applicable

_____ 7. If your answer to the previous question was yes, how often are these updates given? (Check all that apply.)

            _____ Whenever there is an organizing attempt

            _____ At least once a year

_____ On an unscheduled basis

_____ Every year or more

_____ Other

_____ Not applicable

_____   8. Has accountability for directing the Organization's response to a union-organizing attempt been identified prior to any such situation?

       _____ Yes _____ No _____ Not applicable

_____   9. In the event of a union-organizing campaign, is one person accountable for directing the Organization's response?

       _____ Yes _____ No _____ Not applicable

_____   10. What position does the person accountable for directing the Organization's response to a union-organizing attempt hold? (Check just one.)

_____ External labor attorney

_____ Internal labor attorney

_____ Senior human resources manager

_____ The Organization's senior labor relations manager, if not the senior human resources manager

_____ Senior manager in other than human resources

_____ Senior executive of the Organization

_____ No one

_____ Other

_____ Not applicable

_____   11. Is there an individual within the Organization who regularly reviews labor relations regulations, legislation, developments, rulings, and other related activities?

_____ Yes _____ No

_____   12. In preparation for union negotiations are current labor relations regulations, legislation, rulings, and other related activities reviewed?

_____ Yes _____ No

_____   13. In preparation for union negotiations are the managers and supervisors of employees represented by the union asked for comments and recommendations regarding the current contract and its implementation?

_____ Yes _____ No

_____   14. In preparation for union negotiations are grievance and arbitration records reviewed?

_____ Yes _____ No

_____   15. In preparation for union negotiations does someone from the Organization attend an updating seminar or conference on labor relations?

_____ Yes _____ No

_____   16. Are parameters for the Organization's union negotiations established in advance of negotiations?

_____ Yes _____ No

_____   17. Who is the chief spokesperson for the Organization in union negotiations? (Check just one.)

_____ External labor attorney

_____ Internal labor attorney

_____ Senior human resources manager

_____ The Organization's senior labor relations manager

_____ Senior manager in other than human resources

_____ Senior executive of the Organization

_____ Senior manager of the unit covered by the agreement

_____ No one

_____ Other

_____ 18. Who is a member of the Organization's union-negotiating team? (Check all that apply.)

_____ External labor attorney

_____ Internal labor attorney

_____ Senior human resources manager

_____ The Organization's senior labor relations manager

_____ Senior manager in other than human resources

_____ Senior executive of the Organization

_____ No one

_____ Nonhuman resources manager or supervisor

_____ Other

_____ 19. Is a senior Organization manager with decision-making authority always available to the negotiating team?

_____ Yes   _____ No

_____ 20. Is a system in place for calculating the cost of any proposal introduced during union negotiations?

_____ Yes   _____ No

————   21. Are updating meetings conducted for the Organization's managers during union negotiations?

—————— Yes   —————— No

————   22. Does the Organization regularly share information regarding labor relations with other companies in your geographic area and industry? (Check just one.)

—————— Area   —————— Industry

—————— Both   —————— No

————   23. Is there an individual accountable for approving the final settlement of all grievances?

—————— Yes   —————— No

————   24. If your answer to the previous question was yes, who is that individual? (Check just one.)

—————— External labor attorney

—————— Internal labor attorney

—————— Senior human resources manager

—————— The Organization's senior labor relations manager, if not the senior human resources manager

—————— Senior manager in other than human resources

—————— Senior executive of the Organization

—————— No one

—————— Other

————   25. Is an investigation of a grievance conducted within five days of it being filed?

—————— Yes   —————— No

_____   26. When a grievance is filed, is an investigation conducted of the circumstances prior to the first grievance meeting?

_____ Yes   _____ No

_____   27. Are written records made of all grievance investigations?

_____ Yes   _____ No

_____   28. Are the managers and supervisors whose actions are the subject of grievances required to submit or sign written statements of information and facts regarding the grievances?

_____ Yes   _____ No

_____   29. When are statements regarding a grievance taken from the involved managers and supervisors? (Check just one.)

_____ As soon as a grievance is filed

_____ Within five days of a grievance being filed

_____ After the first grievance meeting

_____ Just prior to the last meeting in the grievance procedure

_____ When a grievance is appealed to arbitration

_____ Never

_____ Other

_____   30. Is it the Organization's policy to settle grievances?

_____ Yes   _____ No

_____   31. Are records of all grievances and their resolutions maintained and analyzed?

_____ Yes   _____ No

_____ 32. Are grievances and their proposed settlements reviewed by internal or external labor counsel at any point in the grievance procedure prior to final settlement?

_____ Yes _____ No

_____ 33. At an arbitration hearing, who is spokesperson for the Organization? (Check just one.)

_____ External labor attorney

_____ Internal labor attorney

_____ Senior human resources manager

_____ The Organization's senior labor relations manager, if not the senior human resources manager

_____ Nonhuman resources manager

_____ Senior executive of the Organization

_____ No one

_____ Other

_____ 34. If the Organization has external facilities such as a parking lot, have signs been posted to indicate no soliciting or distribution of literature and limiting who can be on that property?

_____ Yes _____ No

_____ 35. Is there a rule that there can be no solicitation or distribution of literature within the Organization's facilities?

_____ Yes _____ No

_____ 36. On a scale of one to nine (one being low, five being typical, and nine being high), how do you think the human resources department has performed in this category? _____

_____ 37. On a scale of one to nine (one being low, five being typical, and nine being high), how do you think employees of the human resources department feel the human resources department has performed in this category? _____

_____ 38. On a scale of one to nine (one being low, five being typical, and nine being high), how do you think the clients of the human resources department within the Organization feel the human resources department has performed in this category? _____

RECRUITMENT AND SELECTION— INFORMATION GATHERING

Obtaining and evaluating qualified candidates from internal and external sources for positions throughout the Organization.

If this category is not one for which your human resources department is accountable, go directly to the next category beginning on page 53.

_____ 1. Who has the primary accountability for requesting and authorizing the hiring of a new employee? (Check just one in each column.)

Requesting   Approving

_____   _____   Supervisor of the open position

_____   _____   Manager of the open position's supervisor

_____   _____   Senior manager in the department of the open position

_____   _____   Senior human resources manager

_____   _____   Human resources manager accountable for recruitment

_____   _____   Other

_____ 2. Is the requesting and authorizing for hiring a new employee a formal procedure; that is, is it in writing and are approvals required?

_____ Yes   _____ No

_____ 3. Does authorization for hiring a new employee require a position description?

_____ Yes   _____ No

39

_____ 4. Does authorization for hiring a new employee require the position's standards of performance or objectives?

_____ Yes _____ No

_____ 5. Does authorization for hiring a new employee require a statement of the position's specific requirements (competencies, education, experience, and skills, both technical and special)?

_____ Yes _____ No

_____ 6. Is an attempt made to fill positions from within the Organization prior to obtaining candidates from outside the Organization?

_____ Yes _____ No

_____ 7. Does the Organization have a job-posting program?

_____ Yes _____ No

_____ 8. If your answer to the previous question was yes, are attempts made to fill jobs from within the department where the position exists prior to posting to employees throughout the Organization?

_____ Yes _____ No

_____ 9. If your answer to Question 7 was yes, are attempts made to fill jobs through the job-posting program before outside resources are utilized?

_____ Yes _____ No _____ Sometimes

_____ 10. If your answer to Question 7 was yes, which jobs are posted? (Check just one.)

_____ All jobs

_____ Only nonmanagement jobs

_____ Only jobs at certain levels

_____ Only management jobs

_____ Other

_____ 11. If your answer to Question 7 was yes, can the Organization elect to not post a job?

_____ Yes _____ No

_____ 12. If your answer to the previous question was yes, must there be an approved reason for not posting a job?

_____ Yes _____ No

_____ 13. If your answer to Question 11 was yes, who can elect to not post a job? (Check all that apply.)

_____ Supervisor of the open position

_____ Manager of the open position's supervisor

_____ Senior manager in the department of the open position

_____ Senior human resources manager

_____ Human resources manager accountable for recruitment

_____ Other

_____ 14. Does your Organization have a policy regarding promotions?

_____ Yes _____ No

_____ 15. If your answer to the previous question was yes, is that policy in writing?

_____ Yes _____ No

_____   16. If your answer to the previous question was yes, has that policy
                  been communicated to all employees?

                  _____ Yes   _____ No

_____   17. Who determines the methods used for obtaining candidates for
                  open positions? (Check all that apply.)

                  _____ Supervisor of the open position

                  _____ Manager of the open position's supervisor

                  _____ Senior manager in the department of the open posi-
                            tion

                  _____ Senior human resources manager

                  _____ Human resources manager accountable for recruit-
                            ment

                  _____ Other

_____   18. In recruitment advertisements which of the following job partic-
                  ulars are provided? (Check all that apply.)

                  _____ Organization name

                  _____ Position title

                  _____ Location

                  _____ Telephone number

                  _____ Compensation

                  _____ Benefits

                  _____ Position requirements

                  _____ Name of person to contact

                  _____ Confidentiality of contact

_____ How the Organization will respond to replies

_____ "Our employees know of this advertisement" or similar words

_____ Other

_____ Organization does not advertise

_____ 19. Is there a minimum number of candidates interviewed for an open position?

_____ Yes _____ No

_____ 20. Who initially screens candidates? (Check all that apply.)

_____ Supervisor of the open position

_____ Manager of the open position's supervisor

_____ Senior manager in the department of the open position

_____ Senior human resources manager

_____ Human resources manager accountable for recruitment

_____ Human resources department recruiter or screener

_____ Other

_____ 21. What sources are used for external candidates? (Check all that apply.)

_____ Internet

_____ Search firms

_____ Employment agencies

_____ Schools

_____ Consultants

_____ Newspaper advertisements

_____ Professional journal advertisements

_____ Professional associations

_____ Employee recommendations

_____ Job fairs

_____ Outplacement firms

_____ Downsizing/relocating employers

_____ Organization publications

_____ Organization marquees and signs

_____ Other

_____ 22. Does the Organization have an employee referral program?

_____ Yes _____ No

_____ 23. If your answer to the previous question was yes, is the program utilized in hiring for all positions?

_____ Yes _____ No

_____ 24. If your answer to Question 23 was yes, does the program include a cash award for recommending someone who is hired?

_____ Yes _____ No

_____ 25. Does the Organization require all candidates to sign a reference-checking release as a part of an application or as a separate form?

_____ Yes _____ No

_____ 26. Are reference checks made of all candidate's qualifications?

_____ Yes _____ No _____ Sometimes

_____ 27. If your answer to the previous question was yes, when are reference checks for a candidate made? (Check just one.)

_____ When an application/resume is received

_____ Before a first interview

_____ After a first interview

_____ When a candidate is being seriously considered

_____ Prior to a job offer

_____ After a job offer is accepted but prior to hiring

_____ After hiring

_____ Other

_____ 28. If your answer to Question 27 was yes, who conducts such reference checks? (Check all that apply.)

_____ Supervisor of the position

_____ Manager of the supervisor of the position

_____ Senior manager in the department of the open position

_____ Senior human resources manager

_____ Human resources manager accountable for recruitment

_____ Human resources department recruiter or screener

_____ Other

29. If your answer to Question 26 was yes, are written records made
    of all conducted reference checks?

    _____ Yes   _____ No

30. Who determines which candidates to interview? (Check all that
    apply.)

    _____ Supervisor of the open position

    _____ Manager of the open position's supervisor

    _____ Senior manager in the department of the open posi-
              tion

    _____ Senior human resources manager

    _____ Human resources manager accountable for recruit-
              ment

    _____ Human resources department recruiter or screener

    _____ Other

31. Who conducts the initial interview with a candidate? (Check all
    that apply.)

    _____ Supervisor of the open position

    _____ Manager of the open position's supervisor

    _____ Senior manager in the department of the open posi-
              tion

    _____ Senior human resources manager

    _____ Human resources manager accountable for recruit-
              ment

    _____ Human resources department recruiter or screener

    _____ Other

_____ 32. Who of the following interviews a candidate before a hiring decision is made? (Check all that apply.)

       _____ Supervisor of the open position

       _____ Manager of the open position's supervisor

       _____ Senior manager in the department of the open position

       _____ Senior human resources manager

       _____ Human resources manager accountable for recruitment

       _____ Human resources department recruiter or screener

       _____ Other

_____ 33. Are the people who interview a candidate required to make an immediate assessment of the candidate's qualifications for the position?

       _____ Yes _____ No

_____ 34. Are any measurement devices such as tests used?

       _____ Yes _____ No _____ Sometimes

_____ 35. If your answer to the previous question was yes or sometimes, are such devices based on an analysis of the job?

       _____ Yes _____ No

_____ 36. If your answer to Question 34 was yes or sometimes, have such measurement devices been professionally validated?

       _____ Yes _____ No

_____ 37. If your answer to Question 34 was yes, who administers such devices? (Check all that apply.)

      _____ Someone in the open position's department

      _____ Someone in the human resources department

      _____ An external consultant

      _____ Other

_____ 38. If your answer to Question 34 was yes or sometimes, has the person who administers such devices been properly trained or certified?

      _____ Yes _____ No

_____ 39. If your answer to Question 34 was yes or sometimes, have the people who receive the results of such devices been trained in how to interpret the results?

      _____ Yes _____ No

_____ 40. Have all people who interview candidates been trained in the types of questions and actions that are legal?

      _____ Yes _____ No

_____ 41. Have all people who interview candidates been trained in interviewing techniques?

      _____ Yes _____ No

_____ 42. Are requirements identical for internal and external candidates for the same position?

      _____ Yes _____ No

_____ 43. Are all position requirements based on an analysis of the job?

      _____ Yes _____ No

_____   44. If multiple interviews are conducted, are the interview questions coordinated?

_____ Yes   _____ No   _____ Not applicable

_____   45. Does the hiring area have a bulletin board with all legally required notices on display?

_____ Yes   _____ No

_____   46. Are the bulletin board notices in the hiring area regularly reviewed to ensure all notices are on display and are current?

_____ Yes   _____ No

_____   47. Does your Organization require drug testing?

_____ Yes   _____ No

_____   48. If your answer to the previous question was yes, is that policy posted in the hiring area and/or communicated to all candidates?

_____ Yes   _____ No

_____   49. If your answer to Question 48 was yes, are drug tests administered to all candidates prior to employment?

_____ Yes   _____ No

_____   50. Does your Organization require reemployment physical examinations?

_____ Yes   _____ No   _____ Some positions

_____   51. If your answer to the previous question was yes, is that policy posted in the hiring area and/or communicated to candidates?

_____ Yes   _____ No   _____ Not applicable

_____   52. If your answer to Question 50 was yes, are the physical examinations administered to all final candidates prior to employment?

_____ Yes _____ No _____ Some positions

_____   53. Who makes the final decision regarding to hire or not to hire a candidate? (Check just one.)

_____ Supervisor of the open position

_____ Manager of the open position's supervisor

_____ Senior manager in the department of the open position

_____ Senior human resources manager

_____ Human resources manager accountable for recruitment

_____ Other

_____   54. Are all candidates for a position notified of the company's hiring decision?

_____ Yes _____ No

_____   55. Is there a policy governing to which received applications and resumes the Organization will respond?

_____ Yes _____ No

_____   56. To which received resumes and applications does the Organization respond? (Check all that apply.)

_____ Those from walk-in candidates

_____ Those from employment agency/search firm candidates

_____ Those from employee-recommended candidates

_____ Those from candidates responding to advertisements

_____ Those from school- or professional association–recommended candidates

_____ Those from candidates sending unsolicited resumes

_____ Those from Internet candidates

_____ Other

_____ 57. Is descriptive literature available to all candidates regarding the Organization and the open position?

_____ Yes _____ No

_____ 58. Is there an individual within the human resources department accountable for the entire Organization's selection and recruitment programs?

_____ Yes _____ No

_____ 59. Does the Organization participate in job fairs and college recruiting?

_____ Yes _____ No

_____ 60. On a scale of one to nine (one being low, five being typical, and nine being high), how do you think the human resources department has performed in this category? _____

_____ 61. On a scale of one to nine (one being low, five being typical, and nine being high), how do you think employees of the human resources department feel the human resources department has performed in this category? _____

_____ 62. On a scale of one to nine (one being low, five being typical, and nine being high), how do you think the clients of the human resources department within the Organization feel the human resources department has performed in this category? _____

EDUCATION, TRAINING, AND DEVELOPMENT— INFORMATION GATHERING

Providing performance skills training and career development to employees, utilizing both internal and external resources, including providing expertise in assessing education, training, and development needs and identification of high-potential employees.

If this category is not one for which your human resources department is accountable, go directly to the next category beginning on page 63.

_____   1. Is there an individual within the human resources department accountable for the Organization's entire education, training, and development activities?

_____ Yes _____ No

_____   2. Who initiates requests for employee training? (Check all that apply.)

_____ Employee

_____ Employee's supervisor

_____ Manager of employee's supervisor

_____ Senior manager in the employee's department

_____ Senior human resources manager

_____ Human resources manager accountable for training

_____ An external consultant

_____ Other

_____   3. Is training available in any skills unique to the Organization?

_____ Yes _____ No

——————— 4. Is training available for employees desiring to prepare for other positions within the Organization?

——————— Yes ——————— No

——————— 5. Is management or supervisory training available?

——————— Yes ——————— No

——————— 6. Is training available in remedial skills such as English and mathematics?

——————— Yes ——————— No

——————— 7. Do all training programs have clearly established and specific behavioral objectives?

——————— Yes ——————— No

——————— 8. If your answer to the previous question was yes, are the results of training continually compared to the training program's behavioral objectives?

——————— Yes ——————— No

——————— 9. Whether there are training program behavioral objectives or not, are the results of training programs continually monitored and evaluated?

——————— Yes ——————— No

——————— 10. Are follow-up reviews regularly conducted with managers of employees attending training programs to determine the results as reflected on the job?

——————— Yes ——————— No

——————— 11. Is the subject matter of training programs regularly reviewed with the managers of the areas for which the training is conducted?

——————— Yes ——————— No

_____ 12. How often is the subject matter of training programs reviewed to determine relevancy and currentness? (Check all that apply.)

      _____ At least once a year

      _____ Every one to three years

      _____ Every three to five years

      _____ When requested by management

      _____ When there appears to have been a change in the subject matter

      _____ When results of the training are not as planned

      _____ Never

_____ 13. Who identifies the specific training needs of an employee? (Check no more than three.)

      _____ Employee

      _____ Employee's supervisor

      _____ Manager of employee's supervisor

      _____ Senior manager in the employee's department

      _____ Senior human resources manager

      _____ Human resources manager accountable for training

      _____ An external consultant

      _____ Other

_____ 14. How are training needs identified? (Check all that apply.)

      _____ Performance to job standards and objectives

      _____ Performance reviews

_____ Changes in job content

_____ Assessment program

_____ Promotion

_____ Individual employee development objectives

_____ Other

_____ 15. Are the Organization's managers made aware of available training programs?

_____ Yes _____ No

_____ 16. Are employees made aware of available training programs?

_____ Yes _____ No

_____ 17. How are internally conducted training programs obtained? (Check all that apply.)

_____ Purchased from external sources

_____ Developed internally by training professionals

_____ Developed internally by operating departments

_____ Developed externally by consultants

_____ Developed by schools or professional associations

_____ Other

_____ 18. Who conducts internal training programs? (Check all that apply.)

_____ Internal training professionals

_____ Externally contracted people

_____ Internal operating people

_____ Other

_____   19. What types of internal delivery methods are used for training? (Check all that apply.)

       _____ Group training

       _____ Individual coaching

       _____ Individual computer-based training

       _____ Internet or Web-based training

       _____ Rotational job assignments

       _____ Other

_____   20. Does the Organization have the necessary physical facilities dedicated for training?

       _____ Yes   _____ No

_____   21. Does the Organization use external facilities for training?

       _____ Yes   _____ No

_____   22. Are the people who deliver training required to be knowledgeable in the contents of the programs they deliver?

       _____ Yes   _____ No

_____   23. Are the people who deliver training required to have training skills?

       _____ Yes   _____ No

_____   24. Are external seminars and courses considered as training resources?

       _____ Yes   _____ No

_____   25. Is there a single position within the human resources department accountable for maintaining information on external courses and seminars?

       _____ Yes   _____ No

_____   26. If your answer to the previous question was yes, do the Organization employees know who that individual is and/or where the information is available?

                 _____ Yes   _____ No

_____   27. Does the Organization have access to all necessary training delivery equipment such as audiovisual equipment and computers?

                 _____ Yes   _____ No

_____   28. Are the costs of training in each program regularly calculated?

                 _____ Yes   _____ No

_____   29. Are the costs of training charged back to the departments of employees who have been trained?

         _____ Yes   _____ No   _____ Sometimes

_____   30. Is the use of external training resources throughout the Organization coordinated by a position in the human resources department?

                 _____ Yes   _____ No

_____   31. Is a catalog of available Organization training programs published?

                 _____ Yes   _____ No

_____   32. If your answer to the previous question was yes, is the catalog distributed throughout the Organization?

                 _____ Yes   _____ No

_____   33. If your answer to Question 31 was yes, how often is the catalog revised? (Check just one.)

                 _____ Every three months

                 _____ Every six months to one year

_____ Every year

_____ Every one to three years

_____ Whenever requested

_____ Never

_____ Other

_____ 34. Is a catalog of externally available and/or recommended training programs published?

_____ Yes _____ No

_____ 35. If your answer to the previous question was yes, is the catalog distributed throughout the Organization?

_____ Yes _____ No

_____ 36. If your answer to Question 34 was yes, how often is the catalog revised? (Check no more than two.)

_____ Every three months

_____ Every six months to one year

_____ Every year

_____ Every one to three years

_____ Whenever requested

_____ Never

_____ Other

_____ 37. Is a position within human resources accountable for monitoring and maintaining information on developments in the training field?

_____ Yes _____ No

_____   38. If your answer to the previous question was yes, is such informa-
                   tion circulated to training professionals?

                           _____ Yes _____ No

_____   39. Are professional seminars (internal or external) provided to
                   professional trainers to further develop their skills?

                           _____ Yes _____ No

_____   40. Is membership and participation in professional training as-
                   sociations encouraged for the Organization's training profes-
                   sionals?

                           _____ Yes _____ No

_____   41. Is membership in professional training associations paid by the
                   Organization?

                           _____ Yes _____ No

_____   42. Is attendance at professional training conferences paid by the
                   Organization?

                           _____ Yes _____ No

_____   43. Has the possibility of outsourcing part or all of training been
                   considered?

                           _____ Yes _____ No

_____   44. Is there an individual within the human resources department
                   who is available to assist employees in preparing and imple-
                   menting their development plans?

                           _____ Yes _____ No

_____   45. Does the Organization offer a tuition reimbursement program?

                           _____ Yes _____ No

_____ 46. If your answer to the previous question was yes, what items are eligible for reimbursement? (Check all that apply.)

       _____ Tuition

       _____ Books

       _____ Lab fees

       _____ Transportation

       _____ Other

_____ 47. Must the courses or course of study be related to the employee's current job or Organization?

       _____ Yes   _____ No

_____ 48. Is reimbursement based on achieving a certain grade?

       _____ Yes   _____ No

_____ 49. On a scale of one to nine (one being low, five being typical, and nine being high), how do you think the human resources department has performed in this category? _____

_____ 50. On a scale of one to nine (one being low, five being typical, and nine being high), how do you think employees of the human resources department feel the human resources department has performed in this category? _____

_____ 51. On a scale of one to nine (one being low, five being typical, and nine being high), how do you think the clients of the human resources department within the Organization feel the human resources department has performed in this category? _____

EMPLOYEE RELATIONS—INFORMATION GATHERING

The formal policies and procedures governing all conditions of employment, including specific human resources activities not otherwise categorized.

If this category is not one for which your human resources department is accountable, go directly to the next category beginning on page 73.

_____ 1. Is one individual within the human resources department accountable for coordinating all employee relations programs?

_____ Yes _____ No

_____ 2. Have the Organization's employees been told whom that individual is?

_____ Yes _____ No

_____ 3. Are there formal Organizationwide employee relations policies and procedures?

_____ Yes _____ No

_____ 4. If your answer to the previous question was yes, who has a copy of the Organization's formal policies and procedures? (Check all that apply.)

_____ All supervisors

_____ All managers

_____ Human resources

_____ All employees

_____ Other

_____ Individual responsible for employee relations

_____   5. Is there an employee handbook (a book for employees that describes conditions of employment)?

_____ Yes   _____ No

_____   6. If your answer to the previous question was yes, is each employee given the handbook at time of hire?

_____ Yes   _____ No

_____   7. If the Organization issues a handbook to employees, are new pages or a new handbook issued when changes are made?

_____ Yes   _____ No

_____   8. Whether there is an employee handbook or not, for which of the following subjects do new employees receive information? (Check all that apply.)

_____ Organization history

_____ Organization mission

_____ Organization performance objectives and history

_____ Organization financial history

_____ Key people within Organization to contact with questions

_____ Job information

_____ Department information

_____ Rules and regulations

_____ Benefits

_____ Performance reviews

_____ Compensation

_____ Leaving the Organization

_____ Time off

_____ Promotions and transfers

_____ Training and development opportunities

_____ Career opportunities

_____ Other

_____ 9. How often are employee relations policies and procedures reviewed? (Check no more than two.)

_____ At least every six months

_____ Every six months to one year

_____ Every year

_____ Every year to three years

_____ Every three years or more

_____ When requested

_____ When the law requires a change

_____ When the Organization makes a significant change

_____ Never

_____ 10. Are employees supplied (in employee handbooks or otherwise) information about whom to contact in human resources regarding employee relations policies and procedures?

_____ Yes _____ No

_____ 11. Is that information kept current?

_____ Yes _____ No

_____   12. Is there a handbook or other manual for supervisors and managers on how to administer the Organization's policies and procedures?

_____ Yes _____ No

_____   13. If your answer to the previous question was yes, is each supervisor and manager issued a handbook or manual?

_____ Yes _____ No

_____   14. If there is a supervisor/manager handbook or manual, are new pages or a new handbook issued when changes are made?

_____ Yes _____ No

_____   15. Is a file of employee relations decisions for areas not currently covered by established policy and procedure precedents maintained?

_____ Yes _____ No

_____   16. If your answer to the previous question was yes, is that file referred to when employee relations policies and procedures are revised?

_____ Yes _____ No _____ Not applicable

_____   17. Is there an individual within human resources available to counsel employees on personal problems?

_____ Yes _____ No

_____   18. If your answer to the previous question was yes, are employees supplied (in the handbook or otherwise) information on whom that person is and how to contact her?

_____ Yes _____ No

_____   19. If your answer to the previous question was yes, is that information kept current?

_____ Yes _____ No

_____ 20. If your answer to Question 17 was yes, are procedures in place to ensure the confidentiality of employee discussions?

_____ Yes _____ No

_____ 21. If your answer to Question 17 was yes, has the individual conducting the counseling been trained in appropriate techniques?

_____ Yes _____ No

_____ 22. Do new employees receive an orientation program regarding employee relations policies and procedures?

_____ Yes _____ No _____ Sometimes

_____ 23. If your answer to the previous question was yes, when is orientation conducted? (Check just one.)

_____ Prior to hiring

_____ The first day of employment

_____ The first week of employment

_____ The first month of employment

_____ Whenever there are enough new employees

_____ Other

_____ 24. Are exit interviews conducted with or offered to all employees leaving the Organization? (Check just one.)

_____ Conducted _____ Offered _____ No

_____ 25. Does someone within the human resources department conduct the exit interviews?

_____ Yes _____ No

_____ 26. If your answer to Question 24 was yes, to whom is exit interview information sent? (Check all that apply.)

_____ Supervisor of person in position

_____ Manager of supervisor of person in position

_____ Senior human resources manager

_____ Senior manager to whom senior human resources manager reports

_____ Other

_____ 27. Are employee opinion surveys conducted?

_____ Yes _____ No

_____ 28. If your answer to the previous question was yes, how often are employee opinion surveys conducted? (Check just one.)

_____ At least every six months

_____ Every six months to one year

_____ Every year

_____ Every one to three years

_____ Every three years or more

_____ When requested

_____ When a change has been made

_____ Never

_____ 29. If your answer to Question 27 was yes, are the results of employee opinion surveys communicated to employees?

_____ Yes _____ No _____ Sometimes

_____   30. If your answer to Question 27 was yes, who conducts the employee opinion surveys? (Check just one.)

        _____ Someone in human resources

        _____ An external consultant or consulting firm

        _____ Someone from operating management

        _____ Other

_____   31. Is an external employee assistance program, psychological program, or counseling service available for employees?

        _____ Yes _____ No

_____   32. If your answer to the previous question was yes, are employees supplied (in the handbook or otherwise) information on that service and how to contact it?

        _____ Yes _____ No

_____   33. If your answer to the previous question was yes, is that information kept current?

        _____ Yes _____ No

_____   34. If your answer to Question 31 was yes, are procedures in place to ensure the confidentiality of employee discussions?

        _____ Yes _____ No

_____   35. Is there an employee grievance procedure?

        _____ Yes _____ No

_____   36. If your answer to the previous question was yes, is it in writing?

        _____ Yes _____ No

_____ 37. If your answer to the previous question was yes, has the procedure been distributed to all employees?

_____ Yes _____ No

_____ 38. Does the Organization have an open-door policy that allows any employee to talk to any manager within the Organization?

_____ Yes _____ No

_____ 39. If your answer to the previous question was yes, is it in writing?

_____ Yes _____ No _____ Not applicable

_____ 40. If your answer to Question 39 was yes, has it been distributed to all employees?

_____ Yes _____ No _____ Not applicable

_____ 41. If your answer to Question 38 was yes, is the policy followed?

_____ Yes _____ No

_____ 42. Does the Organization have employee behavior rules, guidelines, and regulations?

_____ Yes _____ No

_____ 43. If your answer to the previous question was yes, are they in writing?

_____ Yes _____ No

_____ 44. If your answer to Question 43 was yes, have they been distributed to all employees?

_____ Yes _____ No

_____ 45. Do individual departments have rules, guidelines, and regulations regarding employee behavior?

_____ Yes _____ No

_____   46. If your answer to the previous question was yes, are they in writing?

         _____ Yes   _____ No   _____ Not applicable

_____   47. If your answer to Question 46 was yes, have they been distributed to all employees of the department?

         _____ Yes   _____ No   _____ Not applicable

_____   48. Have individual department rules, guidelines, and regulations been coordinated with Organization rules, guidelines, and regulations?

         _____ Yes   _____ No   _____ Not applicable

_____   49. Does the Organization have a performance improvement and/or disciplinary procedure?

         _____ Yes   _____ No

_____   50. If your answer to the previous question was yes, is it in writing?

         _____ Yes   _____ No

_____   51. If your answer to Question 50 was yes, has it been distributed to all employees?

         _____ Yes   _____ No

_____   52. Does your Organization have a policy regarding termination?

         _____ Yes   _____ No

_____   53. If your answer to the previous question was yes, is that policy in writing?

         _____ Yes   _____ No

_____   54. If your answer to the previous question was yes, has that policy been communicated to all employees?

         _____ Yes   _____ No

_____   55. Has consideration been given to any of the following? (Check all that apply.)

        _____ Flexible hours

        _____ Work at home

        _____ Part-time work

        _____ Job sharing

        _____ Employee wellness program

        _____ Outplacement for terminated employees

        _____ Dress-down days

        _____ Dress code

        _____ Preretirement counseling

        _____ Employment of spouses as a team

        _____ Employment of two people alternately scheduled for one position

_____   56. On a scale of one to nine (one being low, five being typical, and nine being high), how do you think the human resources department has performed in this category? _____

_____   57. On a scale of one to nine (one being low, five being typical, and nine being high), how do you think employees of the human resources department feel the human resources department has performed in this category? _____

_____   58. On a scale of one to nine (one being low, five being typical, and nine being high), how do you think the clients of the human resources department within the Organization feel the human resources department has performed in this category? _____

BENEFITS—INFORMATION GATHERING

The noncash compensation provided to employees of the Organization including, but not limited to, such components as insurances, retirement saving plans, and paid time off, and the systems and support services and communications to successfully deliver the benefits.

If this category is not one for which your human resources department is accountable, go directly to the next category beginning on page 79.

_____   1. Is there a position within the human resources department accountable for the Organization's benefit programs?

                  _____ Yes _____ No

_____   2. Does the Organization have an overall policy regarding benefits?

                  _____ Yes _____ No

_____   3. Is it a published policy?

                  _____ Yes _____ No

_____   4. Are employees supplied (in handbooks or otherwise) information on whom to contact in the human resources department regarding benefits?

                  _____ Yes _____ No

_____   5. Is that information kept current?

                  _____ Yes _____ No

_____   6. Do employees receive descriptions of their benefits at the time of hire?

                  _____ Yes _____ No

_____   7. Is that information kept current?

           _____ Yes   _____ No

_____   8. Are revisions to benefits communicated to employees at the time they occur?

           _____ Yes   _____ No

_____   9. How often are benefits reviewed? (Check no more than two.)

           _____ At least every six months

           _____ Every six months to one year

           _____ Every year

           _____ Every one to three years

           _____ Every three years or more

           _____ When requested

           _____ When there is a necessary change

           _____ Never

_____   10. Are benefit surveys conducted or obtained for the geographic area or industry? (Check just one.)

           _____ Area   _____ Industry   _____ Both

           _____ Neither

_____   11. If your answer to Question 10 was yes, how often are such surveys conducted? (Check just one.)

           _____ Every six months to one year

           _____ Every year

           _____ Every one to three years

_____ Every three years or more

_____ When requested

_____ When there is a necessary change

_____ Never

_____ 12. If your answer to Question 10 was yes, are the results of such surveys communicated to employees?

_____ Yes _____ No

_____ 13. Does the Organization's benefit program agree with its policy?

_____ Yes _____ No

_____ 14. Is there a position in the human resources department or an external firm that maintains current legal information regarding benefits?

_____ Yes _____ No

_____ 15. Is there a position accountable for ensuring all benefit programs meet government requirements?

_____ Yes _____ No

_____ 16. Have studies or surveys been made to determine what type of benefits the Organization's employees want?

_____ Yes _____ No

_____ 17. Has consideration been given to cafeteria benefits?

_____ Yes _____ No

_____ 18. Are the costs of benefits communicated to employees?

_____ Yes _____ No

_____   19. Are mandatory programs such as Social Security and Workers Compensation considered benefits?

_____ Yes   _____ No

_____   20. Have you investigated or considered, or do you offer any of the following? (Check all that apply, but only in one column for each benefit.)

Investigated/
Considered   *Offer*

_____   _____   Organization day care center or assistance

_____   _____   Organization exercise facility or assistance

_____   _____   Organization-dependent day care center or assistance

_____   _____   Paid vacations

_____   _____   Paid time off for illness

_____   _____   Paid time off for personal reasons

_____   _____   Combining of all time off (vacations, sick days, personal days, etc.) into a single employee-controlled bank of days

_____   _____   Portable pension benefits

_____   _____   Financial counseling

_____   _____   Preretirement counseling

_____   _____   Legal assistance

_____   _____   Long-term care benefits

_____ _____ Dress-down days

_____ _____ Short-term disability

_____ _____ Long-term disability

_____ _____ Life insurance

_____ _____ Accidental death and dismember-
ment insurance

_____ _____ Employee contributory retirement
investment program such as a
401k

_____ _____ Employee health insurance

_____ _____ Dependent health insurance

_____ _____ Paid family leave

_____ _____ Dental insurance

_____ _____ Dependent dental insurance

_____ _____ Vision/eyeglasses insurance

_____ _____ Dependent vision/eyeglasses insurance

_____ _____ Prescription drug insurance

_____ _____ Dependent prescription drug insurance

_____ _____ Employee purchase of Organization products/services

_____ 21. Has consideration been given to outsourcing of any or all benefits administration?

_____ Yes _____ No

_____ 22. On a scale of one to nine (one being low, five being typical, and nine being high), how do you think the human resources department has performed in this category? _____

_____ 23. On a scale of one to nine (one being low, five being typical, and nine being high), how do you think employees of the human resources department feel the human resources department has performed in this category? _____

_____ 24. On a scale of one to nine (one being low, five being typical, and nine being high), how do you think the clients of the human resources department within the Organization feel the human resources department has performed in this category? _____

Compensation—Information Gathering

All cash payments to employees and also the systems by which positions are evaluated, salary and wage ranges and bands are determined, and adjustments are made, including commissions, lump sum payments, incentive payments, and bonuses.

If this category is not one for which your human resources department is accountable, go directly to the next category beginning on page 87.

_____ 1. Is there a position within the human resources department accountable for the Organization's compensation program?

_____ Yes _____ No

_____ 2. Does the Organization have an overall policy regarding compensation?

_____ Yes _____ No

_____ 3. Is it a published policy?

_____ Yes _____ No

_____ 4. Are employees supplied (in handbooks or otherwise) information on whom to contact in the human resources department regarding compensation?

_____ Yes _____ No

_____ 5. Is that information kept current?

_____ Yes _____ No

_____ 6. Do employees receive descriptions of the Organization's compensation administration program at the time of hire?

_____ Yes _____ No

_____   7. Is that information kept current?

             _____ Yes   _____ No

_____   8. Are compensation surveys conducted in the geographic area or industry? (Check just one.)

             _____ Area   _____ Industry

             _____ Neither   _____ Both

_____   9. If your answer to the previous question was yes, how often are such compensation surveys conducted? (Check just one.)

             _____ At least every six months

             _____ Every six months to one year

             _____ Every year

             _____ Every one to three years

             _____ Every three years or more

             _____ When requested

             _____ Never

_____   10. If your answer to Question 8 was yes, are the results of such surveys communicated to employees?

             _____ Yes   _____ No

_____   11. Does the Organization's compensation program agree with its policy?

             _____ Yes   _____ No   _____ Not applicable

_____   12. Is there a position in the human resources department that maintains current legal information regarding compensation?

             _____ Yes   _____ No

_____ 13. Is there a position within the human resources department accountable for ensuring all positions are correctly classified as exempt or nonexempt and meeting all other legal requirements for compensation?

_____ Yes _____ No

_____ 14. Is there a formal procedure for evaluating positions?

_____ Yes _____ No

_____ 15. If your answer to the previous question was yes, is the evaluation performed by an individual or a group/committee? (Check just one.)

_____ Individual _____ Group/committee

_____ Other

_____ 16. If your answer to the previous question was individual, who is that individual? (Check just one.)

_____ Position's supervisor

_____ Manager of position's supervisor

_____ Senior manager of department in which position reports

_____ Senior executive of Organization

_____ Position in human resources accountable for compensation

_____ Senior human resources manager

_____ External consultant

_____ Other

_____   17. If your answer to Question 15 was group/committee, who are
                  the members of that group? (Check all that apply.)

                  _____ Position's supervisor

                  _____ Manager of position's supervisor

                  _____ Senior manager of department in which position re-
                            ports

                  _____ Senior executive of Organization

                  _____ Position in human resources accountable for compen-
                            sation

                  _____ Senior human resources manager

                  _____ External consultant

                  _____ Other

_____   18. How often is a position's evaluation reviewed? (Check all that
                  apply.)

                  _____ Whenever a new position description is prepared

                  _____ Once a year

                  _____ Every one to three years

                  _____ Every three years or more

                  _____ When requested by its supervisor

                  _____ When requested by its department manager

                  _____ Never

_____   19. Is every position assigned a wage, wage range, or wage band?

                  _____ Yes   _____ No

_____ 20. If your answer to the previous question was yes, is every employee informed of her or his wage, wage range, or wage band?

_____ Yes _____ No

_____ 21. Is there a formal plan for the regular review of each employee's wages for a possible adjustment?

_____ Yes _____ No

_____ 22. Is the wage review separate from any other performance review?

_____ Yes _____ No

_____ 23. If your answer to the previous question was yes, by how long are wage and performance reviews separated? (Check just one.)

_____ One week to one month

_____ One to two months

_____ Two to three months

_____ Three to six months

_____ More than six months

_____ No separation

_____ 24. Are guidelines provided to supervisors for wage adjustments?

_____ Yes _____ No

_____ 25. Which of the following are considered in developing wage adjustment guidelines? (Check all that apply.)

_____ Inflation/cost of living

_____ Employee performance

_____ Position on wage range or band

_____ Amount and time of last increase

_____ Other

_____   26. Is there a program to ensure internal equity among employees' compensation? (Check just one.)

       _____ Yes   _____ No

       _____ Under special conditions

_____   27. Are wage adjustments allowed outside of the normal period?

       _____ Yes   _____ No   _____ Under special conditions

_____   28. Who initiates and approves an employee's wage adjustment? (Check just one in the Initiates column and all that apply in the Approves column.)

       Initiates   *Approves*

       _____   _____   Employee

       _____   _____   Employee's supervisor

       _____   _____   Manager of employee's supervisor

       _____   _____   Senior manager of employee's department

       _____   _____   Senior executive of Organization

       _____   _____   Individual in human resources accountable for compensation

       _____   _____   Senior human resources manager

       _____   _____   Other

_____   29. Does the Organization have a bonus or gain-sharing program?

       _____ Yes   _____ No

_____ 30. If your answer to the previous question was yes, are the eligibility requirements written and communicated to all employees?

_____ Yes _____ No

_____ 31. If your answer to Question 29 was yes, is the bonus based on performance of the individual, department, or Organization? (Check all that apply.)

_____ Individual _____ Department

_____ Organization _____ None

_____ 32. If your answer to Question 29 was yes, is any portion of the bonus discretionary?

_____ Yes _____ No

_____ 33. If your answer to Question 29 was yes, is there a procedure to ensure the equal treatment of employees with respect to a bonus payment?

_____ Yes _____ No

_____ 34. What types of compensation, in addition to regular wages, gain sharing, and bonuses, has the Organization investigated or considered? (Check all that apply.)

_____ Stock options

_____ Sales commissions

_____ Deferred compensation

_____ Lump sum, single-year wage adjustments

_____ Team or work group compensation

_____ Individual piecework payment

_____ Individual wage adjustment tied to individual performance

_____   35. On a scale of one to nine (one being low, five being typical, and nine being high), how do you think the human resources department has performed in this category? _____

_____   36. On a scale of one to nine (one being low, five being typical, and nine being high), how do you think employees of the human resources department feel the human resources department has performed in this category? _____

_____   37. On a scale of one to nine (one being low, five being typical, and nine being high), how do you think the clients of the human resources department within the Organization feel the human resources department has performed in this category? _____

HUMAN RESOURCES PLANNING—INFORMATION GATHERING

The collection and analysis of data providing long-term (strategic) and short-term (tactical) plans and forecasts to meet the department's and Organization's missions, including such activities as succession planning, leadership development, and recruiting schedules.

If this category is not one for which your human resources department is accountable, go directly to the next category beginning on page 93.

_____ 1. Is there an individual within the human resources department accountable for analyzing the current and projected personnel requirements of the Organization?

_____ Yes _____ No

_____ 2. Does the human resources department produce a projected personnel requirements plan for the Organization?

_____ Yes _____ No

_____ 3. If your answer to the previous question was yes, how often is such a plan prepared? (Check just one.)

_____ Every six months

_____ Every year

_____ Every one to two years

_____ Every three or more years

_____ When requested

_____ 4. If your answer to Question 2 was yes, who supplies information to the human resources department for determining the Organization's projected personnel requirements? (Check all that apply.)

_____ Individual department heads

_____ Human resources

_____ External sources

_____ Senior Organization managers

_____ Consultants

_____ No one

_____ 5. Are the Organization's projected personnel requirements used in planning recruitment activities?

_____ Yes _____ No

_____ 6. Are the Organization's projected personnel requirements used in planning the training and development programs to be offered?

_____ Yes _____ No

_____ 7. Are the Organization's projected personnel requirements coordinated with the Organization's tactical plans?

_____ Yes _____ No

_____ 8. Are the Organization's projected personnel requirements coordinated with the Organization's strategic plans?

_____ Yes _____ No

_____ 9. Are the Organization's projected personnel requirements reflected in the Organization's budget?

_____ Yes _____ No

_____ 10. Does the human resources department produce a management succession chart?

_____ Yes _____ No

_____   11. If your answer to the previous question was yes, how often is the chart prepared? (Check just one.)

_____ Every six months

_____ Every year

_____ Every one to two years

_____ Every three or more years

_____ When requested

_____ Never

_____   12. If your answer to Question 10 was yes, is the management succession chart considered in making promotion decisions?

_____ Yes   _____ No

_____   13. If your answer to Question 10 was yes, who identifies the people to place on the management succession chart? (Check all that apply.)

_____ Individual department heads

_____ Human resources

_____ External sources

_____ Senior Organization managers

_____ External consultants

_____ No one

_____   14. Have replacements been identified for all key positions?

_____ Yes   _____ No

_____ 15. Are replacements for positions considered from functional areas other than that of the position?

                 _____ Yes   _____ No

_____ 16. If an employee is identified as a replacement for another position, is he notified?

                 _____ Yes   _____ No

_____ 17. Are employees identified as replacements for other positions supplied any training and development to prepare them in advance for such positions?

                 _____ Yes   _____ No

_____ 18. Are rotational assignments used to prepare employees identified as replacements for other positions?

                 _____ Yes   _____ No

_____ 19. Are development objectives assigned to individual employees identified as replacements for other positions?

                 _____ Yes   _____ No

_____ 20. Are individual employee career objectives considered in identifying replacement employees?

                 _____ Yes   _____ No

_____ 21. Are tools such as assessment centers used to identify promotional potential?

                 _____ Yes   _____ No

_____ 22. Are human resources department personnel plans an integral part of the Organization's strategic planning process?

                 _____ Yes   _____ No

_____ 23. Is the senior human resources manager involved in the Organization's strategic planning process?

_____ Yes   _____ No

_____ 24. Does the Organization's strategic plan include a section on human resources and/or its projected personnel requirements?

_____ Yes   _____ No

_____ 25. Are human resources personnel plans an integral part of the Organization's tactical planning process?

_____ Yes   _____ No

_____ 26. Is the senior human resources manager involved in the Organization's tactical planning process?

_____ Yes   _____ No

_____ 27. Does the Organization's tactical plan include a section on human resources and/or its projected personnel requirements?

_____ Yes   _____ No

_____ 28. Has the human resources department identified logical job families and/or career paths for developing employees?

_____ Yes   _____ No

_____ 29. If your answer to the previous question was yes, have these job families/career paths been communicated to appropriate employees and candidates?

_____ Yes   _____ No

_____ 30. Does the human resources department provide career-planning assistance to employees?

_____ Yes   _____ No

_____   31. Is a representative of human resources involved in any merger or acquisition consideration and/or analysis?

_____ Yes _____ No _____ Not applicable

_____   32. On a scale of one to nine (one being low, five being typical, and nine being high), how do you think the human resources department has performed in this category? _____

_____   33. On a scale of one to nine (one being low,; five being typical, and nine being high), how do you think employees of the human resources department feel the human resources department has performed in this category? _____

_____   34. On a scale of one to nine (one being low, five being typical, and nine being high), how do you think the clients of the human resources department within the Organization feel the human resources department has performed in this category? _____

Organization Development— Information Gathering

Improving communication and understanding in the Organization in order to produce effective, functioning management and employee teams; establishing or changing to a desired culture; responding to changing conditions; and analyzing and influencing Organization personnel, systems, structures, policies, and rewards to ensure synergy and maximize internal consistency.

If this category is not one for which your human resources department is accountable, go directly to the next category beginning on page 103.

_____ 1. Is there an individual within the human resources department accountable for coordinating the Organization development activities of the Organization?

_____ Yes _____ No

_____ 2. Does an individual within the human resources department continually review current trends and techniques of Organization development?

_____ Yes _____ No

_____ 3. Has the Organization identified a desired culture?

_____ Yes _____ No

_____ 4. If your answer to the previous question was yes, is it in writing?

_____ Yes _____ No

_____ 5. If your answer to Question 3 was yes, has it been communicated to the Organization's managers?

_____ Yes _____ No

_____ 6. Is there a consistent culture throughout the Organization?

_____ Yes _____ No

_____ 7. Has the Organization attained its desired culture?

_____ Yes _____ No

_____ 8. If your answer to the previous question was no, have actions been taken to attain the desired culture in all Organization areas?

_____ Yes _____ No

_____ 9. Does the Organization have a philosophy of Organization structure?

_____ Yes _____ No

_____ 10. If your answer to the previous question was yes, is it in writing?

_____ Yes _____ No

_____ 11. If your answer to Question 9 was yes, has it been communicated to the Organization's managers?

_____ Yes _____ No

_____ 12. Is there a consistent Organization structure throughout the Organization?

_____ Yes _____ No

_____ 13. Does the human resources department provide expertise in ensuring the Organization's structures agree with its philosophy?

_____ Yes _____ No

_____ 14. If your answer to the previous question was no, have actions been taken to attain the desired Organization structure in all Organization areas?

_____ Yes _____ No

15. Are Organization development considerations a part of the Organization's strategic planning process?

_____ Yes _____ No

16. Are Organization development considerations a part of the Organization's tactical planning process?

_____ Yes _____ No

17. Are proposed Organization changes reviewed with respect to the desired culture and Organization structure?

_____ Yes _____ No

18. Are surveys and analysis conducted of the Organization structure and its effectiveness?

_____ Yes _____ No

19. If your answer to the previous question was yes, how frequently are they conducted? (Check no more than two.)

_____ Every six months

_____ Every year

_____ Every one to two years

_____ Every three or more years

_____ When requested

_____ When there is a significant change impacting the Organization

_____ When an Organization structure problem is identified

_____ Never

_____   20. Are surveys and analyses of the Organization's culture and its effectiveness conducted?

_____ Yes   _____ No

_____   21. If your answer to the previous question was yes, how frequently are they conducted? (Check no more than two.)

_____ Every six months

_____ Every year

_____ Every one to two years

_____ Every three or more years

_____ When requested

_____ When there is a significant change impacting the Organization

_____ When a culture problem is identified

_____ Never

_____   22. Is training provided for managers and supervisors in Organization effectiveness?

_____ Yes   _____ No

_____   23. Is communication within the Organization regularly reviewed to determine its relationship to the desired Organization structure and culture?

_____ Yes   _____ No

_____   24. In planning communication to employees is someone from Organization development allowed to review it?

_____ Yes   _____ No

_____ 25. Are procedures in place to identify and resolve any Organization conflicts among departments?

_____ Yes _____ No

_____ 26. Has training in how to prepare for and conduct effective meetings been provided to the Organization's managers?

_____ Yes _____ No

_____ 27. Have the frequency and quality of the Organization meetings been analyzed? (Check just one.)

_____ Frequency _____ Quality

_____ Both _____ Neither

_____ 28. Have employees been trained in the effective use of voice mail and e-mail?

_____ Yes _____ No

_____ 29. Do the ways employees use voice mail and e-mail support the Organization's desired culture?

_____ Yes _____ No

_____ 30. Is there an Organization policy regarding personal use of e-mails and the Internet?

_____ Yes _____ No _____ Do not know

_____ 31. If your answer to the previous question was yes, is that policy in writing?

_____ Yes _____ No

_____ 32. If your answer to Question 30 was yes, has the e-mail and voice mail policy been communicated to all employees?

_____ Yes _____ No

————————   33. Have facilities such as lunchrooms, parking places, and offices been reviewed in terms of the desired culture?

—————— Yes   —————— No

————————   34. Are proposed changes in conditions of employment reviewed in terms of the desired culture prior to implementing them?

—————— Yes   —————— No

————————   35. Are Organization and/or department meetings of employees encouraged?

—————— Yes   —————— No

————————   36. Have departments been encouraged to identify their internal and external customers?

—————— Yes   —————— No

————————   37. Does the Organization believe in providing quality customer service to both internal and external customers?

—————— Yes   —————— No

————————   38. Have employees been provided training in improving the quality of customer service?

—————— Yes   —————— No

————————   39. If the Organization provides parking, are any of the spaces identified for specific groups or types of individuals?

—————— Yes   —————— No

————————   40. If your answer to the previous question was yes, for whom are spaces identified? (Check all that apply.)

—————— All employees

—————— Senior managers of the Organization

_____ All managers of the Organization

_____ Employee of the month

_____ Visitors

_____ Employees frequently visiting the facility during the day such as messengers

_____ Employees with disadvantages such as impaired mobility

_____ Other

_____   41. If you identified one or more groups of employees for the previous question, which group(s) has significantly better parking space? (Check all that apply.)

_____ All employees

_____ Senior managers of the Organization

_____ All managers of the Organization

_____ Employee of the month

_____ Visitors

_____ Employees frequently visiting the facility during the day such as messengers

_____ Employees with disadvantages such as impaired mobility

_____ Other

_____   42. If your answer to Question 39 was yes, which group(s) is assigned the spaces closest to the building's entrance? (Check all that apply.)

_____ Senior managers of the Organization

_____ All managers of the Organization

_____ Employee of the month

_____ Visitors

_____ Employees frequently visiting the facility during the day such as messengers

_____ Employees with disadvantages such as impaired mobility

_____ Other

_____ 43. Does the Organization have a code of business conduct?

_____ Yes _____ No

_____ 44. If your answer to the previous question was yes, which of the following are required to sign it? (Check all that apply.)

_____ All employees

_____ All managers

_____ Senior managers of the Organization

_____ Nonemployees doing business with the Organization who work on its premises

_____ Other

_____ 45. If you identified any group in the previous question, when are they required to sign the code of business conduct?

_____

_____

_____ 46. If you answered the previous question with a time, are the people ever asked to re-sign the agreement?

_____ Yes _____ No

_____ 47. Is training offered to employees in how to deal positively with change?

_____ Yes _____ No

_____ 48. Is assistance provided to the Organization in analyzing the effectiveness of work teams?

_____ Yes _____ No

_____ 49. Is training provided for the improvement of team performance?

_____ Yes _____ No

_____ 50. On a scale of one to nine (one being low, five being typical, and nine being high), how do you think the human resources department has performed in this category? _____

_____ 51. On a scale of one to nine (one being low, five being typical, and nine being high), how do you think employees of the human resources department feel the human resources department has performed in this category? _____

_____ 52. On a scale of one to nine (one being low, five being typical, and nine being high), how do you think the clients of the human resources department within the Organization feel the human resources department has performed in this category? _____

Diversity and Equal Employment Opportunity—Information Gathering

Developing and implementing workforce programs to maximize employment of productive people with different characteristics, qualifications, and talents while recognizing the legal requirements and social responsibilities of equal treatment for all employees and the actions necessary to ensure those requirements are met.

If this category is not one for which your human resources department is accountable, go directly to the next category beginning on page 111.

_____ 1. Is there an individual within the human resources department accountable for ensuring the Organization fulfills all equal employment laws and regulations?

_____ Yes _____ No

_____ 2. Does the Organization have an equal employment opportunity policy?

_____ Yes _____ No

_____ 3. If your answer to the previous question was yes, is that policy in writing?

_____ Yes _____ No

_____ 4. If your answer to Question 2 was yes, has that policy been distributed or communicated to all employees?

_____ Yes _____ No

_____ 5. Have all supervisors and managers been trained in the proper implementation of the Organization's equal employment opportunity policy?

_____ Yes _____ No

———————— 6. Does the Organization have a grievance procedure for employees to redress perceived violations of the Organization's equal employment opportunity policy?

————— Yes ————— No

———————— 7. If your answer to the previous question was yes, is that procedure in writing?

————— Yes ————— No

———————— 8. If your answer to Question 6 was yes, has the equal employment opportunity policy been communicated to all employees?

————— Yes ————— No

———————— 9. Have all supervisors and managers been trained in the proper implementation of the Organization's equal employment grievance procedure?

————— Yes ————— No

———————— 10. Are employee equal opportunity employment grievances researched to obtain the facts of the situation?

————— Yes ————— No

———————— 11. If your answer to the previous question was yes, are the results of such research communicated to the grieving employee?

————— Yes ————— No

———————— 12. Does the employee have the ability to appeal a determination regarding her or his equal employment opportunity grievance?

————— Yes ————— No

———————— 13. Are equal employment opportunity grieving employees ensured of no retribution for filing a grievance?

————— Yes ————— No

_____   14. Does the Organization have a sexual harassment policy?

                _____ Yes   _____ No

_____   15. If your answer to the previous question was yes, is that policy in writing?

                _____ Yes   _____ No

_____   16. If your answer to Question 14 was yes, has that policy been distributed or communicated to all employees?

                _____ Yes   _____ No

_____   17. Have all supervisors and managers been trained in the proper implementation of the Organization's sexual harassment policy?

                _____ Yes   _____ No

_____   18. Does the Organization have a procedure for employees to redress perceived violations of the Organization's sexual harassment policy?

                _____ Yes   _____ No

_____   19. If your answer to the previous question was yes, is that procedure in writing?

                _____ Yes   _____ No

_____   20. If your answer to Question 18 was yes, has that procedure been communicated to all employees?

                _____ Yes   _____ No

_____   21. Have all supervisors and managers been trained in the proper implementation of the Organization's sexual harassment grievance procedure?

                _____ Yes   _____ No

22. Are employee sexual harassment grievances researched to obtain the facts of the situation?

_____ Yes _____ No

23. If your answer to the previous question was yes, are the results of such research communicated to the grieving employee?

_____ Yes _____ No

24. Does the employee have the ability to appeal a determination regarding her or his sexual harassment grievance?

_____ Yes _____ No

25. Are sexual harassment grieving employees ensured of no retribution for filing a grievance?

_____ Yes _____ No

26. Have supervisors and managers been trained in what constitutes sexual harassment?

_____ Yes _____ No

27. Have nonmanagement employees been trained in what constitutes sexual harassment, the Organization's sexual harassment policy, and the grievance procedure?

_____ Yes _____ No

28. Do all of the Organization's advertisements for employment identify the Organization as an equal opportunity employer?

_____ Yes _____ No

29. Have all search firms and employment agencies used by the Organization been informed in writing that the Organization is an equal opportunity employer?

_____ Yes _____ No

_____ 30. Have all required equal opportunity posters been prominently displayed for all employees and candidates to see?

_____ Yes _____ No

_____ 31. Have all required sexual harassment posters been prominently displayed for all employees and candidates to see?

_____ Yes _____ No

_____ 32. Have employee opinions on equal employment opportunity and sexual harassment been surveyed separately or as a part of a general employee opinion survey?

_____ Yes _____ No

_____ Do not survey such information

_____ 33. If your answer to the previous question was yes, how frequently are these surveys conducted? (Check no more than two.)

_____ Every six months

_____ Every year

_____ Every one to two years

_____ Every three or more years

_____ When requested

_____ Never

_____ 34. Are employment statistics regularly reviewed to determine if there are any areas of seemingly unequal treatment?

_____ Yes _____ No

_____ 35. Have all selection devices (tests, interviews, etc.) been reviewed to ensure they are job-related, valid, and nondiscriminatory?

_____ Yes _____ No _____ Not applicable

_____   36. Has the employment application form been reviewed to ensure it is job-related, valid, legal, and nondiscriminatory?

_____ Yes _____ No

_____   37. Are employee transfer, assignment, demotion, termination, and promotion decisions reviewed to ensure they are nondiscriminatory?

_____ Yes _____ No

_____   38. Are reports on compliance with equal employment and sexual harassment policies and grievance procedures regularly supplied to senior managers of the Organization?

_____ Yes _____ No

_____   39. Does the Organization accommodate disadvantaged and/or disabled people whenever possible?

_____ Yes _____ No

_____   40. Do the Organization's facilities meet requirements for disadvantaged employees and visitors?

_____ Yes _____ No

_____   41. Does the Organization have continuous access to internal and/or external legal counsel for sexual harassment and equal employment compliance? (Check just one.)

_____ External legal counsel

_____ Internal legal counsel

_____ Both _____ Neither

_____   42. Is the legal counsel utilized for sexual harassment and equal employment compliance a specialist in these areas?

_____ Yes _____ No

_____   43. On a scale of one to nine (one being low, five being typical, and nine being high), how do you think the human resources department has performed in this category? _____

_____   44. On a scale of one to nine (one being low, five being typical, and nine being high), how do you think employees of the human resources department feel the human resources department has performed in this category? _____

_____   45. On a scale of one to nine (one being low, five being typical, and nine being high), how do you think the clients of the human resources department within the Organization feel the human resources department has performed in this category? _____

SAFETY AND ENVIRONMENT—
INFORMATION GATHERING

The training, communication, and leadership required to provide a safe working environment; to provide an appropriate level of employee involvement and responsibility for implementing safe practices, using safety equipment, and complying with Organization safety rules and practices; and to ensure that federal, state, and local safety and environmental requirements are met.

    If this category is not one for which your human resources department is accountable, go directly to the next category beginning on page 119.

_____   1. Is there an individual within the human resources department accountable for ensuring the safety of employees and for fulfilling safety laws and regulations?

                               _____ Yes   _____ No

_____   2. Does the Organization have a policy regarding safety and environmental conditions?

                                 _____ Yes   _____ No

_____   3. If your answer to the previous question was yes, is that policy in writing?

                                 _____ Yes   _____ No

_____   4. If your answer to Question 2 was yes, has that policy been communicated to all employees?

                                 _____ Yes   _____ No

_____   5. Are records maintained on the number of accidents, days lost due to accidents, first aid visits, and alleged accidents?

                                 _____ Yes   _____ No

_____   6. Are regular reports prepared on accident severity and fre-
                 quency?

                         _____ Yes _____ No

_____   7. If your answer to the previous question was yes, to whom are
                 such reports sent? (Check all that apply.)

                         _____ Individual department heads

                         _____ Human resources

                         _____ External sources

                         _____ Senior Organization managers

                         _____ External consultants

                         _____ No one

_____   8. Do bulletin boards have posted all required legal safety and en-
                 vironmental notices?

                         _____ Yes _____ No

_____   9. Do you have a safety committee?

                         _____ Yes _____ No

_____   10. If your answer to Question 9 was yes, who are the members of
                 the safety committee? (Check all that apply.)

                         _____ Individual department employees

                         _____ Individual department supervisors and managers

                         _____ Human resources employees

                         _____ External sources such as insurance carrier representa-
                                   tives

                         _____ Senior Organization managers

_____ External consultants

_____ Other

_____   11. Are safety and environmental inspections conducted on a regular basis?

        _____ Yes _____ No

_____   12. If your answer to the previous question was yes, how often are they conducted? (Check all that apply.)

        _____ Every month

        _____ Every six months

        _____ At least once a year

        _____ Every year or more

        _____ When requested

        _____ Whenever an accident occurs

        _____ Whenever required by the government

_____   13. If your answer to Question 11 was yes, who conducts the inspections? (Check all that apply.)

        _____ Individual department employees

        _____ Individual department heads

        _____ Human resources

        _____ External sources such as insurance carrier representatives

        _____ Senior Organization managers

        _____ External consultants

_____   14. Are reports of safety and environmental inspections issued?

        _____ Yes _____ No

_____   15. If your answer to the previous question was yes, to whom are such reports sent? (Check all that apply.)

        _____ Department employees

        _____ Department heads

        _____ Human resources

        _____ External sources such as insurance companies

        _____ Senior Organization managers

        _____ External consultants

        _____ No one

_____   16. Have the Organization's supervisors and managers been trained in safety and environmental regulations and practices?

        _____ Yes _____ No

_____   17. Is a person trained in first aid available on Organization premises?

        _____ Yes _____ No

_____   18. If your answer to the previous question was yes, when is first aid available? (Check just one.)

        _____ Whenever employees are working

        _____ During normal business hours including scheduled overtime

        _____ During normal business hours excluding scheduled overtime

        _____ At specified times during the day or week

        _____ At nonscheduled times

_____ 19. Is there a supply of first aid materials available in all work areas?

_____ Yes _____ No

_____ 20. If your answer to the previous question was yes, have all employees been informed as to its location?

_____ Yes _____ No

_____ 21. If your answer to Question 17 was yes, has a competent professional identified what supplies should be available?

_____ Yes _____ No

_____ 22. If your answer to Question 19 was yes, are the supplies regularly checked to ensure they are all there and current?

_____ Yes _____ No

_____ 23. Have managers and supervisors been trained in what actions to take in case of an accident?

_____ Yes _____ No

_____ 24. Has a hospital been identified to use in case of an accident?

_____ Yes _____ No

_____ 25. Are a hospital's telephone number and location posted and available for all employees?

_____ Yes _____ No

_____ 26. Has an ambulance service or other transportation for use in case of an accident been identified?

_____ Yes _____ No

_____ 27. Has a physician been identified for notification in case of an accident?

_____ Yes _____ No

_____ 28. Is a physician's telephone number posted and available for all employees?

_____ Yes _____ No

_____ 29. Is insurance information for treatment of an injured employee available for the hospital, doctor, and ambulance?

_____ Yes _____ No

_____ 30. Are all plans for new and refurbished facilities reviewed for safety and environmental compliance before construction?

_____ Yes _____ No

_____ 31. Are all new and refurbished facilities inspected for safety and environmental compliance before being occupied?

_____ Yes _____ No

_____ 32. Are all new and repaired equipment inspected for safety and environmental compliance prior to being put into use?

_____ Yes _____ No

_____ 33. Does the individual accountable for safety have the authority to immediately, without other approvals, stop any unsafe or environment-harming action or activity?

_____ Yes _____ No

_____ 34. Are accidents immediately investigated?

_____ Yes _____ No

_____ 35. Are accident statistics collected and analyzed by department or work group?

_____ Yes _____ No

_____ 36. Are Organization accident statistics compared with statistics from similar industries and companies in the same geographic area?

_____ Yes _____ No

_____ 37. Does the Organization have its environment (light, sound, air, and other) inspected for compliance with legal levels and good working conditions?

_____ Yes _____ No

_____ 38. If your answer to the previous question was yes, how often are environmental inspections conducted? (Check no more than two.)

_____ Every month

_____ Every six months

_____ At least once a year

_____ Whenever there are changes to the operations

_____ 39. Have individual employees been trained in what to do in case of an accident?

_____ Yes _____ No

_____ 40. Is there an individual within the human resources department or an external service accountable for staying current with appropriate safety and environmental legislation and trends?

_____ Yes _____ No

_____ 41. Is the Organization's Workers Compensation insurance carrier utilized for assistance in maintaining a safe and healthy workplace?

_____ Yes _____ No

_____ 42. Does the Organization make available individual safety equipment such as safety shoes and glasses, make partial payment for such items, or make arrangements for discounts on purchase of such items? (Check just one.)

_____ Provides   _____ Partial payment

_____ Discounts   _____ No action

_____ 43. Has consideration been given to the safety of employees working at home?

_____ Yes _____ No

_____ 44. On a scale of one to nine (one being low, five being typical, and nine being high), how do you think the human resources department has performed in this category? _____

_____ 45. On a scale of one to nine (one being low, five being typical, and nine being high), how do you think employees of the human resources department feel the human resources department has performed in this category? _____

_____ 46. On a scale of one to nine (one being low, five being typical, and nine being high), how do you think the clients of the human resources department within the Organization feel the human resources department has performed in this category? _____

Security—Information Gathering

Maintaining and protecting the Organization's employees, assets, and human resources documents, information, and facilities.

If this category is not one for which your human resources department is accountable, go directly to the next category beginning on page 125.

_____ 1. Is there an individual within the human resources department accountable for the Organization's security program?

_____ Yes _____ No

_____ 2. Is entrance to all Organization facilities controlled?

_____ Yes _____ No

_____ 3. Is a record of all nonemployees entering or requesting permission to enter Organization facilities maintained?

_____ Yes _____ No

_____ 4. Are employees required to have identification cards or badges?

_____ Yes _____ No

_____ 5. If your answer to the previous question was yes, do the identification cards or badges include photographs?

_____ Yes _____ No

_____ 6. Are employees allowed to be on Organization premises without identification?

_____ Yes _____ No

_____ 7. Are employee IDs collected at termination and is access ability terminated?

_____ Yes _____ No

_____   8. Are visitors required to have identification?

                    _____ Yes _____ No

_____   9. Is a procedure in place for what to do in case of a person enter-
                 ing the Organization's facilities without permission?

                    _____ Yes _____ No

_____   10. If your answer to the previous question was yes, have supervisors
                 and managers been trained in what to do in case of a person
                 entering the Organization's facilities without permission?

                    _____ Yes _____ No

_____   11. Have the local police visited the Organization's facilities to re-
                 view security and establish procedures in case of an emergency?

                    _____ Yes _____ No

_____   12. Has the local fire department visited the Organization's facili-
                 ties to review fire prevention conditions and establish proce-
                 dures in case of a fire?

                    _____ Yes _____ No

_____   13. Does the Organization have a procedure for evacuating the
                 premises in case of a fire or other emergency?

                    _____ Yes _____ No

_____   14. Have the Organization's managers been trained in what to do
                 in case of a fire or an emergency?

                    _____ Yes _____ No

_____   15. Has the Organization conducted a fire drill?

                    _____ Yes _____ No

_____ 16. Is the Organization's fire fighting equipment checked for working conditions on a regular basis?

_____ Yes _____ No

_____ 17. Have the appropriate employees (managers, switchboard operators, receptionists) been trained in what to do in case of a bomb scare or other threat?

_____ Yes _____ No

_____ 18. Have procedures been established with the local fire department in case it is called?

_____ Yes _____ No

_____ 19. Is there a security system or personnel in place when the facilities are closed?

_____ Yes _____ No

_____ 20. Have appropriate managers to contact in case of an emergency been identified?

_____ Yes _____ No

_____ 21. If your answer to the previous question was yes, are their telephone numbers available to all employees and to the police and the fire department?

_____ Yes _____ No

_____ 22. Is access to all employee records controlled?

_____ Yes _____ No

_____ 23. Are employee records maintained in locked files?

_____ Yes _____ No

_____   24. Are people eligible to review employee records required to sign for such records?

_____ Yes   _____ No

_____   25. Are employee records allowed to leave the premises?

_____ Yes   _____ No

_____   26. Are there separate files for general employee information and confidential information?

_____ Yes   _____ No

_____   27. Are security systems regularly reviewed?

_____ Yes   _____ No

_____   28. If your answer to the previous question was yes, how often are they reviewed? (Check no more than two.)

_____ Every month

_____ Every six months

_____ At least once a year

_____ Every year or more

_____ When requested

_____ Whenever there is a security breach

_____ Whenever required by the government

_____   29. Does the Organization have a confidentiality agreement?

_____ Yes   _____ No

_____ 30. If your answer to the previous question was yes, are any of the following required to sign it? (Check all that apply.)

    _____ All nonmanagement employees

    _____ All managers other than senior managers

    _____ Senior managers of the Organization

    _____ All employees who have access to confidential information

    _____ External people doing business with the Organization who have access to confidential information

    _____ Other

_____ 31. If you identified any group in the previous question, when are they required to sign the confidentiality agreement? (List all that apply.)

_____

_____

_____

_____

_____ 32. If you answered the previous question with a time, are the people ever asked to re-sign the agreement?

    _____ Yes   _____ No

_____ 33. Has consideration been given to outsourcing any or all security activities?

    _____ Yes   _____ No

_____ 34. Does the Organization have a policy on who can provide reference checks on former employees and what information can be provided?

    _____ Yes   _____ No

_____ 35. Are all managers aware of the reference check policy?

    _____ Yes _____ No _____ Not applicable

_____ 36. Who has the authority to provide reference checks for former employees? (Check all that apply.)

    _____ Former employee's supervisor

    _____ Manager of the former employee's supervisor

    _____ Someone in human resources

    _____ No one

_____ 37. Is there a procedure requiring proper authorization for the removal and return of any Organization property from the premises?
    _____ Yes _____ No

_____ 38. Is there a procedure for ensuring the confidentiality and security of any information or equipment taken off the Organization's premises?

    _____ Yes _____ No

_____ 39. On a scale of one to nine (one being low, five being typical, and nine being high), how do you think the human resources department has performed in this category? _____

_____ 40. On a scale of one to nine (one being low, five being typical, and nine being high), how do you think the employees of the human resources department feel the human resources department has performed in this category? _____

_____ 41. On a scale of one to nine (one being low, five being typical, and nine being high), how do you think the clients of the human resources department within the Organization feel the human resources department has performed in this category? _____

EQUIPMENT AND FACILITIES—INFORMATION GATHERING

Providing the necessary equipment and facilities to fulfill the human resources mission and provide optimum service to the Organization.

If this category is not one for which your human resources department is accountable, go directly to the next category beginning on page 129.

_____ 1. Have the physical facilities of the human resources department been designed for the work it is to accomplish and the number of people involved?

_____ Yes _____ No

_____ 2. Are private areas available for interviews and employee consultations?

_____ Yes _____ No

_____ 3. Is the human resources area convenient to employees?

_____ Yes _____ No

_____ 4. Has an area been allocated for the reception of job candidates?

_____ Yes _____ No

_____ 5. If your answer to the previous question was yes, is there a space with tables or desks for completion of applications?

_____ Yes _____ No _____ Not applicable

_____ 6. Is there a bulletin board in the area used for receiving candidates that contains all legal and other employment notices?

_____ Yes _____ No

_____ 7. Do the environmental conditions of the human resources area (heat, light, and sound) support employee comfort and the work of the department?

_____ Yes _____ No

_____ 8. Are all supplies required by the human resources department stored in the area and easily accessed by human resources department employees?

_____ Yes _____ No

_____ 9. Is one individual accountable for maintaining adequate human resources department supply inventory levels?

_____ Yes _____ No

_____ 10. Is there a meeting room available in the area for human resources department use?

_____ Yes _____ No

_____ 11. Which of the following equipment has been considered and/or is available? (Check only one column for each item.)

Considered *Available*

_____ _____ Fax

_____ _____ Photocopier

_____ _____ Individual desk PCs

_____ _____ Individual laptop PCs

_____ _____ Telephone voice mail

_____ _____ Central department telephone number

_____ _____ Employee beepers

_____ _____ Cellular or digital telephones

_____ 12. If there is a fax, is it used exclusively by human resources?

_____ Yes _____ No

_____ 13. If there is a department computer printer, is it in a secure location within the human resources department?

_____ Yes _____ No

_____ 14. Is mail addressed to the human resources department opened in a central mail-receiving area before delivery?

_____ Yes _____ No

_____ 15. Does outgoing mail from the human resources department leave the department in sealed envelopes?

_____ Yes _____ No

_____ 16. Does each human resources department employee have a separate telephone and number?

_____ Yes _____ No

_____ 17. If there is voice mail, have human resources department employees been instructed to answer their telephones except when in meetings or away?

_____ Yes _____ No

_____ 18. If there is voice mail, do messages include how to reach a live person?

_____ Yes _____ No

_____ 19. Is there a policy regarding equipment for employees who work at home?

_____ Yes _____ No _____ Not applicable

_____   20. If your answer to the previous question was yes, is there a written procedure on how the policy is to be implemented?

_____ Yes   _____ No   _____ Not applicable

_____   21. On a scale of one to nine (one being low, five being typical, and nine being high), how do you think the human resources department has performed in this category? _____

_____   22. On a scale of one to nine (one being low, five being typical, and nine being high), how do you think employees of the human resources department feel the human resources department has performed in this category? _____

_____   23. On a scale of one to nine (one being low, five being typical, and nine being high), how do you think the clients of the human resources department within the Organization feel the human resources department has performed in this category? _____

Documentation and Information Systems— Information Gathering

Preparing, storing, and maintaining employee records and information, including computerized human resources information systems, and meeting federal, state, and local requirements.

If this category is not one for which your human resources department is accountable, go directly to the next category beginning on page 135.

_____ 1. Is there an individual within the human resources department accountable for ensuring employee documentation meets all legal requirements?

_____ Yes _____ No

_____ 2. Has employee documentation been reviewed to ensure individual privacy rights are not violated?

_____ Yes _____ No

_____ 3. Is an individual allowed to review all documentation regarding him?

_____ Yes _____ No _____ Not applicable

_____ 4. If your answer to the previous question was no, is there an identified reason for not allowing full employee review?

_____ Yes _____ No

_____ 5. Which employee notifications for poor or otherwise unacceptable performance are kept in a confidential file—current performance data and/or past performance data? (Check just one.)

_____ Current _____ Past _____ Neither

_____ 6. Are employee reference checks kept in a separate file?

_____ Yes _____ No _____ Not applicable

129

_____   7. Are employee test results and medical information kept in a separate restricted file?

_____ Yes   _____ No   _____ Not applicable

_____   8. Which of the following employee statistics are regularly calculated? (Check all that apply.)

_____ Employee turnover

_____ Employee absences

_____ Employee lateness

_____ Employee first aid visits

_____ Training costs

_____ Employee accident frequency

_____ Employee accident severity

_____ Employee accident lost time

_____ Employee benefit costs

_____ Employee productivity

_____ Average compensation increases

_____ Recruiting cost per employee hired

_____ Average benefit cost per employee

_____ Other

_____   9. How often are such reports calculated? (Check no more than two.)

_____ Every month

_____ Every three months

_____ Every six months

_____ At least once a year

_____ Every year or more

_____ When requested

_____ Whenever required by the government

_____ Never

_____ 10. To whom are such reports sent? (Check all that apply.)

_____ Individual department heads

_____ Human resources

_____ External sources such as insurance companies

_____ Senior company managers

_____ Consultants

_____ No one

_____ 11. Does someone within the human resources department analyze such statistics?

_____ Yes _____ No

_____ 12. Is there a formal human resources information system that maintains all employee information?

_____ Yes _____ No

_____ 13. Is employee information computerized?

_____ Yes _____ No

_____ 14. Is access to the human resources information system controlled?

_____ Yes _____ No

_____ 15. If an employee with access to the human resources information system leaves the department, is that individual's access canceled, voided, or terminated?

_____ Yes _____ No

_____ 16. If your answer to the previous question was yes, is the system run on a department PC or on a mainframe, network, or server located outside the department? (Check just one.)

_____ Department PC

_____ Mainframe, network, or server located outside the human resources department

_____ 17. If your answer to the previous question was outside the department, is the system protected so that only qualified human resources personnel may access it?

_____ Yes _____ No

_____ 18. If your answer to Question 13 was no, has the possibility of using a computerized system been considered?

_____ Yes _____ No

_____ 19. Is there a procedure for updating employee information?

_____ Yes _____ No

_____ 20. How frequently are employees requested to update their personal information? (Check just one.)

_____ Every month

_____ Every six months

_____ At least once a year

_____ Every year or more

_____ Never

_____ 21. Are comparisons of employee statistics made with similar companies or other companies in the area?

_____ Yes _____ No

_____ 22. If your answer to the previous question was yes, does the human resources department conduct any analyses of differences?

_____ Yes _____ No _____ Not applicable

_____ 23. Has the possibility of outsourcing employee information been considered?

_____ Yes _____ No

_____ 24. On a scale of one to nine (one being low, five being typical, and nine being high), how do you think the human resources department has performed in this category? _____

_____ 25. On a scale of one to nine (one being low, five being typical, and nine being high), how do you think employees of the human resources department feel the human resources department has performed in this category? _____

_____ 26. On a scale of one to nine (one being low, five being typical, and nine being high), how do you think the clients of the human resources department within the Organization feel the human resources department has performed in this category? _____

SUMMARY—INFORMATION GATHERING

You have now answered all the audit's questions in the categories of human resources applicable to your situation. Now, taking what you know of your human resources department and its performance into consideration, answer the following questions.

_____ 1. On a scale of one to nine (one being low, five being typical, and nine being high), how well do you think the human resources department has performed in fulfilling its role and mission in the Organization? _____

_____ 2. On a scale of one to nine (one being low, five being typical, and nine being high), how well do you think the employees of the human resources department feel human resources has performed in fulfilling its role and mission in the Organization? _____

_____ 3. On a scale of one to nine (one being low, five being typical, and nine being high), how well do you think clients of the human resources department within the Organization feel human resources has performed in fulfilling its role and mission in the Organization? _____

STEP TWO—
EVALUATION

You have now completed Step One of the audit process. You have gathered the appropriate information about the human resources department. The next step is to evaluate that information.

To accomplish this you are going to use numerical ratings for your answers. To assist you in understanding the basis for the ratings, a short explanation is provided. However, the purpose of this audit is not to deal with every possible situation and discuss every activity in depth. This is a general audit of the function—an audit designed to identify areas for further consideration and investigation. It is similar to a consultant's first visit, in which an attempt is made to discover in what areas the function appears to be performing well and in what areas it may need improvement.

To determine the correct ratings for each of your answers you need to use two sets of pages at one time (Step One—Information Gathering and Step Two—Evaluation).

For example, the following is the first question in Step One. It is from page 3 of the Department Mission—Information Gathering.

_____   1. Does your Organization have an identical function unit accountable for human resources activities?

_____X_____ Yes   _____ No

Note that the question has been answered "Yes."

The following is the rating for the answer and a brief explanation from page 139 of the Department Mission—Evaluation.

Every Organization has a primary reason for existing—a specific mission to fulfill. This is true whether an Organization is profit making, not-for-profit, or a division of government. To assist in fulfilling its mission, an Organization requires a wide variety of activities—activities devoted to the use of the Organization's assets: people, money, information, supplies, and equipment. In smaller Organizations these activities may be combined, but in midsize and larger Organizations each of these areas requires full-time professionals to produce optimum performance. There are few, if any, Organizations that can successfully fulfill their missions without people, so the functional area devoted to the Organization's people—to obtaining and maintaining qualified people—is of vital importance.

There should be an identified functional unit accountable for the human re-sources activities of the Organization.

<u>   9   </u> Yes   <u>   1   </u> No

Since in our example the answer is "Yes," a 9 has been written on the short line in front of the question in the Department Mission—Information Gathering.

You proceed in this manner for all the Step One questions. Check your answers. Write the appropriate number on the short line preceding the question.

You may disagree with some of the ratings and the basis for them. In fact, you may feel that the exact opposite of a suggested answer is true because of the way your department or Organization operates. In those situations, mark the question with a note by the rating. In Step Three—Analysis, you can make any necessary adjustments. For this evaluation step, just enter the ratings for your answer and identify questions that may require adjustments.

DEPARTMENT MISSION—EVALUATION

If this category is not one for which your human resources department is accountable, go directly to the next category beginning on page 147.

1. Every Organization has a primary reason for existing—a specific mission to fulfill. This is true whether an Organization is profit making, not-for-profit, or a division of government. To assist in fulfilling its mission, an Organization requires various activities, activities devoted to the use of the Organization's assets: people, money, information, supplies, and equipment. In smaller Organizations the accountability for these activities may be combined into a single position, but in midsize and larger Organizations, each of these areas requires full-time professionals to produce optimum performance. There are few, if any, Organizations that can successfully fulfill their missions without people, so the functional area devoted to obtaining and maintaining qualified people is of vital importance. There should be an identified functional unit accountable for the human resources activities of the Organization.

__9__ Yes __1__ No

2. In addition to being an identified functional unit, human resources should be clearly defined as a department or division of the Organization rather than a part of an area dealing with other functional activities.

__9__ Yes __1__ No

3. Just as the Organization as a whole has a primary purpose for its existence—a specific mission—so too should the human resources department. The mission should be written as an unambiguous statement of the overall object or purpose for the human resources department within the Organization. It should be a statement that provides guidance and direction for all human resources activities.

__8__ Yes __1__ No

4. A mission statement that is not published can be subject to many interpretations. To be effective the human resources department mission statement should be written and published; that is, copies should be distributed and avail-

able for use. If you have no mission statement, give yourself 3 points for this question.

___8___ Yes ___1___ No

5. The human resources department mission statement should be communicated to all employees within the department. This communication should be more than just the distribution of the statement. It should include a thorough discussion of its implications for the department's performance. As one Advisory Board member commented, "It is significant when each employee of a human resources department has a copy of the department's mission statement on prominent display and can discuss it intelligently."

___8___ Yes ___1___ No

6. A human resources department mission is important not only to the members of the human resources department but also to the rest of the Organization. The mission provides other employees with a clear statement of the role of human resources. It allows for coordination of the activities of the other functional areas and helps to identify any areas of dual accountability or areas not assigned to any department.

___7___ Yes ___1___ No

7. Our Advisory Board believes a human resources mission statement should be prepared by the senior manager of human resources and other managers of the department. Nonmanagement employees of human resources also can provide input.

Once prepared, the human resources department mission statement should be reviewed by as many other people within the Organization as possible. However, because the senior manager of the human resources department and the other department managers have developed the mission, they have been assigned no points for the review.

The Organization's senior executive and/or the person to whom the human resources senior manager reports should be the one to approve the human resources mission statement. Next, the board of directors and other senior operating managers should approve it.

If you do not prepare or have a mission (answered no to Question 7), give yourself 6 points.

Prepares   *Reviews*   *Approves*

___0___   ___1___   ___3___   Senior executive of the Organization and/or person to whom senior human resources manager reports

0	1	1	Organization's board of directors
2	0	0	Senior human resources manager
2	1	0	Human resources department managers
1	1	0	Human resources nonmanagement employees
1	1	1	Senior managers in other than human resources
0	1	0	Other

8. With new developments in technology, expanding markets, revised government regulations, globalization of trade, and changing customer needs, change is most definitely accelerating external changes, as well as internally inspired changes, requiring an Organization to review its activities and direction continually. Its individual functional areas and departments must do the same. The human resources department should revisit its mission on a regular basis to ensure the department is meeting the needs of the Organization. If you have no mission statement, give yourself 2 points for this question. Otherwise, use the following table to score points.

____4____ Once a year

____6____ Every one to three years

____6____ Every three to five years

____2____ More than every five years

____1____ Never

9 and 10. If the human resources department mission is not coordinated with the mission of the entire Organization, the department may be pursuing an objective that has little to do with or contradicts the mission of the Organization. It is important that the mission of the human resources department be developed in conjunction with the Organization's mission and that there be a clear relationship between the two. The fulfillment of the human resources department mission should contribute directly to the achievement of the Organization's mission.

9. ____9____ Yes ____1____ No

10. ___9___ Yes   ___1___ No

11. This question deals directly with the importance and functionality of the human resources department mission statement. Our Advisory Board feels strongly that the department's mission statement should be regularly used to assist in decisions regarding department operations. If you have no mission statement, give yourself 3 points for this question.

___1___ Never

___3___ Sometimes

___6___ Usually

___8___ Always

12. Because the Advisory Board believes the human resources department mission statement is something to be used on a regular basis, the Board also believes when situations occur that differ or conflict with the mission, either the mission is not being used as a guide, or it is being superseded. In either case (unless there is a compelling reason that requires revision of the mission), any difference is an area of concern for the human resources department. If you have no mission statement, give yourself 3 points for this question.

___8___ Never

___6___ Rarely

___2___ Sometimes

___1___ Often

___1___ Always

13. To be effective, the human resources department mission should be specific, clear, and unambiguous. It should state the relationship between the human resources department and the balance of the Organization, distinguish the activities of the human resources department from those of all other functional areas, and describe the general areas of accountability and performance for human resources. If you have no mission statement, give yourself 3 points for this question.

___8___ Yes   ___1___ No

14. The logical extension of a mission statement is a strategic plan. Although time periods for such plans vary, generally a period of three years or more is considered long-term as opposed to short-term (tactical plans) that cover one to two years. Strategic plans detail the mission statement by providing a delineation of activities for the human resources department that enables it to achieve its mission. Strategic plans provide more detailed directions for the department's operation.

<u>   8   </u> Yes   <u>   2   </u> No

15, 16, and 17. Here the rationale is similar to that used for the questions about the mission statement. The plan should be in writing to ensure a common understanding and eliminate misinterpretation. Likewise, it should be communicated to all human resources department employees along with discussions to ensure complete understanding of contents and impact on department performance. The plan also should be communicated to other employees of the Organization to assist in coordinating the activities of all functional areas and fulfilling the Organization's strategic plans. If you have no strategic plan (answered no to Question 14), give yourself 2 points for each of these questions.

15. <u> 8 </u> Yes <u> 1 </u> No

16. <u> 7 </u> Yes <u> 2 </u> No

17. <u> 6 </u> Yes <u> 3 </u> No

18. Due to the relatively long time horizon of a strategic plan, there is sometimes a tendency to not review performance to the strategic plan. When this occurs the strategic plan ceases to be a useful document. Our Advisory Board believes that the human resources department performance to its strategic plan should be a regular review activity occurring at least annually. If you have no strategic plan (answered no to Question 14), give yourself 2 points for this question.

<u> 4 </u> Every six months

<u> 8 </u> Once a year

<u> 8 </u> Every one to three years

<u> 4 </u> Every three to five years

_____2_____ More than every five years

_____1_____ Never

19. The same review and approval process used for the mission statement is desirable for the strategic plan. The human resources strategic plan should be prepared by the senior manager of human resources and other department managers. Nonmanagement employees of human resources also can provide input.

Once prepared, the human resources department strategic plan should be reviewed by as many other people within the Organization as possible. Because the senior manager of the human resources department and the other department managers have developed the strategic plan, they have been assigned no points for the review.

The Organization's senior executive and/or the person to whom the human resources senior manager reports should be the one to approve the human resources strategic plan. Next the board of directors and other senior operating managers should approve it.

If you do not prepare or have a human resources strategic plan (answered no to Question 14), give yourself 6 points.

Prepares	*Reviews*	*Approves*	
0	1	3	Senior executive of the Organization and/or person to whom senior human resources manager reports
0	1	1	Organization's board of directors
2	0	0	Senior human resources manager
2	1	0	Human resources department managers
1	1	0	Human resources nonmanagement employees
1	1	1	Senior managers in other than human resources
0	1	0	Other

20 and 21. Here again the desired answers are similar to those desired for the human resources department's mission statement. If the human resources

department's strategic plan is not coordinated with the strategic plan of the entire Organization, the department may be pursuing an objective that has little to do with those of the Organization. It is important that the human resources department's strategic plan be developed in conjunction with the Organization's strategic plan. The department's strategic plan should be one part of the Organization's strategic plan. Fulfillment should contribute directly to the achievement of the Organization's strategic plan. If you do not prepare or have a human resources strategic plan (answered no to Question 14), give yourself 3 points for each of these two questions.

20. ____8____ Yes ____1____ No

21. ____8____ Yes ____1____ No

22 and 23. If the human resources department strategic plan is the elaboration of the mission statement, it must both be coordinated with the mission statement and agree with it. Otherwise, the department will only achieve its mission by coincidence. If you do not prepare or have a human resources strategic plan (answered no to Question 14), give yourself 4 points for each of these two questions.

22. ____9____ Yes ____1____ No

23. ____9____ Yes ____1____ No

24, 25, and 26. Whatever number you used to answer each of these questions is the rating for that question.

DEPARTMENT ORGANIZATION—EVALUATION

If this category is not one for which your human resources department is accountable, go directly to the next category beginning on page 161.

1. The first step in department organization is to identify the key result areas for the human resources department (the main activities to be accomplished). These areas should represent activities similar to the categories of this entire human resources audit.

_____9_____ Yes   _____1_____ No

2. Generally, a key result area is assigned to a specific position. However, in some cases more than one position may be accountable for a key result area. For example, two managers might be accountable for the key result area of recruiting—one for university recruiting and the other for all other recruiting. In such a case, it is important that the differences in accountability within the key result area be specified. (This comment refers to different positions and not to a number of people within the same position.) In other cases, a single position may be assigned more than one key result area, such as a manager accountable for both compensation and benefits. The important point is that there is an assigned accountability for all the human resources department's identified key result areas. If the key result areas for human resources have not been identified (that is, you answered no to Question 1), give yourself 1 point for this question.

_____1_____ None

_____2_____ Some

_____3_____ About half

_____7_____ Most

_____9_____ All

3 through 6. In some cases human resources department key result areas may be assigned outside the department. For example, an Organization may assign a portion of benefits administration to another department such as finance,

or a human resources department may be assigned key result areas generally considered to belong to other functional areas of the Organization. Payroll would be an example here. The important point to remember is not that human resources has all key result areas within its department's accountability, but rather that the human resources department be able to control its key result areas; know which of its areas, if any, are assigned to other functional areas or departments; and know why such assignment has occurred. With that knowledge, you will be able to determine whether this is appropriate to the needs of your Organization and properly maintain the ability to meet your mission and fulfill your strategic plan.

3. ____6____ Yes ____1____ No

4. ____8____ Yes ____1____ No ____5____ Not applicable

5. ____8____ Yes ____1____ No ____5____ Not applicable

6. ____8____ Yes ____1____ No ____5____ Not applicable

7. A relatively recent development has been the outsourcing of some human resources department key result areas. Generally this has occurred when the vendor can supply unique skills or provide a lower implementation cost. However, sometimes there have been other considerations in outsourcing, such as improving legal compliance, improving service, and increasing employee assistance. Here the question has been asked in the broadest way. Other questions in the audit address specific activities and categories as possibilities for outsourcing.

Our Advisory Board believes the important point is not whether or not outsourcing is done. The Board believes it is important to consider all alternatives. The points awarded for your answer reflect this thinking.

____6____ Yes ____3____ No

8. If there is a separate functional unit within the Organization identified as being accountable for human resources activities, that unit or department should have a single management position accountable for its activities. Exceptions to this might occur. For example, in some Organizations labor relations may be a separate activity; in others, Organization development may be a separate activity. In those situations, a single management position might not be accountable for all the human resources activities. However, whatever the Organization identifies as its human resources function should be headed by a single management position. In some Organizations the senior manager of human resources may also be

the manager of other activities. For example, a vice president of administration may be the senior manager for both office services and human resources.

_____9_____ Yes _____1_____ No

9 and 10. The management level of the senior human resources manager reveals much about the importance of the function to the Organization. Our Advisory Board believes employees of the Organization are one of its most important assets. Because human resources is such an important function, we believe the senior manager of human resources should report directly to the senior executive of the Organization.

In some traditional line/staff organizations, staff departments may be separated from line departments. In those situations, our Advisory Board believes the senior human resources manager should be on the same level as the senior executive of all other staff departments.

9. _____9_____ Same as senior management positions in other departments

_____6_____ Lower than senior management positions in other departments

_____5_____ Higher than senior management positions in other departments

_____5_____ Nonmanagement levels in our Organization

10. _____8_____ A senior operating management position

_____7_____ A senior staff management position

_____9_____ The senior executive position in the Organization

_____5_____ Other

11 and 12. In addition to assigning key result areas to positions, the assignment of activities and reporting relationships is required. Positions and reporting relationships should be identified and documented. Generally, such documentation takes the form of an Organization chart. However, any form is acceptable if easily understood.

11. _____8_____ Yes _____1_____ No

12. _____7_____ Yes _____2_____ No

13 and 14. The documented Organization structure, whether a chart or other format, is a tool to be used by both human resources department employees

and the balance of the Organization. It is probably of more use to human resources department employees—it specifies who does what and who works for whom. The rest of the Organization can benefit by knowing the same information, but employees also can contact the human resources department and allow the department to direct them to the correct position.

13. ___7___ Yes ___1___ No

14. ___6___ Yes ___3___ No

15. Organizations should be designed around their roles and missions. In the case of a human resources department, the Organization structure should be based on key result areas and not the abilities of existing department employees. Employee abilities should be considered during the staffing process.

___8___ Key result areas ___2___ Employees' abilities ___3___ Other

16. Just as it is important for the Organization and the human resources department to have mission statements, it is also important for each position within the human resources department to have a mission statement or overall objective. A position's mission statement or overall objective should be based on the primary purpose of the position. In most cases, this will be the key result area or portion of a key result area assigned to the position.

___8___ Yes ___2___ No

17. Positions and their missions need to be clearly defined in writing. This allows all parties (supervisor of the position, employee in the position, candidates for the position, etc.) to have a clear understanding of the position's role in the Organization, its reporting relationships, and the mission of the human resources department.

___8___ Yes ___2___ No

18. To be clear and effective, position descriptions need to include certain basic information. Give yourself 2 points for each item you identified as being included in the human resources department position description. Give yourself 4 points total for this question if you do not have position descriptions.

___2___ Position title

___2___ Department

___2___ Reporting relationships

___2___ Responsibilities or tasks

___2___ Authorities

___2___ Competencies or requirements

19. One of the principles of good organization is *unity of command*. This principle states that a position should report to no more than one other position for the same key result area or responsibility. Being accountable to two or more positions for the same responsibility generally reduces the chance of high performance and increases confusion and frustration. For example, a recruiter should not be accountable to both an operating manager and a human resources manager for selection procedures. However, the recruiter could be accountable to a human resources manager for selection procedures and to an operating manager for filling positions—two different responsibilities.

If you answered yes to this question, give yourself 7 points. If you answered no but the position reports to more than one other position for separate key result areas or responsibilities, give yourself 7 points. Any other no answer receives 3 points.

20. Organizations tend to be more effective when decisions are made as close to their need as possible. Having to seek higher authority adds time and expense so, ideally, decision-making authority is delegated to the lowest possible level.

___7___ Yes ___3___ No

21. As indicated in the response to Question 16, it is important for an employee to have a copy of his position description. If your answer to Question 16 was yes, use the scoring below. If your answer to Question 16 was negative, give yourself 3 points for this question.

___8___ Yes ___1___ No

22. Change impacts individual positions as well as the Organization and the human resources department. If you do not have written position descriptions, give yourself 3 points for your answer to this question.

___6___ Once a year

___7___ Every one to three years

___6___ Every three to five years

___4___ More than every five years

___1___ Never

23. Position descriptions are primarily a tool for the supervisor of a position and the employee in that position. Position descriptions have other uses, but the scoring below for the Reviews column reflects the primary use.

The scoring for the Approves column reflects the primary use of position descriptions, but it also recognizes secondary interests. Because the person in the position and the supervisor of the position prepare the position description, they are not given points for approving it. If you do not have written position descriptions, give yourself 4 points for this question.

Prepares   Approves

Prepares	Approves	
0	2	Senior human resources manager
2	0	Person in the position
3	0	Supervisor of person in the position
0	3	Manager of supervisor of person in the position
0	0	Senior manager to whom senior human resources manager reports
0	0	Position or compensation evaluation committee
0	0	Other

24. The Advisory Board believes the primary use of position descriptions should be for setting standards or objectives for the position. Standards and objectives are statements or measures of what a person in the position is to accomplish; they communicate exactly what the person in the position is to do and, simultaneously the position itself. If setting standards or objectives was your answer, give yourself 4 points. If you used words similar to "to communicate the job" give yourself 3 points. If you responded with words similar to "compensation, evaluation, or hiring," give yourself 2 points. If you responded with anything else, give yourself 1 point. If you do not have written position descriptions, give yourself 4 points for this question.

25. Assigning two or more *positions* the same responsibilities indicates the positions are the same and should not be identified separately. However, this question does not refer to *people* in the same position. For example, it is possible to have three employees all identified as recruiters and all with the same responsibilities.

_____1_____ Yes _____7_____ No

26 and 27. These two questions refer to the assigning of the same responsibilities to two or more different positions. If that is a reality, you should know what those positions and responsibilities are, to whom they are assigned, and why. If you do not have two or more positions assigned the same responsibilities (you answered no to Question 25), give yourself 4 points for each of these two questions.

26. _____6_____ Yes _____2_____ No

27. _____5_____ Yes _____2_____ No

28. A human resources department serves all other departments and employees within the Organization. Service is most effective when the clients (other departments and employees) know whom to contact.

_____8_____ Yes _____1_____ No

29. Standards of performance are statements of the conditions that will exist when a responsibility is being performed satisfactorily. Standards of performance are therefore extensions of specific job responsibilities. Objectives are more general statements of what is to be accomplished by the person in a position. They may be based on specific responsibilities or on the position's mission or overall objective.

_____8_____ Yes _____2_____ No

30 and 31. As with position descriptions, standards of performance and objectives should be in writing to avoid misinterpretation and misunderstanding, and each employee should know and have a copy of his standards of performance/ objectives. If there are no standards of performance or objectives, give yourself 3 points for each of these two questions.

30. ____7____ Yes ____1____ No

31. ____7____ Yes ____1____ No

32. Because of the explanation provided for the previous question, the ratings shown below should be self-explanatory. If you do not have standards of performance or objectives, give yourself 5 points for your answer to this question.

Prepares   *Approves*

____0____	____2____	Senior human resources manager
____2____	____0____	Person in the position
____3____	____0____	Supervisor of person in the position
____0____	____3____	Manager of supervisor of person in the position
____0____	____0____	Senior manager to whom senior human resources manager reports
____0____	____0____	Position or compensation evaluation committee
____0____	____0____	Other

33. Standards of performance and objectives serve several Organization needs. Our Advisory Board sees them primarily as tools for an employee and his supervisor, but they also can produce desired results for the department, employee, and Organization. If you do not have standards of performance or objectives, give yourself 5 points for this question.

____3____ Achieve department performance objectives

____2____ Salary adjustment

____2____ Hiring

____2____ Bonus consideration

____2____ Employee development

____1____ Promotion or assignment

    __1__ Planning

    __1__ Other

34. The requirements for a job change for many reasons, some organizational, some departmental, and some individual. Revised budgets or sales projections, an increase or decrease in department employees, and development of the employees' performance abilities all produce a need for revised standards or objectives. In most cases, an annual review is appropriate. If you do not have standards of performance or objectives, give yourself 5 points for this question.

    __0__ Never

    __2__ Monthly

    __2__ Once a quarter

    __2__ Every six months

    __2__ Once a year

    __1__ Other

35. Since standards of performance and objectives are measures of what the person in a position is to accomplish, they form the basis for performance reviews, that is, how well the employee has accomplished the position's standards of performance and objectives. The following scores reflect this idea and the one expressed in the explanation to the previous question. If you do not have standards of performance or objectives, give yourself 5 points total for this question.

Prepares	Conducts	Approves	
2	2	0	Employee's supervisor
0	0	2	Manager of employee's supervisor
0	0	2	Senior human resources manager
2	0	1	Employee
0	0	1	Other

36. If standards of performance and objectives are the requirements of the job and if they are communicated to the employee at the beginning of an appraisal period, the employee should know exactly how he is performing (one of the benefits of written measures). Even so, if the supervisor is required to prepare a written evaluation, the employee deserves to see it. If you do not have written performance evaluations, give yourself 3 points for this question.

____8____ Yes   ____1____ No

37. Having the employee sign a copy of his performance evaluation is an excellent way to ensure the employee has seen it. However, the employee's signature should indicate only that. It should not be a statement of agreement unless the employee is allowed to disagree and state why. If you do not have written performance evaluations, give yourself 3 points for this question.

____7____ Yes   ____2____ No

38. Who maintains a copy of an employee's performance review depends somewhat on what purpose(s) the review serves. The most important point is that there is a secure location in which the review will be maintained. If you do not have written performance evaluations, give yourself 3 points total for this question.

____3____ Employee's supervisor

____1____ Manager of employee's supervisor

____0____ Senior human resources manager

____2____ Employee

____2____ Employee's file in human resources department

____1____ Other

39 through 46. Earlier several questions pertained to strategic plans (long-term plans). These questions refer to tactical or short-term plans. Tactical plans are generally for one year, although in some situations they may be for as short as six months or as long as eighteen months. It depends on the business cycle for the Organization and rapidity and frequency of change.

39. ___9___ Yes ___1___ No

For the following questions, give yourself 3 points each if you have no tactical plan (answer to Question 39 was no).

40. ___5___ Yes ___1___ No

41. ___5___ Yes ___2___ No

42. ___4___ Yes ___3___ No

43. ___1___ Never

___3___ Every month

___3___ Every quarter

___3___ Once a year

___3___ Other

44. For the following question, give yourself 5 points each if you have no tactical plan (answer to Question 39 was no).

Prepares	Reviews	Approves	
0	1	3	Senior executive of the Organization and/or person to whom senior human resources manager reports
0	1	1	Organization's board of directors
2	0	0	Senior human resources manager
2	1	0	Human resources department managers
1	1	0	Human resources nonmanagement employees
1	1	1	Senior managers in other than human resources
0	1	0	Other

For the following questions, give yourself 3 points each if you have no tactical plan (answer to Question 39 was no).

45. ___5___ Yes ___1___ No

46. ___5___ Yes ___1___ No

47 and 48. Ideally, a tactical plan is a direct outgrowth of a strategic plan, so there should be coordination between the two plans.
  If your answer to Question 39 was yes, use the following scoring:

47. ___4___ Yes ___2___ No

48. ___5___ Yes ___3___ No

If your answer to Question 39 was no and/or if your department and/or Organization do not have strategic plans, give yourself 3 points for your answer to each of Questions 47 and 48.

49. A budget should be the financial statement of a plan. The human resources department should have an annual budget based on its annual or tactical plan. If you have a budget but no annual or tactical plan, give yourself 7 points for this question. If you have an annual or tactical plan and no budget, give yourself 5 points for this question. If you have both an annual/tactical plan and an annual budget, give yourself 9 points for this question. If you have no annual or tactical plan and no budget, give yourself 1 point for your answer to this question.

50. To be effective management tools budgets need to indicate planned expenses by type, key result area, and position or other functional assignment. If you do not have a budget, give yourself 2 points for this question.

                    ___7___ Yes ___2___ No

51. The budget of the human resources department should be prepared by the department employees but coordinated and approved by representatives of the entire Organization. If you do not have a budget, give yourself 5 points for this question.

Prepares   Reviews   Approves

___0___   ___1___   ___3___   Senior executive of the Organization and/or person to whom senior human resources manager reports

0	1	1	Organization's board of directors
2	0	0	Senior human resources manager
2	1	0	Human resources department managers
1	1	0	Human resources nonmanagement employees
1	1	1	Senior managers in other than human resources
2	2	1	Someone from a financial function of the Organization
0	1	0	Other

52. Performance to budget reports should be received at least monthly. If longer, it becomes difficult to identify needed corrective action and take such action. If you do not have a budget, give yourself 5 points total for this question.

___0___ Never

___8___ Every month

___5___ Every quarter

___2___ Once a year

___2___ Other

53. Each manager within the human resources department should be required to analyze the results and variances of his or her area of accountability as indicated in a performance to budget report. If you do not have a budget, give yourself 5 points for this question.

___8___ Yes ___1___ No

54, 55, and 56. Whatever number you used to answer each of these questions is the rating for that question.

DEPARTMENT EMPLOYEES—EVALUATION

If this category is not one for which your human resources department is accountable, go directly to the next category beginning on page 171.

1. No matter how well-planned the human resources department, it is not an operating reality until staffed with employees. If the organization of the department is well-developed and published, it should be followed. However, adjustments may be required due to the abilities of employees currently in the department.

<u>   7   </u> Yes   <u> 3 </u> No

2. Unless your human resources department has been established recently, you probably have a mix of seniority. One factor that could affect your answer is a recent reduction in workforce, which most likely would result in few employees with low seniority. If either the recent formation of the department or a reduction in workforce has affected seniority, give yourself 3 points. Otherwise, give yourself 6 points if at least 75 percent of your department employees have been in the department for one year or more, and give yourself 3 points if less than 75 percent of your department employees have been in the department for one year or more.

3. If your human resources department is staffed with people who are not technically qualified, there is a serious training problem and probably a problem with the selection process. You can always afford (in fact many would suggest it is desirable) to have a percentage of your department's personnel in the learning/development stage of their careers. However, human resources is too important to an Organization to be staffed by a large percentage of unqualified people. If your answer was 90 percent or above, give yourself 8 points. If your answer was at least 75 percent but less than 90 percent, give yourself 6 points. If your answer was at least 60 percent but less than 75 percent, give yourself 5 points. If your answer was less than 60 percent, give yourself 3 points.

4. The explanation for this question is similar to that given for developing and approving position descriptions and standards of performance/objectives. The position description describes the position's purpose and its responsibilities, and standards of performance and objectives delineate the specifics of what is to be accomplished by a person in the position. The qualifications should be the specific education, competencies, skills, and experience a person requires to perform the job as designed.

Establishes   Approves

4	0	Position's supervisor
2	2	Manager of supervisor of person in the position
1	1	Senior manager to whom top human resources manager reports
0	0	Compensation evaluation committee
0	0	Other

5. All positions within the human resources department should be filled unless an employee has recently left the department and a new employee has not yet been hired. If your answer was 100 percent, give yourself 8 points. If it was between 90 percent and 100 percent, give yourself 7 points. Any other answer receives 3 points.

6. Nonmanagement positions within the human resources department should be filled within thirty days and management positions within sixty days with the possible exception of the senior management position of the department. If your answer for nonmanagement was less than thirty days, give yourself 6 points. If it was between thirty and sixty days, give yourself 4 points. If it was more than sixty days, give yourself 2 points. If you have no open nonmanagement positions, give yourself 5 points.

If your management answer (other than for the senior manager position in the department) was less than one month, give yourself 6 points. If it was between one and three months, give yourself 4 points. If it was between three and six months, give yourself 4 points. If it was greater than six months, give yourself 2 points. If you have no open management positions, give yourself 5 points.

If the open management position was for the senior manager position of the human resources department, and your answer was less than three months, give yourself 6 points. If it was between three and six months, give yourself 4 points. If it was between six and nine months, give yourself 4 points. If it was greater than nine months, give yourself 2 points.

7. Assuming a budget exists for the human resources department, and it reflects the number of positions required to meet the department's objectives, the supervisor of the open position should be the one to request the new employee while simultaneously notifying the manager to whom she reports. Decision mak-

ing should be delegated to the lowest possible level within the department. The following scoring reflects that philosophy.

___6___ Supervisor of the position

___8___ Manager of position's supervisor

___4___ Senior manager in the human resources department

___1___ Senior manager to whom senior human resources manager reports

___1___ Other

8. For newly created positions, positions probably not included in a current approved budget, the approval process should differ. The addition of a new position and employee has an impact on a number of areas. Use the following scoring:

___4___ Supervisor of the position

___6___ Manager of position's supervisor

___8___ Senior manager in the human resources department

___2___ Senior manager to whom senior human resources manager reports

___1___ Other

9. The supervisor of the position is the most important person to interview candidates for the position, but human resources serves the entire Organization, so having others interview the candidate is an excellent way of obtaining information about the candidate's probable success in the position. It is also a good way for the candidate to obtain information on how well the position fits her career objectives.

___4___ Supervisor of the open position

___2___ Manager of position's supervisor

___1___ Senior human resources manager

___1___ Other human resources managers

_____0_____ Senior manager to whom top human resources manager reports

_____2_____ Human resources department employees in similar positions

_____1_____ Managers of client departments

_____1_____ Other

10. Every human resources department and every Organization operates somewhat differently. Human resources department employees generally are in positions that administer and interpret employee programs, solve employee-related problems, and establish conditions of employment. A department orientation program is an ideal way to acquaint new employees with the specifics of these activities.

_____7_____ Yes   _____2_____ No

11 and 12. To obtain and retain qualified employees, compensation is a major factor. For all department employees, it is important that compensation be competitive with other Organizations in the geographic area. For managers and professionals, industry competitiveness is also important because this group will move to new geographic areas for work more frequently than nonmanagement employees.

11. _____8_____ Yes   _____1_____ No

12. _____8_____ Yes   _____1_____ No

13 and 14. There are no correct answers to these two questions for all Organizations and all human resources departments. Turnover varies by industry, geographic area, and Organization growth or decline. Absenteeism varies by these same factors. Type of work, amount of overtime, shift work, and days of week also affect absenteeism rates. The important point is that you were able to answer these questions, that you know what the department turnover and absences are. If you were able to answer these questions, give yourself 7 points for each question you answered. If you were unable to answer these questions, give yourself 2 points for each question you could not answer.

15 through 20. A recent article suggested that human resources professionals can become outdated in their knowledge and skill levels within five years. The solution appears to be in-service training and development programs, participation in professional associations, attendance at professional conferences, and

reading professional journals and books. The scoring reflects the belief that to encourage and support these activities and the continual professionalism of the human resources department is healthy for the department and beneficial for the individual.

15.   ___7___ Yes   ___2___ No

16. Association dues   ___7___ Yes   ___3___ No

    Conference registrations   ___6___ Yes   ___3___ No

17.   ___6___ Yes   ___2___ No

18.   ___5___ Yes   ___3___ No

19.   ___5___ Yes   ___3___ No

20.   ___7___ Yes   ___2___ No

21. Generally, the more knowledgeable of the operations of the Organization's other departments human resources department employees are, the more effective they can be in providing service to the entire Organization. Rotational assignments (varying from attending other department staff meetings to providing human resources services from a client department location to a temporary assignment to other than a human resources position) provide such knowledge and often improve the quality and speed of human resources services.

                      ___8___ Yes   ___2___ No

22. Likewise, nonhuman resources department personnel can benefit from temporary assignments to human resources. Such assignments contribute to a better understanding of each other's work and improved communication.

                      ___8___ Yes   ___3___ No

23. Ideally, your answer should be 100 percent. All human resources department employees should have specific goals for their individual development, including new department employees. If your answer was 100 percent, give yourself 8 points. If your answer was between 90 percent and 100 percent, give yourself 7 points. If your answer was less than 90 percent, give yourself 4 points.

24 and 25. Performance reviews should be primarily for developing employees and improving performance. Employees should be developed to successfully

fulfill the requirements of their current position, remain current with developments in their profession, and prepare for meeting their individual career objectives. If compensation is a part of performance reviews, it becomes the dominant factor. Therefore, even though an employee's performance is a part of any compensation review, our Advisory Board believes the two reviews should be separate.

24. ____9____ Yes   ____2____ No

25. One week to one month   ____4____

    One to two months   ____6____

    Two to three months   ____7____

    Three to six months   ____8____

    More than six months   ____2____

    No separation   ____2____

26. Good human resources planning should include an employee replacement document for at least the key positions of the human resources department. Such a document should indicate which replacement employees are available and what training and/or experience they require. It should also indicate where it will be necessary to fill positions from outside the department or even outside the Organization.

                    ____6____ Yes ____2____ No

27. If your human resources department has an employee replacement document, it should be realistic and used when replacements are necessary. The exception is when such documents are prepared only for emergency situations. If the document was created solely for emergencies or you do not have such a document (a no answer to Question 26), give yourself 2 points. However, if your document is a planning document for the department and your answer was 100 percent, give yourself 6 points. If your answer was between 90 percent and 100 percent, give yourself 5 points. If your answer was between 80 percent and 90 percent, give yourself 4 points. If your answer was between 70 percent and 80 percent, give yourself 3 points. If your answer was less than 70 percent, give yourself 2 points.

28. As with similar planning documents, a replacement document needs to recognize all the changes that can impact it, so it requires regular review and

updating. If you do not have such a document (a no answer to Question 26) give yourself 2 points.

    0   Never

    2   Every six months

    6   Once a year

    4   Every one to three years

    1   More than every three years

    4   Whenever someone leaves the department

    1   Other

29. A replacement document should be primarily for the use of the human resources department. However, it also should be coordinated with the Organization's plans and similar documents to ensure proper integration and appropriate use by all employees. (Check just one.)

    4   Department only   4   Organizationwide

    6   Both

30. Exit interviews can provide valuable information for improving departmental operations. Often, departing employees provide insights not otherwise obtainable. Not conducting such interviews with all departing employees deprives the department of such information.

    8   Yes   1   No

31. The supervisor of a departing employee should always speak with that employee, but the formal exit interview generally is best conducted by someone other than a close working colleague. Generally, it should be a neutral person not involved with the employee's activities.

In most cases, employees departing from departments or the Organization are best interviewed by human resources employees. In the case of departing human resources employees, the exit interview should be conducted by someone outside the department.

However, the result of the exit interview should be shared and reviewed by those people who can benefit from the information. If you do not conduct exit interviews, give yourself 4 points total for this question.

Conducts   Reviews

Conducts	Reviews	
__2__	__2__	Supervisor of employee
__2__	__2__	Manager of employee's supervisor
__2__	__1__	Other human resources department personnel
__1__	__3__	Senior human resources manager
__2__	__2__	Other

32. Our Advisory Board believes the first action to be taken with an employee not performing as required is to conduct a performance review. Such a review will provide an opportunity for the supervisor to obtain information as to the cause of the problem. The development objectives can be established, training provided, or assignments changed to bring the employee up to standard performance.

If a performance review does not work, then an oral warning followed by a written warning and, if necessary, discharge can take place. Our Advisory Board believes it is the supervisor's responsibility always to try to develop the employee. Other actions should only be taken when development efforts prove impossible. But in all cases, follow-up actions should be based on creating a satisfactorily performing employee and not as punishment. For that reason, giving the employee time off is not a positive approach. In some cases, transferring the employee to another job in the Organization or department may be the best action, but it should only be used when the employee clearly is in an unsuitable position.

__2__ Performance review conducted

__2__ Employee issued an oral warning

__2__ Employee issued a written warning

__1__ Employee discharged

__0__ Employee given disciplinary time off

__2__ Employee transferred to another job

33. Our Advisory Board was split on the answer to this question. Some believe probationary periods are a thing of the past. They point out that probationary periods often limit the quality of employees you can hire. One member commented, "A really good candidate may currently have a job. Why should he or she make an irrevocable decision (leaving her current employment) when you are only willing to make a conditional decision (probationary period). After all, you can discharge an employee who is not performing—with or without a probationary period."

Others who support a probationary period feel it provides time in the position for both the Organization and the employee to decide if it is the right position for the employee.

<u>   7   </u> Yes   <u>   7   </u> No

34 through 37. Whether or not the Organization has specific rules, guidelines, and regulations regarding employee behavior, there are almost always situations unique to a human resources department that require additional rules or guidelines. These should be clearly stated in writing, given to all employees, and enforced consistently.

34. <u>   7   </u> Yes   <u>   2   </u> No

If there are no human resources rules, guidelines, and regulations, give yourself 3 points for each of the following three questions.

35. <u>   7   </u> Yes   <u>   1   </u> No

36. <u>   5   </u> Yes   <u>   2   </u> No

37. <u>   8   </u> Yes   <u>   1   </u> No

38. Certification in several areas of human resources is available through professional Organizations such as the Society for Human Resource Management. Certification generally requires a combination of experience and knowledge as demonstrated on a standardized examination. This can be further evidence of a desired level of professionalism and can assist employees in maintaining current knowledge in their field.

<u>   6   </u> Yes   <u>   2   </u> No

39, 40, and 41. Whatever number you used to answer each of these questions is the rating for that question.

LABOR RELATIONS—EVALUATION

If this category is not one for which your human resources department is account-able, go directly to the next category beginning on page 181.

1. This question can be answered in a number of ways. It depends to some extent on what "establishes" means to you. However, our Advisory Board believes the most important condition is that labor relations policy is established by the Organization and not by an external individual or group.

If you are answering the questions in this category, labor relations must be an area for which the human resources department of your Organization is ac-countable. That being the case, human resources should have a major role in determining labor relations policy. Ideally such policy should be developed by human resources with senior management involvement and approval. Labor attor-neys, whether internal or external, should provide information and advice. In some situations, an Organization's internal labor attorney is a member of the human resources department and accountable for labor relations. If that is your situation, the internal attorney can be considered a human resources labor rela-tions employee.

_____4_____ External labor attorney

_____7_____ Internal labor attorney

_____9_____ Senior human resources manager

_____9_____ The Organization's senior labor relations manager, if not the senior human resources manager

_____5_____ Senior manager in other than human resources

_____6_____ Senior executive of the Organization

_____8_____ A team, group, or committee of the Organization

_____0_____ No one

_____2_____ Other

2. Although an Organization should be accountable for establishing its labor relations policy, as indicated in the above answer, it needs to have input from legal counsel, a source of professional information regarding the legal ramifications of labor relations decisions and possible directions to achieve the Organization's objectives. The legal counsel can be internal, external, or a combination of both.

    __8__ External legal counsel   __8__ Internal legal counsel

    __9__ Both   __0__ Neither

3. The field of labor relations is becoming increasingly complex. New court decisions, arbitration decisions, and legislation impacting labor relations occur almost constantly. The Organization should have the services of a legal counsel who devotes full time to the area and has in-depth training in the field.

                __9__ Yes   __1__ No

4. Labor relations decisions should be made by human resources with significant decisions reviewed with senior management. Legal counsel opinions and suggestions should be obtained, as in the case of establishing labor relations policy. This conforms to the Organization principle of keeping decision-making authority as close to implementation as possible and contributes to speedy resolution of problems.

    __4__ External labor attorney

    __6__ Internal labor attorney

    __8__ Senior human resources manager

    __8__ The Organization's senior labor relations manager, if not the senior human resources manager

    __4__ Senior manager in other than human resources

    __4__ Senior executive of the Organization

    __4__ A team, group, or committee

    __1__ No one

    __2__ Other

5. There should be an established policy and established procedures for what to do in the event of an attempt by a union to organize employees. These should have been communicated to all managers. Failure to have knowledgeable and trained managers in this area can, in certain circumstances, lead to decisions in a union organizational drive that have adverse consequences for the Organization.

      __8__ Yes   __1__ No   __6__ Not applicable

6 and 7. There are several important reasons for regularly updating managers on the Organization's policy and procedures regarding union-organizing attempts. One is that a policy on unions is not used on a regular basis by managers, so they need to be refreshed. The second is that managers change; some leave and new ones are hired. Another reason for updates is that changes to the policy and procedures may occur. A regular schedule for updating managers is desirable, and special updating is required whenever there is an actual union-organizing attempt.

6. __7__ Yes   __2__ No   __5__ Not applicable

7. __4__ Whenever there is an organizing attempt

    __4__ At least once a year

    __3__ On an unscheduled basis

    __2__ Every year or more

    __2__ Other

    __6__ Not applicable

8, 9, and 10. In order to coordinate all activities and provide a consistent approach and spokesperson, one individual should be in charge of the Organization's reaction to a union-organizing campaign. That individual should have been identified prior to any such attempt, so if an attempt does occur, that person is ready to take control and has had the opportunity to prepare.

Whoever is selected should have the necessary knowledge and experience. In addition, the individual should have access to a committee or specialized individuals who can provide assistance. It is best if this person is from the Organization and is accountable for labor relations. External people are best used for advice and suggestions. The senior executive should never be this individual.

8. ___6___ Yes ___2___ No ___4___ Not applicable

9. ___8___ Yes ___1___ No ___6___ Not applicable

10. ___4___ External labor attorney

___6___ Internal labor attorney

___6___ Senior human resources manager

___6___ The Organization's senior labor relations manager, if not the senior human resources manager

___4___ Senior manager in other than human resources

___2___ Senior executive of the Organization

___1___ No one

___4___ Not applicable

11. Regardless of whether external labor relations counsel is used, an Organization should have someone inside the Organization who maintains current information on labor relations regulations, legislation, rulings, and other related activities.

___7___ Yes ___2___ No

12, 13, and 14. To have a successful labor contract, facts and negotiation decisions from a number of sources must be reviewed. These sources include current labor relations regulations, legislation, rulings, and other related external activities; the managers and supervisors of employees represented by the union; and the grievances and arbitration decisions arising from the Organization's current contract with the union.

12. ___8___ Yes ___2___ No

13. ___8___ Yes ___2___ No

14. ___8___ Yes ___2___ No

15. Another source of information for contract negotiations is an updating seminar or conference. Here the latest activities and trends can be reviewed.

___6___ Yes ___2___ No

16. Once all information has been obtained and reviewed, the Organization should establish clear parameters for negotiations. These parameters should include what the Organization must obtain and what it wants but can live without. Also included should be responses to anticipated union requests, the financial cost of probable union demands, and the financial limitations on any settlement.

<u> 8 </u> Yes   <u> 2 </u> No

17. The chief spokesperson for the Organization should be someone from within the Organization, ideally the human resources manager accountable for labor relations. It should not be the senior executive of the Organization.

<u> 5 </u> External labor attorney

<u> 7 </u> Internal labor attorney

<u> 9 </u> Senior human resources manager

<u> 9 </u> The Organization's senior labor relations manager, if not the senior human resources manager

<u> 6 </u> Senior manager in other than human resources

<u> 0 </u> Senior executive of the Organization

<u> 5 </u> Senior manager of the unit covered by the agreement

<u> 0 </u> No one

<u> 4 </u> Other

18. It is rare that union contract negotiations are conducted by a single Organization representative. Generally there is a team with one spokesperson. The members of the team should be those individuals who can contribute significantly to the outcome by providing immediate and knowledgeable advice and information. In some negotiations, because of the specialized nature of a bargaining position or an item of negotiation, one or more team members may be added for that item. The senior executive of the Organization should not be on the team.

<u> 1 </u> External labor attorney

<u> 2 </u> Internal labor attorney

_____2_____ Senior human resources manager

_____2_____ The Organization's senior labor relations manager

_____1_____ Senior manager in other than human resources

_____0_____ Senior executive of the Organization

_____0_____ No one

_____2_____ Nonhuman resources manager or supervisor

_____2_____ Other

19. Although the senior executive of the Organization should not be on the negotiating team, that individual or another senior manager with decision-making authority should always be available to the team. This provides a procedure and a source for immediate decision making that often can contribute to a more desirable outcome.

_____7_____ Yes   _____2_____ No

20. The negotiating team needs to be able to respond to proposals as rapidly as possible. The team needs to know which proposals to immediately discard and which to pursue. Quick and accurate calculations can contribute to this type of decision making.

_____7_____ Yes   _____2_____ No

21. The Organization's management needs to be aware of the general directions of negotiations. Also, they can provide information on proposals and discussions that may develop within the negotiation meetings.

_____7_____ Yes   _____2_____ No

22. There are geographic area trends in employee rewards and conditions of employment. Because an Organization competes with other local organizations for employees, the compensation and benefits practices and other conditions of employment in the region are important. Also, industries tend to follow certain trends in their labor relations. The unions recognize this and continually seek such information.

_____4_____ Area _____4_____ Industry

_____8_____ Both _____2_____ No

23 and 24. As with union-organizing campaigns and negotiations, there needs to be a single individual accountable for the settlement of all grievances. This allows for consistency in settlements. That individual should be an employee of the Organization but should never be the senior executive of the Organization.

23. _____8_____ Yes _____1_____ No

24. _____4_____ External labor attorney

_____6_____ Internal labor attorney

_____8_____ Senior human resources manager

_____8_____ The Organization's senior labor relations manager, if not the senior human resources manager

_____4_____ Senior manager in other than human resources

_____0_____ Senior executive of the Organization

_____0_____ No one

_____2_____ Other

25 and 26. Ideally an investigation is conducted as soon as a grievance is filed, but certainly no more than five days following its filing and always prior to a first meeting regarding the grievance. It is impossible to deal with a grievance without information, and the longer you wait to collect that information, the less likely it will be accurate.

25. _____7_____ Yes _____2_____ No

26. _____8_____ Yes _____1_____ No

27. Written records should be made of all grievance investigations. They should be made immediately following, if not during, the investigations.

_____8_____ Yes _____1_____ No

28 and 29. Generally, a grievance involves the actions of a manager and/or supervisor. The investigation should always obtain, as soon as possible, their understanding of the situation and any facts they may know. Often grievances end at an arbitration hearing, and the decisions made by an arbitrator can have a far-reaching impact on the Organization. Our Advisory Board believes managers and supervisors involved in the circumstances that led to a grievance should be considered as witnesses in a possible legal proceeding. Their statements should be signed to ensure a record of the facts as close in time to the incident as possible. Such statements can also assist in later testimony. These statements should be taken, recorded, and signed as soon as possible after the grievance is filed.

28. ___8___ Yes ___1___ No

29. ___8___ As soon as a grievance is filed

___7___ Within five days of a grievance being filed

___5___ After the first grievance meeting

___2___ Just prior to the last meeting in the grievance procedure

___1___ When a grievance is appealed to arbitration

___0___ Never

___2___ Other

30. Grievances are generally best settled as soon as possible. This is not to imply that they should be settled other than in a desirable way just to settle them fast, but grievances are costly procedures and the sooner settled the better.

___7___ Yes ___2___ No

31. Records of grievance meetings and settlements are necessary to ensure consistency of responses and administration. They also provide valuable information when preparing for contract negotiations.

___8___ Yes ___1___ No

32. All proposed grievance settlements should be reviewed with legal counsel to understand any precedents they may be setting, and how the settlements relate to current labor trends, rules, and legislation.

___7___ Yes ___1___ No

33. Our Advisory Board believes it is generally best for the Organization to be represented at an arbitration hearing by an employee of the Organization. However, arbitration hearings are quasi-legal procedures, so often it is better to use legal counsel trained in such procedures.

____6____ External labor attorney

____7____ Internal labor attorney

____8____ Senior human resources manager

____8____ The Organization's senior labor relations manager, if not the senior human resources manager

____4____ Nonhuman resources manager

____0____ Senior executive of the Organization

____0____ No one

____2____ Other

34 and 35. There is some differing of opinion by the Advisory Board regarding these questions, but the majority of our Board believes such limitations should be posted. All agree posting should be done only with approval of the Organization's labor counsel.

34. ____8____ Yes ____5____ No

35. ____8____ Yes ____3____ No

36, 37, and 38. Whatever number you used to answer each of these questions is the rating for that question.

Recruitment and Selection—Evaluation

If this category is not one for which your human resources department is accountable, go directly to the next category beginning on page 195.

1. The supervisor of the open position should be the one to request the new employee while simultaneously notifying the manager to whom she reports. Decision making should be delegated to the lowest possible level within the department. The following scoring reflects that philosophy.

Requesting *Approving*

__8__	__4__	Supervisor of the open position
__4__	__8__	Manager of the open position's supervisor
__2__	__6__	Senior manager in the department of the open position
__2__	__4__	Senior human resources manager
__2__	__2__	Human resources manager accountable for recruitment
__2__	__2__	Other

2. The request and authorization for hiring a new employee should be a formal procedure. It should be in writing with proper approvals. Like so many activities of an Organization, a formal procedure assists in eliminating misunderstandings.

__8__ Yes __2__ No

3. The document that can provide the greatest assistance in hiring an employee is a position description. A position description provides a standard document of required qualifications and competencies for every position. In addition,

it communicates the type of responsibilities and authorities the position has been delegated.

_____8_____ Yes _____2_____ No

4. The second most useful document in the hiring process is the standards of performance or objectives for the position. While the position description describes the job, the standards/objectives describe exactly what is expected of a person in the position. This is of great benefit in describing to a candidate what is to be accomplished.

_____6_____ Yes _____2_____ No

5. The standards of performance/objectives specify what is to be accomplished and the competencies, education, experience, and skills required provide the information necessary to evaluate a candidate's qualifications.

_____7_____ Yes _____1_____ No

6. Our Advisory Board believes the best source of candidates is within the Organization. These are people who have already "bought in to" the Organization's mission and culture. Generally, it is assumed such candidates will be those seeking promotion, but often a lateral move can benefit both the employee and the Organization. The main reason not to attempt to fill positions from within the Organization is that experiences, skills, knowledge, or style required are not available among existing employees.

_____6_____ Yes _____2_____ No

7. A job-posting program provides a formal procedure for first considering internal employees for open positions.

_____7_____ Yes _____2_____ No

8. Although job posting is an ideal way to obtain candidates from within the Organization, our Advisory Board believes first consideration should be given to those employees of a department in which an open position occurs. If you do not have a job-posting program, give yourself 4 points for this question.

_____6_____ Yes _____1_____ No

9. Although our Advisory Board believes the best source of candidates for a position is within the Organization (within the department first), there is an ex-

ception when the required experiences, skills, knowledge, or style are not available among existing employees. The Board believes job posting should be used unless there is a need to hire from outside the Organization. If you do not have a job-posting program, give yourself 3 points for this question.

___6___ Yes ___1___ No ___4___ Sometimes

10. If you have a job-posting program, the best approach is to post all jobs. When only selected jobs are posted, the job-posting program, which should be seen by employees as a benefit, is instead seen as a relatively unfair procedure. If you do not have a job-posting program, give yourself 3 points for your answer to this question.

___7___ All jobs

___5___ Only nonmanagement jobs

___5___ Only jobs at certain levels

___6___ Only management jobs

___3___ Other

11 and 12. Generally the Organization should have the authority to not post a job, but the concerns mentioned in the explanations to previous questions should always be considered in making such a decision, and any such decision should be based on specific reasons. If you do not have a job-posting program, give yourself 4 points for each of these two questions.

11. ___6___ Yes ___2___ No

12. ___6___ Yes ___1___ No

13. If a decision is made to not post a job, at least two individuals should approve the decision: the manager of the open position's supervisor and the human resources manager accountable for recruiting. If you do not have a job-posting program, or you do have a job-posting program that requires all jobs to be posted, give yourself 5 points for this question.

___1___ Supervisor of the open position

___3___ Manager of the open position's supervisor

____2____ Senior manager in the department of the open position

____1____ Senior human resources manager

____2____ Human resources manager accountable for recruitment

____2____ Other

14. The Organization should have a written policy on promotions. It might contain a statement such as:

Positions are filled from within the Organization whenever they are promotions unless the required qualifications are unavailable.

An employee must be in his current position at least six months before being considered for another position.

The key point is that there is a policy developed as a guideline for internal promotions.

____8____ Yes   ____1____ No

15 and 16. As with all Organization policies, once developed it should be written and communicated to those affected. In the case of promotions, all employees of the Organization might be affected at some time. If you do not have a policy on promotions, give yourself 3 points for each of these two questions.

15. ____7____ Yes   ____2____ No

16. ____7____ Yes   ____2____ No

17. As a general rule, the methods used to obtain candidates should be determined by the person doing the recruiting. Generally that person should be someone in the human resources department. The exception is when the supervisor of the open position or the manager of that supervisor knows of sources for the unique skills required, or has external relationships that will benefit the Organization. However, even in these cases, the use of the source should be by the person obtaining candidates.

____1____ Supervisor of the open position

____1____ Manager of the open position's supervisor

____1____ Senior manager in the department of the open position

_____1_____ Senior human resources manager

_____5_____ Human resources manager accountable for recruitment

_____2_____ Other

18. Ideally, advertisements for open positions will produce candidates who are qualified for the position, so the more information provided, the better the chance of obtaining candidates.

_____3_____ Organization name

_____3_____ Position title

_____3_____ Location

_____2_____ Telephone number

_____2_____ Compensation

_____1_____ Benefits

_____3_____ Position requirements

_____2_____ Name of person to contact

_____1_____ Confidentiality of contact

_____1_____ How the Organization will respond to replies

_____1_____ "Our employees know of this advertisement" or similar words

_____1_____ Other

_____8_____ Organization does not advertise

19. Our Advisory Board does not believe there should be a minimum number of candidates, other than the number necessary to find and obtain a qualified employee. Therefore, if the first candidate has the qualifications and accepts the position, no other candidates need to be seen.

_____1_____ Yes   _____6_____ No

20. Screening candidates is the sorting of candidates into groups of qualified and unqualified. This screening may consist solely of a review of resumes and applications, initial interviews, or both.

____2____ Supervisor of the open position

____1____ Manager of the open position's supervisor

____0____ Senior manager in the department of the open position

____0____ Senior human resources manager

____1____ Human resources manager accountable for recruitment

____2____ Human resources department recruiter or screener

____2____ Other

21. To some extent the sources of candidates for a specific position depend on the position. All sources should be used, with the specific ones selected based on the requirements of the position. Give yourself 1 point for each source you checked.

22. Employee referral programs generally produce excellent candidates. Usually the candidates already know something about the Organization and are favorably disposed toward it. Also, there appears to be a tendency among employees to recommend well-qualified people who will reflect favorably on the employee making the recommendation.

____7____ Yes   ____2____ No

23 and 24. Employee referral programs, like job-posting programs, appear to be most effective when used for all positions. However, if they are not used for certain positions, that fact should be stated clearly in the description of the program. Referral programs normally provide a cash reward to a recommending employee if the recommended individual is hired and stays with the Organization for a specified period of time. If you do not have an employee referral program, give yourself 3 points for each of these two questions.

23. ____7____ Yes   ____1____ No

24. ____7____ Yes   _____ No

25. In recent years there have been several legal decisions regarding reference checking of candidates. Some of these decisions have upheld the right to

check references but others have penalized Organizations for any negative impact such actions may have had on candidates. The most professional, ethical, and safe approach is to have a reference check release form signed by a candidate prior to conducting any reference checks. Actually, this is a good approach even if the Organization does not normally conduct reference checks.

_____8_____ Yes   _____1_____ No

26 and 27. As a general rule, at least the key qualifications of a candidate should be checked or verified. However, such checks should probably be made only when a candidate is being seriously considered or prior to a job offer. There may be some references, such as for the current job, that are not conducted until after the employee is hired. If you do not conduct reference checks, give yourself 4 points for Question 27.

26. _____7_____ Yes   _____2_____ No   _____4_____ Sometimes

27. _____0_____ When an application/resume is received

_____1_____ Before a first interview

_____1_____ After a first interview

_____6_____ When a candidate is being seriously considered

_____7_____ Prior to a job offer

_____5_____ After a job offer is accepted but prior to hiring

_____4_____ After hiring

_____2_____ Other

28. The ideal person to conduct reference checks is the individual accountable for recruiting. This person generally has been trained in what to ask for and how to ask it. In some cases the supervisor of the open position or his manager may do the reference checking if it is of a highly technical nature, or if one of them has a contact with the person to be called. Even then, reference checks should be done under the guidance of the recruiter. If you do not conduct reference checks, give yourself 4 points for this question.

_____2_____ Supervisor of the position

_____4_____ Manager of the supervisor of the position

_____1_____ Senior manager in the department of the open position

_____1_____ Senior human resources manager

_____4_____ Human resources manager accountable for recruitment

_____3_____ Human resources department recruiter or screener

_____2_____ Other

29. There should be a written record of all reference checks. At a minimum it should contain time of check, who was talked to, what was said, and who performed the check. This ensures that no misunderstandings occur and provides evidence in the event of a later claim or charge. If you do not conduct reference checks, give yourself 3 points for this question.

_____7_____ Yes _____1_____ No

30. There should be at least two parties involved in determining which candidates to interview: someone from human resources (preferably the individual involved in filling the position) and someone in the department where the open position is. The human resources person should base her recommendation on the candidate's qualifications for success as an employee of the Organization and an initial evaluation of job qualifications. Someone from the position's department should base his recommendation on specific job qualifications, understanding of the position, and ability to perform the work.

_____3_____ Supervisor of the open position

_____2_____ Manager of the open position's supervisor

_____1_____ Senior manager in the department of the open position

_____1_____ Senior human resources manager

_____3_____ Human resources manager accountable for recruitment

_____2_____ Human resources department recruiter or screener

_____2_____ Other

31. The initial interview is a screening to determine the qualifications of a candidate.

_____2_____ Supervisor of the open position

_____1_____ Manager of the open position's supervisor

_____0_____ Senior manager in the department of the open position

_____0_____ Senior human resources manager

_____1_____ Human resources manager accountable for recruitment

_____2_____ Human resources department recruiter or screener

_____2_____ Other

32. At the very least the individual in human resources accountable for filling the position and the supervisor of the position should interview the candidate prior to hiring. Ideally, the manager of the open position's supervisor also will interview the candidate. Others may provide additional insight but generally are not required interviewers. In some cases, depending on the position's level within the Organization, internal relationships or unique skills may require other interviews.

_____3_____ Supervisor of the open position

_____2_____ Manager of the open position's supervisor

_____1_____ Senior manager in the department of the open position

_____1_____ Senior human resources manager

_____2_____ Human resources manager accountable for recruitment

_____2_____ Human resources department recruiter or screener

_____2_____ Other

33. An assessment of the candidate's qualifications against the position's requirements tends to be more accurate when it is performed immediately after the interview. However, this does not have to be an assessment accompanied by a

final decision. The important point is to capture the information before other activities and time affect how the candidate is perceived.

_____7_____ Yes _____2_____ No

34. There are certain skills and competencies best determined by standardized measurement devices. (If your Organization has positions with such requirements, these devices should be used unless there is a more accurate method to make such determinations.) However, measurement devices should be used only when they are the best method for determining such information and they meet all legal requirements.

_____6____ Yes ___3___ No ___6____ Sometimes

35 and 36. In the explanation to the previous question, the need to ensure such measurement devices met legal requirements was mentioned. Actually, these requirements are the correct way to use tests. First, tests should be used only when they measure actual job requirements. The professional method for determining job requirements is to conduct a job analysis. Second, the tests should be valid instruments; that is, you should be able to demonstrate they are accurate in what they claim to measure, and such validity should be determined specifically for the job within your Organization. If you do not use such measuring devices, give yourself 3 points for your answer to each of these two questions.

35. _____7_____ Yes ____1____ No

36. _____7_____ Yes ____1____ No

37 and 38. To be valid and reliable (error free) measurement devices need to be administered in a consistent way. All candidates should receive exactly the same instructions, have the same environment and, when required, the same time to complete the test. The person administering tests should be properly trained and/or certified. The test requirements may dictate somewhat who can administer the test, but generally someone in human resources is best. An external consultant may be required for some tests; however, someone in the open position's department is the least desirable. If you do not use such measuring devices, give yourself 6 points for each of these two questions.

37. ____2____ Someone in the open position's department

____7____ Someone in the human resources department

_____6_____ An external consultant

_____2_____ Other

38. _____7_____ Yes _____1_____ No

39. Anyone receiving test results needs to have been thoroughly trained in what the test measures, how that measurement relates to the job and job success, and the importance of keeping such personal information confidential. Moreover, test results should be restricted to only those with a need to know.

_____7_____ Yes _____1_____ No

40 and 41. Anyone conducting interviews should be trained in interviewing techniques. Interviewers need to know what actions and questions are legal and which are not legal, and what types of questions will obtain the type of information required.

40. _____8_____ Yes _____1_____ No

41. _____7_____ Yes _____2_____ No

42. Requirements should be based on the needs of the job. Requirements should not change based on the source of candidates. Requirements should only change when it has been determined that candidates who meet existing requirements cannot be obtained.

_____7_____ Yes _____1_____ No

43. Position requirements should be part of a position description and should have been the product of a job analysis.

_____6_____ Yes _____2_____ No

44. Multiple interviews can be most effective if the information each interviewer is seeking has been planned and coordinated before the interview. This means the questions asked should have been coordinated. Otherwise, the results can be counterproductive. The Organization could appear to the candidate as not knowing what it is doing in the selection process, and interviewers could fail to obtain important information.

_____7_____ Yes _____2_____ No _____5_____ Not applicable

45 and 46. You need to check federal, state, and local requirements to be sure you have all legally required notices posted where they can be viewed by candidates. To ensure you continue to be in compliance, you need to regularly review requirements.

45. _____7_____ Yes _____1_____ No

46. _____6_____ Yes _____2_____ No

47, 48, and 49. Drug testing of candidates is still somewhat controversial. However, if you use drug testing as a condition of employment, you should test all candidates at the same time in the hiring process. The hiring area should contain a notice about your drug-testing practice, or a written notice should be supplied to all candidates. If your Organization does not require drug testing, give yourself 6 points for each of Questions 47, 48, and 49.

47. _____8_____ Yes _____2_____ No

48. _____6_____ Yes _____2_____ No

49. _____8_____ Yes _____1_____ No

50, 51, and 52. Our Advisory Board members were split on their answers to these questions. Some recommended physicals and some did not. Make sure you have a job-related reason for requiring physical examinations. Assuming there is one, notice to candidates should be given, and all appropriate candidates given physicals.

50. _____8_____ Yes _____8_____ No _____8_____ Some positions

51. _____6_____ Yes _____2_____ No _____4_____ Not applicable

52. _____6_____ Yes _____1_____ No _____4_____ Some positions

53. Although many may have input, and in some cases approval of the decision, the final decision regarding hiring should be made by the supervisor of the position.

_____8_____ Supervisor of the open position

_____6_____ Manager of the open position's supervisor

___4___ Senior manager in the department of the open position

___2___ Senior human resources manager

___2___ Human resources manager accountable for recruitment

___2___ Other

54. It is important to remember that all candidates are also potentially candidates for other positions and/or customers of the Organization. All candidates should be treated in the most professional way possible. As one of our Advisory Board members commented, "The selection process provides an excellent method for creating a favorable Organization image."

___7___ Yes ___2___ No

55 and 56. Staying with the philosophy expressed in the explanation to the previous question, applications and resumes provide an excellent opportunity for public relations. An Organization should never pass up such an opportunity. This is true even when candidates do not know to whom they are sending their resumes. The Organization should have a policy covering this activity and should apply it consistently.

55. ___8___ Yes ___2___ No

56. ___1___ Those from walk-in candidates

___1___ Those from employment agency/search firm candidates

___2___ Those from employee-recommended candidates

___2___ Those from candidates responding to advertisements

___2___ Those from school- or professional association–recommended candidates

___1___ Those from candidates sending unsolicited resumes

___2___ Those from Internet candidates

57. The hiring process is a dual search for information. The Organization is attempting to seek information about a candidate in order to make a selection

decision, but the candidate also needs information to make a decision to accept an offered job. In addition, candidates provide an ideal opportunity to build a positive Organization image.

_____7_____ Yes   ____2____ No

58. Recruiting is one of the most significant contributions a professional human resources department can make to an Organization's continued success. Someone should be accountable for it.

_____9_____ Yes   ____1____ No

59. Job fairs and college recruiting provide two things: candidates directly out of school and still another opportunity for positive public relations.

_____6_____ Yes   ____3____ No

60, 61, and 62. Whatever number you used to answer each of these questions is the rating for that question.

Education, Training, and Development—Evaluation

If this category is not one for which your human resources department is accountable, go directly to the next category beginning on page 205.

1. Next to recruiting and selection, education, training, and development is the category in which a professional human resources department can make significant contributions to an Organization's continued success. It requires that someone be accountable for it.

<u> 9 </u> Yes   <u> 1 </u> No

2. Anyone should be able to initiate a training request if he has a way of knowing what training is required and by whom.

<u> 2 </u> Employee

<u> 3 </u> Employee's supervisor

<u> 2 </u> Manager of employee's supervisor

<u> 1 </u> Senior manager in the employee's department

<u> 1 </u> Senior human resources manager

<u> 2 </u> Human resources manager accountable for training

<u> 1 </u> An external consultant

<u> 2 </u> Other

3. If an Organization requires any unique skills, it probably has to train employees in these skills. If that is the case, such training needs should be recognized and training made available.

<u> 8 </u> Yes   <u> 2 </u> No

4. Training should be available for both learning the requirements of a new job when hired and maintaining competence in a current job. It should also be available for preparing for other positions within the Organization.

_____7_____ Yes _____2_____ No

5. In addition to training for specific jobs, training should be offered in management and supervisory skills. Training should include the policies and procedures of the Organization as well as general management skills such as leadership and decision making.

_____8_____ Yes _____1_____ No

6. In today's environment, obtaining employees is difficult due to the low unemployment rate. As a result, candidates often do not have the required basic skills for a job. Organizations that offer remedial training often have discovered a new source of candidates.

_____7_____ Yes _____2_____ No

7. Any training program should include specific behavioral objectives as part of its design. These objectives should be measurable, and the program tested to ensure it fulfills objectives.

_____8_____ Yes _____2_____ No

8. Training programs designed with specific (measurable) behavioral objectives can measure whether or not employees participating in the training have obtained those objectives. Measurements should be taken following every training program. If you do not have behavioral objectives for your training programs, give yourself 5 points for your answer to this question.

_____8_____ Yes _____1_____ No

9. Even if your training programs do not have specific behavioral objectives, attempts should be made to ensure what they are offering is effective. If the employees are not learning from a training program, it is a waste of time.

_____8_____ Yes _____1_____ No

10. In almost all cases, training is meant to improve job performance, so the ultimate measure of a training program's effectiveness is improved performance on the job. This type of activity should be a regular component of all training.

_____8_____ Yes _____1_____ No

11. In today's environment of rapid technological developments, training program subject matter quickly can become outdated. Protection against this can be accomplished by a regular review of subject matter.

_____9_____ Yes _____2_____ No

12. In addition to ensuring subject matter is up-to-date, training programs also need to be reviewed regularly for relevancy to the job and the Organization; how often depends on the subject matter and how fast its technology changes. Every training program should be reviewed at least every two years, and whenever a change affects its subject matter.

_____1_____ At least once a year

_____3_____ Every one to three years

_____1_____ Every three to five years

_____2_____ When requested by management

_____4_____ When there appears to have been a change in the subject matter

_____4_____ When results of the training are not as planned

_____0_____ Never

13. Probably the two individuals who can best identify the training needs of an employee are the employee and his supervisor.

_____2_____ Employee

_____3_____ Employee's supervisor

_____2_____ Manager of employee's supervisor

_____1_____ Senior manager in the employee's department

_____1_____ Senior human resources manager

_____2_____ Human resources manager accountable for training

_____3_____ An external consultant

_____2_____ Other

14. Individual employee training needs for the current position are best identified through performance to job standards and objectives reviews. However, training needs for other positions or due to job or subject matter changes require other approaches. Give yourself 2 points for each item you checked.

15 and 16. Both the Organization's managers and employees need to be made aware of what training is available, when and where it is available, and how to enroll.

15. _____8_____ Yes   _____1_____ No

16. _____8_____ Yes   _____1_____ No

17. There is no one correct way to obtain training programs. If you have a large training department, you may have qualified developers on staff. Otherwise, you may be looking externally. In some cases specific development skills that can only be found in one source are required. You should be open to using all available resources depending on the specific training required. Give yourself 2 points for each source you checked.

18. Training programs should be conducted by the most appropriate qualified person. However, although training professionals are the most skilled in training techniques, our Advisory Board has a slight leaning toward nontrainers, particularly those from the actual work area of the program's subject matter.

_____3_____ Internal training professionals

_____2_____ Externally contracted people

_____3_____ Internal operating people

_____2_____ Other

19. The methods used to conduct training should reflect the subject matter and number of employees to be trained at any one time. The important point is that you deliver the training by whatever method is best suited for the situation. Give yourself 2 points for each method you checked.

20 and 21. Here the key is to have necessary facilities available either within the Organization or externally. Without proper facilities the effectiveness of training can be reduced dramatically.

20. ___8___ Yes ___1___ No

21. ___6___ Yes ___2___ No

22. Whoever conducts training should be knowledgeable of the subject matter and its implementation on the job.

___8___ Yes ___2___ No

23. Trainers should possess the skills of training others in the subject matter as well as the subject matter expertise.

___9___ Yes ___2___ No

24. It is rare that an Organization can provide for every training and development need, so the use of external resources is a good way to augment internal training programs.

___7___ Yes ___2___ No

25. One of the problems with using external seminars and courses is making the necessary information about them available. This is generally best accomplished when all such information is in one location. Therefore, a single individual accountable for obtaining and maintaining that information contributes to its effective use.

___6___ Yes ___3___ No

26. Having such external seminar and course information collected and centralized can only be effective when the employees know where it is maintained and how to access it.

___7___ Yes ___2___ No

27. Like facilities and methods, the proper delivery equipment needs to be available.

___7___ Yes ___1___ No

28. Training is very inexpensive if it provides what is needed, but if it fails, it can be a very expensive activity. Training professionals should calculate the cost of each training program by individual trained. That information can be used to determine whether the training program is worth the effort, and whether or not similar results can be obtained less expensively by other means.

_____8_____ Yes   _____2_____ No

29. Many Organizations have the cost of training charged back to the departments of the employees being trained. Their theory is that this results in the training being evaluated by the user in terms of its cost and benefit. However, other Organizations feel training is an Organizationwide activity and thus a cost to be shared by all.

_____6_____ Yes   _____2_____ No   _____6_____ Sometimes

30. The use of external training resources, whether attendance at seminars or contracting of consultants, is most effective when coordinated by a single individual. Otherwise there is often duplication and unnecessary costs.

_____7_____ Yes   _____2_____ No

31. One of the most effective ways to communicate an Organization's training program availability is to publish a catalog. The catalog is usually similar to those published by schools. It indicates courses, their objectives, their availability, and enrollment procedures.

_____6_____ Yes   _____1_____ No

32 and 33. If you publish a catalog, it is most effective when it is distributed throughout the Organization. However, catalogs demand regular review and revision to ensure they remain relevant, with up-to-date information. If you do not publish a catalog, give yourself 3 points for each of these two questions.

32. _____7_____ Yes   _____2_____ No

33. _____4_____ Every three months

_____6_____ Every six months to one year

_____7_____ Every year

___4___ Every one to three years

___1___ Whenever requested

___0___ Never

___2___ Other

34. Although not as often offered, a catalog of generally used external courses and seminars can be useful.

___6___ Yes ___2___ No

35 and 36. A catalog of external courses and seminars is most effective when distributed throughout the Organization and updated regularly. If you do not publish a catalog, give yourself 3 points for each of these two questions.

35. ___6___ Yes ___3___ No

36. ___2___ Every three months

___4___ Every six months to one year

___6___ Every year

___1___ Every one to three years

___2___ Whenever requested

___0___ Never

___2___ Other

37. In recent years there have been major changes in the training and development field. Individualized courses are now offered through personal computers. Courses are available over the Internet. Global conferencing and workshops are possible through satellite links, and increasing use has been made of simulations for training. These trends have all the signs of continuing and accelerating. They demand that someone monitor and identify those developments that are of the most benefit to the Organization.

___7___ Yes ___1___ No

38. Information is only useful if it is known by the people who can directly benefit from it. If you do not monitor developments in the field, give yourself 3 points for this question.

<u>   7   </u> Yes   <u> 1 </u> No

39. Professional trainers require development activities to remain current. They need to keep skilled in the developments of the field and ensure their current skills are being used for maximum effectiveness.

<u>   8   </u> Yes   <u> 2 </u> No

40, 41, and 42. These three questions all relate to the continued development of trainers. Membership and participation in professional associations and conferences are approaches to improve and ensure currency of skills. Membership should be encouraged and paid for by the Organization.

40. <u> 7 </u> Yes   <u> 2 </u> No

41. <u> 7 </u> Yes   <u> 3 </u> No

42. <u> 6 </u> Yes   <u> 3 </u> No

43. Outsourcing is becoming an attractive alternative in many human resources areas. Training is an area that may offer possibilities for outsourcing, although training that tends to be for unique activities or subject matter often does not lend itself to outsourcing. Likewise, training that requires a full-time staff is often best kept within the Organization. The key point here is that the possibility of outsourcing has been examined and an informed decision made.

<u>   8   </u> Yes   <u> 3 </u> No

44. Many employees can benefit in their development by a discussion with a knowledgeable professional in the training and development field—someone who can provide direction to meeting development objectives. The most logical place within an Organization for this type of activity is human resources.

<u>   7   </u> Yes   <u> 2 </u> No

45. There are many advantages to a tuition reimbursement program. It improves the knowledge of current employees. It assists in retaining employees, and it develops people for future growth in the Organization.

<u>   8   </u> Yes   <u> 2 </u> No

46. Tuition reimbursement programs differ by industry, area, and individual Organization. Cost is a factor, but as a general rule, the more items covered, the stronger the benefits of the program to both the individual and the Organization. If you do not have a tuition reimbursement program, give yourself 4 points for this question.

___5___ Tuition

___2___ Books

___2___ Lab fees

___1___ Transportation

___1___ Other

47. Some Organizations believe any learning can be a benefit to the Organization and so they do not limit the course or courses of study that are reimbursable. Other Organizations require a direct relationship to the current job or to the Organization. If you do not have a tuition reimbursement program, give yourself 3 points for this question.

___7___ Yes   ___5___ No

48. Almost all programs require evidence of successful completion in order for the employee to obtain reimbursement.

___7___ Yes   ___1___ No

49, 50, and 51. Whatever number you used to answer each of these questions is the rating for that question.

EMPLOYEE RELATIONS—EVALUATION

If this category is not one for which your human resources department is accountable, go directly to the next category beginning on page 217.

1. Almost all categories in this audit include a similar question. All of these categories are important to a successful human resources department, so each needs to have an individual within the department who is primarily accountable for that key result area.

<u> 9 </u> Yes   <u> 1 </u> No

2. Because employee relations covers most conditions of employment, it is an area in which employees often have questions or require assistance. They need to know who to contact within human resources.

<u> 9 </u> Yes   <u> 1 </u> No

3. Consistency, equality of treatment, and fairness are the concerns most employees express with respect to conditions of employment. Worries are best alleviated when they are covered by policies and procedures written and applied equally to all.

<u> 9 </u> Yes   <u> 1 </u> No

4. An Organization's policies and procedures should reside in the human resources department, but also in the hands of those employees who administer them, the management of the Organization. Nonmanagement employees need to know policy and procedures, but generally there are better formats such as employee handbooks. If you do not have formal policies and procedures, give yourself 4 points total for this question.

<u> 3 </u> All supervisors

<u> 3 </u> All managers

<u> 3 </u> Human resources

_____1_____ All employees

_____2_____ Other

_____1_____ Individual responsible for employee relations

5. As mentioned in the answer to the previous question, an employee handbook is an ideal format in which to communicate the general employment conditions of the Organization to employees.

_____9_____ Yes _____1_____ No

6 and 7. An employee handbook must be in the hands of the employees to be useful. A handbook should be given to each employee when he joins the Organization. It must be updated whenever a change is made. If you do not have an employee handbook, give yourself 3 points for each of these two questions.

6. _____9_____ Yes _____1_____ No

7. _____8_____ Yes _____1_____ No

8. Our Advisory Board thinks all these subjects are important, but the scoring indicates which ones we believe are absolute musts for communication to employees.

_____1_____ Organization history

_____1_____ Organization mission

_____1_____ Organization performance objectives and history

_____1_____ Organization financial history

_____2_____ Key people within Organization to contact with questions

_____2_____ Job information

_____2_____ Department information

_____2_____ Rules and regulations

_____2_____ Benefits

_____2_____ Performance reviews

_____2_____ Compensation

_____1_____ Leaving the Organization

_____2_____ Time off

_____1_____ Promotions and transfers

_____1_____ Training and development opportunities

_____1_____ Career opportunities

_____2_____ Other

9. Individual policies and procedures require a review whenever a significant change occurs. However, even when there are no changes, all policies and procedures should be reviewed on a regular basis.

_____1_____ At least every six months

_____2_____ Every six months to one year

_____3_____ Every year

_____1_____ Every one to three years

_____0_____ Every three years or more

_____1_____ When requested

_____2_____ When the law requires a change

_____2_____ When the Organization makes a significant change

_____0_____ Never

10 and 11. This actually may be more than one individual. For example, one person in human resources may be identified as the contact regarding benefits, and another may be identified for compensation questions. Employees need to know who to contact and the information needs to be kept current. If that infor-

mation is by position rather than individual name, it does not require revision as often.

10. __8__ Yes __1__ No

11. __8__ Yes __1__ No

12. Formal policies and procedures generally do not describe all the details for proper administration, so a manual describing administrative procedures can be of great assistance to supervisors and can be helpful in preventing employee problems.

__8__ Yes __1__ No

13 and 14. Here the explanation is similar to that given for other written materials. Every supervisor who may administer policies and procedures needs to have a copy of the manual. To remain effective, the manual must be kept current. If you do not have such a manual, give yourself 3 points for each of these two questions.

13. __8__ Yes __1__ No

14. __8__ Yes __1__ No

15 and 16. No matter what level of detail is covered in policies, procedures, and administration manuals, situations will arise that require interpretations and decisions. To ensure consistency and prepare information for later revisions, interpretation and decision records need to be maintained and referred to at the appropriate times.

15. __8__ Yes __1__ No

16. __8__ Yes __1__ No __3__ Not applicable

17. Increasingly, Organizations are identifying an individual who is available to counsel employees on personal problems. Sometimes this is an external professional who is only available at scheduled times. Sometimes it is an individual employee of the human resources department who, in large Organizations, performs the activity full-time, and, in smaller organizations, part-time. In some cases, it is a referral to an external counselor. The objective is to provide employees a source

for assistance with personal problems that might otherwise interfere with job performance.

_____7_____ Yes _____2_____ No

18 and 19. If your Organization provides employees assistance with personal problems, they need to know how to obtain it, and that information needs to be kept current. If you do not offer such assistance, give yourself 3 points for each of these two questions.

18. _____6_____ Yes _____1_____ No

19. _____6_____ Yes _____1_____ No

20 and 21. To be effective, counseling for personal problems must be handled in a professional and ethical manner. This requires complete confidentiality of the information and assurances that the counselor is properly qualified. Due to the need for confidentiality, Organizations often prefer their own personnel not be identified as the counselor. Allowing a nonqualified individual to counsel has the potential of harming the employee. If you do not offer such assistance, give yourself 3 points for each of these two questions.

20. _____6_____ Yes _____1_____ No

21. _____6_____ Yes _____1_____ No

22. Every Organization has different employee policies, procedures, benefits, and structures. Employees can function more efficiently when they know these. The most effective method of communication (along with an employee handbook) is an orientation program. Such a program, whether conducted on an individual or group basis, provides an opportunity for the Organization to ensure all important information is covered, and it provides new employees an opportunity to ask questions.

_____8_____ Yes _____2_____ No _____4_____ Sometimes

23. The most effective time to conduct a new employee orientation is somewhat close to the employee's date of hire. Some Organizations feel orientation is most effective a week or month after hire. The first day offers so much that is new that it is better to allow the employee time to adjust to the Organization's environment before reviewing all details, the thinking goes. Other Organizations feel a new employee should be exposed to all conditions of employment before

actually reporting to the work assignment. If you do not conduct orientation programs, give yourself 3 points for your answer to this question.

____6____ Prior to hiring

____8____ The first day of employment

____7____ The first week of employment

____6____ The first month of employment

____4____ Whenever there are enough new employees

____2____ Other

24. Exit interviews can provide useful information, particularly to the human resources department. Often departing employees will communicate information that might otherwise be kept quiet.

____8____ Conducted   ____6____ Offered   ____1____ No

25. As both a regular operating procedure and common courtesy, a departing employee's supervisor should talk with him, but formal exit interviews are better conducted by someone else. Human resources generally is the ideal department.

____8____ Yes   ____3____ No

26. Whatever information is gained from a departing employee should be distributed to the appropriate management. This is the only way it can be useful in improving employee conditions of employment.

____3____ Supervisor of person in position

____3____ Manager of supervisor of person in position

____3____ Senior human resources manager

____2____ Senior manager to whom senior human resources manager reports

____2____ Other

27. Exit interviews are an excellent way to obtain opinions regarding conditions of employment, but they are from people who will no longer be a part of the Organization. Information from current employees is generally best obtained through employee opinion surveys.

_____8_____ Yes _____2_____ No

28. Employee opinion surveys are most useful when conducted on a somewhat regular basis. To some extent, their frequency is dependent on changes occurring, the results of a previous survey, and revisions to conditions of employment, but the following scoring is generally appropriate:

_____4_____ At least every six months

_____5_____ Every six months to one year

_____7_____ Every year

_____8_____ Every one to three years

_____5_____ Every three years or more

_____4_____ When requested

_____6_____ When a change has been made

_____0_____ Never

29. Studies indicate that to be effective the results obtained through employee opinion surveys need to be communicated to all employees. If not, future surveys tend to lose their reliability. Ideally some type of discussion from the Organization's management is included with the communication about the results. If you do not conduct employee opinion surveys, give yourself 3 points for this question.

_____8_____ Yes _____1_____ No _____3_____ Sometimes

30. Studies indicate employee opinion surveys are most reliable when conducted by nonemployees of the Organization. If you do not conduct employee opinion surveys, give yourself 3 points for this question.

_____5_____ Someone in human resources

_____7_____ An external consultant or consulting firm

_____3_____ Someone from operating management

_____2_____ Other

31. Employee assistance programs (EAPs) provide an external psychological resource for employees. Along with counseling on personal problems, an EAP is a good way to assist employees to remain effective.

_____8_____ Yes _____2_____ No

32, 33, and 34. These three questions all have to do with communicating the EAP and ensuring it is conducted professionally and ethically. If you do not have an EAP, give yourself 3 points for each of these three questions.

32. _____6_____ Yes _____2_____ No

33. _____6_____ Yes _____2_____ No

34. _____7_____ Yes _____1_____ No

35. Regardless of how well an Organization is managed, sooner or later there will be employees who have complaints or grievances. Attempting to handle these informally may be a noble objective, but it can lead to an employee's insecurity or feeling that the complaint is not being handled in a satisfactory manner. Studies indicate that lacking a formal grievance procedure, even when it is seldom used, can be a significant factor in employee discontent.

_____8_____ Yes _____1_____ No

36 and 37. These two question have to do with ensuring all employees know of the grievance procedure. If you do not have a grievance procedure, give yourself 3 points for each of these two questions.

36. _____8_____ Yes _____1_____ No

37. _____7_____ Yes _____2_____ No

38. An open-door policy allows any employee to talk with any management member (in some cases with limited management members). It is designed to ensure employees that their individual views are of interest and concern. It also is designed to ensure employees that they may be heard outside their departments. Some Organizations think a grievance procedure eliminates the need for an open-

door policy. Some Organizations think such a policy is ineffective, and some feel employees view it cynically. Still, many have an open-door policy and are pleased with its results.

___6___ Yes ___2___ No

39 and 40. These two question have to do with ensuring all employees know of the open-door policy.

39. ___6___ Yes ___2___ No ___3___ Not applicable

40. ___6___ Yes ___2___ No ___3___ Not applicable

41. The worst condition for employee relations is to have a good-sounding policy and then not follow it. Actually, this is one reason some Organizations cite employee cynicism to an open-door policy—it sounds good but management does not follow it. If you do not offer an open-door policy, give yourself 3 points for this question.

___6___ Yes ___1___ No

42. An Organization needs general rules, guidelines, and regulations for its employees. These should describe the behavior that is desired and the behavior that is not permitted. They also should indicate the seriousness of the various nondesirable behaviors. Lacking such rules, guidelines, and regulations, employees may be encouraged to decide for themselves what behaviors are acceptable. Employees in different departments of the Organization may be treated differently and there will be little consistency in enforcement.

___8___ Yes ___1___ No

43 and 44. These two questions deal with ensuring all employees know the Organization's rules, guidelines, and regulations. If your Organization does not have rules, guidelines, and regulations, give yourself 3 points for each of these two questions.

43. ___8___ Yes ___1___ No

44. ___8___ Yes ___1___ No

45 through 48. If the Organization's rules, guidelines, and regulations do not cover all areas of employee behavior for a department, the individual depart-

ment should have additional ones. Department rules, guidelines, and regulations should be in writing, distributed to all department employees, and coordinated with the Organization's rules, guidelines, and regulations to ensure there are no conflicts or differences.

45. ___7___ Yes ___2___ No

If your answer to Question 45 was yes, use the following scoring. If it was no, and the question is not applicable, give yourself 3 points for each of the next three questions.

46. ___7___ Yes ___1___ No ___3___ Not applicable

47. ___7___ Yes ___1___ No ___3___ Not applicable

48. ___8___ Yes ___1___ No ___3___ Not applicable

49. To ensure the fair and equal treatment of employees, there should be an established performance improvement/disciplinary procedure. Ideally the procedure is one designed to correct employee behavior and not to punish. It also should be one that begins with a discussion and moves to increasing actions. It should be administered consistently. It should provide a documented record of what happens. It should be viewed as a positive and constructive approach to employee relations.

___9___ Yes ___1___ No

50 and 51. These questions relate to ensuring the communication of an Organization's conditions of employment. If you do not have such a procedure, give yourself 3 points for each of these two questions.

50. ___8___ Yes ___1___ No

51. ___8___ Yes ___1___ No

52. Even if an Organization does not anticipate terminations of any type (layoffs, discharges, facility closing), it should have a formal policy covering the treatment of employees in such an event.

___9___ Yes ___1___ No

53 and 54. As with all important employee relations policies, a termination policy should be in writing and communicated to all employees.

53. ____7____ Yes ____2____ No

54. ____7____ Yes ____2____ No

55. This audit cannot cover every possible variation of employee relations programs or practices. Employee relations functions have grown significantly in some Organizations. Whether any of these new areas are appropriate or of interest to your Organization is not as important as that you are aware of them, and have considered them as part of your Organization's approach.

Give yourself 1 point for your answer to each item you have considered.

56, 57, and 58. Whatever number you used to answer each of these questions is the rating for that question.

BENEFITS—EVALUATION

If this category is not one for which your human resources department is accountable, go directly to the next category beginning on page 223.

1. Here is another important activity of human resources. As with similar categories, it requires that someone be specifically accountable for it.

<u>9</u> Yes <u>1</u> No

2. An Organization should have some type of overall policy regarding benefits. Two examples of a policy statement are:

Our policy is to offer benefits that are equal to or superior to those offered by other Organizations in the geographic area.

Our policy is to provide minimum benefits but a higher wage than what is offered by other Organizations in this area.

<u>8</u> Yes <u>2</u> No

3. If a benefits policy exists, it should be published and communicated to employees. If you do not have a benefits policy, give yourself 3 points for your answer to this question.

<u>8</u> Yes <u>3</u> No

4 and 5. There are probably more employee questions regarding benefits than any other condition of employment—particularly by new employees. Employees need to know whom within human resources to contact with questions, and that information needs to be kept current.

4. <u>8</u> Yes <u>1</u> No

5. <u>8</u> Yes <u>2</u> No

6. Generally benefits are one of the key concerns new employees have. Actually, in many cases employees will want the information prior to accepting a job offer, but even so, they should also receive information when they join the Organization. Some Organizations delay providing this information for a week or a

month. They provide the new employees an opportunity to adjust to the Organization's environment first, believing employees will then be more receptive to benefits details. Some Organizations who have benefits waiting periods wait until the end of such periods before explaining benefits.

_____9_____ Yes _____1_____ No

7 and 8. Benefits information must be kept current and employees immediately notified of any change. In some cases employees will need to be notified in advance of changes.

7. _____8_____ Yes _____1_____ No

8. _____8_____ Yes _____1_____ No

9. There are many reasons for reviewing specific benefits: new laws or regulations or changes by a benefits carrier such as an insurance company. At a minimum benefits should be reviewed every one to three years.

_____2_____ At least every six months

_____2_____ Every six months to one year

_____4_____ Every year

_____6_____ Every one to three years

_____3_____ Every three years or more

_____2_____ When requested

_____3_____ When there is a necessary change

10. Benefits surveys conducted by the Organization in its geographic area or industry, and information supplied by another Organization for an area or industry, provide valuable information. They indicate how well a benefits policy is being met, how competitive the benefits package is, and what new benefits are offered by others.

_____7_____ Area _____6_____ Industry _____8_____ Both _____2_____ Neither

11. Even if an Organization only reviews benefits every one to three years, having annual benefits survey information provides a basis for reviews, including

annual trends. If you do not conduct or obtain benefits surveys, give yourself 2 points for your answer to this question.

___2___ Every six months to one year

___7___ Every year

___8___ Every one to three years

___4___ Every three years or more

___2___ When requested

___2___ When there is a necessary change

___0___ Never

12. Whatever the results of a benefits survey, they should be communicated to employees. If they are not, employees will develop their own opinions on the competitiveness of your Organization's benefits. Generally, factual information is better and more favorable than opinion. Also, if the Organization has a benefits policy and has communicated it to employees, communicating the results of benefits surveys provides an indication of how well the Organization is meeting its policy. If you do not conduct or obtain benefits surveys, give yourself 3 points for this question.

___6___ Yes ___2___ No

13. If you have a benefits policy, the Organization's benefits program should be in agreement. Otherwise, something is seriously amiss. If you have no benefits policy, give yourself 3 points for this question.

___8___ Yes ___1___ No

14. The past decade has seen an increasing number of new laws, regulations, and court decisions that have affected benefits, and there is little reason to assume this trend will not continue or accelerate. Someone needs to be in the communications cycle to ensure the Organization always has the latest information.

___6___ Yes ___1___ No

15. The previous question dealt with ensuring the Organization has the latest information regarding laws, regulations, and court decisions that impact bene-

fits. This question has to do with recommended actions to ensure compliance with those laws, regulations, and court decisions.

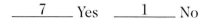

      7   Yes   1   No

16. Many employee opinion surveys ask for employee opinions regarding the Organization's current benefits, but few seem to question how important the benefits being offered are to employees. Having such information can be very helpful in designing and reviewing the Organization's benefits program. However, it is important that the procedure used to obtain such information is not construed by employees as a vote on benefits.

      6   Yes   2   No

17. Cafeteria benefits programs assign a specific amount of money to an employee to purchase whatever benefits best meet his needs. This approach is not necessarily the best for all Organizations, but where it fits, it is usually seen by most employees as an advantage, and it can provide the Organization with better benefits cost control. The important point is that you know of this approach and have considered its possibilities for your Organization.

      8   Yes   2   No

18. Many Organizations believe it is important to communicate the cost of benefits to employees, especially with the higher cost of benefits today. These Organizations want to ensure the employee understands how much is being spent on their behalf. Some even issue statements once a year.

      6   Yes   2   No

19. Such governmentally required benefits as Social Security and Workers Compensation insurance are paid in part or full by the Organization. Although at one time these were relatively modest costs, they now represent significant amounts. They are benefits, and most Organizations want to remind employees that the Organization is paying for these benefits.

      6   Yes   2   No

20. There are many benefits programs unique to specific Organizations. There are some that will work only in a single Organization. Ideas on what are considered appropriate or desirable employee benefits continue to evolve. The important point is to know what is occurring and what the trends are, and to

examine the merits of each type of benefit for your employees. Our Advisory Board believes that at a minimum you should be aware of and have considered the benefits listed in this question. Give yourself 1 point for each one you have investigated, considered, or offer.

21. Many Organizations have found it to be cost-effective to outsource some or all of their benefits administration. The simplest approach is to outsource employee insurance administration, but there are vendors who will handle the entire benefits program. The important point is not whether you outsource benefits administration or not, but whether you have considered outsourcing and have made an informed decision.

<u>   8   </u> Yes   <u>   2   </u> No

22, 23, and 24. Whatever number you used to answer each of these questions is the rating for that question.

Compensation—Evaluation

If this category is not one for which your human resources department is accountable, go directly to the next category beginning on page 231.

1. As with similar categories of human resources, compensation demands that someone be specifically accountable for it.

<u>   9   </u> Yes <u>   1   </u> No

2. An Organization should have some type of overall policy regarding compensation such as:

Our policy is to pay the competitive rate for similar jobs in our geographic area.

Our policy is to pay 80 percent of the competitive rate and provide performance bonuses that can raise total compensation to 150 percent of the competitive rate.

<u>   8   </u> Yes <u>   2   </u> No

3. If a compensation policy exists it should be published so it can be communicated to employees. If you do not have a compensation policy, give yourself 3 points for this question.

<u>   8   </u> Yes <u>   1   </u> No

4 and 5. There are many employee questions regarding compensation. Employees need to know whom within human resources to contact with these questions, and that information needs to be kept current.

4. <u>   7   </u> Yes <u>   2   </u> No

5. <u>   7   </u> Yes <u>   2   </u> No

6. Compensation is one of the key concerns new employees generally have. Actually, in many cases, employees will want the information prior to accepting a job offer, but even so, they also should receive information when they join the Organization. Some Organizations delay providing this information for a week

or a month. Their reasoning is that new employees need time to adjust to the Organization's environment first, and will then be more receptive to the details of their compensation program.

____7____ Yes ____2____ No

7. Compensation information must be kept current and employees immediately notified of any change. In some cases, advance notification of changes is required.

____7____ Yes ____2____ No

8. Compensation surveys conducted by the Organization in its geographic area or industry and the information supplied by another Organization for the area or industry provide valuable information. They indicate how well a compensation policy is being met, how competitive compensation is, and what new benefits are being offered by competitors. They also indicate what type of increases are being projected by other Organizations.

____8____ Area ____8____ Industry

____9____ Both ____2____ Neither

9. There are many reasons for surveying compensation. In general, such surveys should be conducted annually to stay current and to obtain information on trends and increases.

____4____ At least every six months

____6____ Every six months to one year

____8____ Every year

____6____ Every one to three years

____3____ Every three years or more

____2____ When requested

____0____ Never

10. Whatever the results of a compensation survey, they should be communicated to employees. If they are not, the employees will develop their own opinions

on other Organizations' compensation rates. Generally, factual information is better and more favorable than opinion. Also, if the Organization has a compensation policy and has communicated it to employees, communicating the results of a compensation survey provides an indication of how well the Organization is meeting its policy. If you do not conduct or obtain compensation surveys, give yourself 3 points for this question.

      __7__ Yes   __2__ No

11. If you have a compensation policy, the Organization's compensation administration should be in agreement. Otherwise, something is seriously amiss.

      __7__ Yes   __1__ No   __3__ Not applicable

12. The past decade has seen an increasing number of new laws, regulations, and court decisions that have affected compensation, and there is little reason to assume this trend will not continue or accelerate. Someone needs to be in the communications cycle to ensure the Organization always has the latest information.

      __7__ Yes   __2__ No

13. The previous question dealt with ensuring the Organization has the latest information regarding laws, regulations, and court decisions that impact compensation. This question has to do with the recommended actions to ensure compliance with those laws, regulations, and court decisions.

      __8__ Yes   __1__ No

14. However positions are evaluated to determine their worth to the Organization and their compensation, the evaluation procedure needs to be formalized. Only then can consistency and equality be achieved.

      __8__ Yes   __2__ No

15. The correct answer here depends on the type of system you use. Generally, a group or committee is more accurate and acceptable. If your answer to the previous question was no, give yourself 3 points for your answer to this question.

      __6__ Individual   __7__ Group/committee   __4__ Other

16. If your answer to Question 14 was no or your answer to the previous question was Group/committee, give yourself 0 points for this question. Otherwise use the following scoring:

____1____ Position's supervisor

____2____ Manager of position's supervisor

____3____ Senior manager of department in which position reports

____0____ Senior executive of Organization

____7____ Position in human resources accountable for compensation

____6____ Senior human resources manager

____6____ External consultant

____3____ Other

17. If your answer to Question 15 was Individual, give yourself 0 points for this question. Otherwise use the following scoring:

____2____ Position's supervisor

____1____ Manager of position's supervisor

____2____ Senior manager of department in which position reports

____0____ Senior executive of Organization

____4____ Position in human resources accountable for compensation

____3____ Senior human resources manager

____2____ External consultant

____2____ Other

18. There are a number of occasions when a position should be evaluated. When it is first established and whenever there is an action that may change its value to the Organization are the two most important occasions.

____2____ Whenever a new position description is prepared

____1____ Once a year

_____3_____ Every one to three years

_____2_____ Every three years or more

_____1_____ When requested by its supervisor

_____2_____ When requested by its department manager

_____0_____ Never

19. Every position should have a specified wage, wage range, or wage band. This should specify what that position is to be paid.

_____9_____ Yes _____1_____ No

20. Every employee deserves to know what the wage, wage range, or wage band of her position is.

_____9_____ Yes _____1_____ No

21. Unless positions are covered by a contract that addresses compensation increases, wages need to be reviewed and adjusted, if required, on a regular basis. These adjustments should recognize changes in the position, employee performance, and inflationary pressures.

_____9_____ Yes _____1_____ No

22 and 23. Performance reviews should be used primarily for developing employees to successfully fulfill the requirements of their current position, remain current with developments in their professions, and prepare for meeting their individual career objectives. If compensation is a part of a performance review, it becomes the dominant factor. Therefore, even though an employee's performance is a part of any compensation review, our Advisory Board feels the two reviews should be separated.

22. _____9_____ Yes _____2_____ No

23. _____4_____ One week to one month

_____6_____ One to two months

_____7_____ Two to three months

___8___ Three to six months

___2___ More than six months

___2___ No separation

24. If guidelines are not provided to supervisors for wage adjustments, the results will only be consistent, equal, and fair by coincidence.

___9___ Yes   ___1___ No

25. Wage adjustments should be based on the four items in the list. If you do not provide wage adjustment guidelines, give yourself 3 points for your answer to this question.

___2___ Inflation/cost of living

___3___ Employee performance

___3___ Position on wage range or band

___2___ Amount and time of last increase

___2___ Other

26. The Organization's compensation policy and program should be designed to ensure equality of treatment. However, it is good to have some type of program or system in place to monitor wages and ensure the policy is met.

___8___ Yes   ___1___ No   ___7___ Under special conditions

27. No policy or compensation program should lack the flexibility to recognize unusual performance and reward unusual efforts. However, as a general rule, wage adjustments outside of normal reviews should be kept at a minimum.
Under special conditions

___3___ Yes   ___5___ No

28. Our Advisory Board believes human resources should provide a recommendation with respect to annual wage adjustments that recognizes current economic conditions, employee and Organization performance, and budget realities, and that agrees with the Organization's compensation philosophy. The Board be-

lieves an actual increase should be awarded by the supervisor with appropriate approvals. This is the basis for the following:

Initiates	*Approves*	
3	0	Employee
8	1	Employee's supervisor
6	2	Manager of employee's supervisor
4	2	Senior manager of employee's department
2	0	Senior executive of Organization
2	2	Human resources position accountable for compensation
2	1	Senior human resources manager
2	2	Other

29. Bonuses and gain-sharing programs provide ways for employees to participate in the success of the Organization and improve Organization performance. In addition, they have motivational value.

_____8_____ Yes _____2_____ No

30. If you have a bonus or gain-sharing program, our Advisory Board feels it will be most effective when the eligibility requirements are identified and communicated to employees. If you do not have a bonus or gain-sharing program, give yourself 3 points for your answer to this question.

_____8_____ Yes _____2_____ No

31. Bonuses and gain-sharing programs are most effective when they are tied to employee productivity and performance. If you do not have a bonus or gain-sharing program, give yourself 4 points for your answer to this question.

_____4_____ Individual _____2_____ Department

_____4_____ Organization _____2_____ None

32. Our Advisory Board recognizes that many senior level manager and executive bonuses are discretionary. However, The Board believes all bonuses are most effective and fairest when the eligibility criteria and amounts are formalized.

     5   Yes   7   No

33. If your Organization does have discretionary bonuses or gain-sharing programs, there needs to be some method or system to monitor the results for fair and equal treatment.

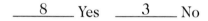

     8   Yes   3   No

34. As with benefits, there are many types of compensation. Some are unique to specific industries and Organizations. The important point is that you are aware of the different compensation programs and have considered the merits of all in terms of your Organization's compensation policy. Give yourself 1 point for your answer to each item you checked.

35, 36, and 37. Whatever number you used to answer each of these questions is the rating for that question.

HUMAN RESOURCES PLANNING—EVALUATION

If this category is not one for which your human resources department is accountable, go directly to the next category beginning on page 237.

1. As with all previous categories covered by this audit, human resources planning requires that someone in human resources be accountable for it.

<u>   9   </u> Yes <u>   2   </u> No

2. Human resources's primary mission within an Organization is to obtain and retain qualified employees. Human resources planning is the function within the Organization that should be supplying personnel projections of numbers of employees and competencies required.

<u>   8   </u> Yes <u>   1   </u> No

3. In some circumstances, especially fast-moving situations, projections may be required within a short time frame, but generally personnel plans should be provided annually. If you do not provide such plans to the Organization, give yourself 2 points for this question.

<u>   2   </u> Every six months

<u>   3   </u> Every year

<u>   2   </u> Every one to two years

<u>   1   </u> Every three or more years

<u>   3   </u> When requested

4. Information for personnel projections should be obtained from all functions and departments. If you do not provide such plans to the Organization, give yourself 2 points for this question.

<u>   3   </u> Individual department heads

<u>   2   </u> Human resources

___1___ External sources

___3___ Senior Organization managers

___1___ Consultants

___0___ No one

5. Personnel projections identify the specific competencies or positions re-quired and when they are required, and they include a comparison with current employees and their abilities. They are then adjusted for probable turnover. This produces a detailed plan that should be used for recruiting. If you do not provide such plans to the Organization, give yourself 3 points for this question.

___8___ Yes ___1___ No

6. The comparison of projected competency needs with those of current em-ployees also identifies areas in which training will be required and when. If you do not provide such plans to the Organization, give yourself 3 points for this ques-tion.

___7___ Yes ___1___ No

7. Human resources personnel projections should be both a product of the Organization's tactical plans and a contributor to them. If you do not provide such plans, give yourself 3 points for this question.

___8___ Yes ___2___ No

8. Depending on the time horizons of personnel projections, they should be coordinated with the Organization's strategic plans. If you do not provide such plans, give yourself 3 points for this question.

___8___ Yes ___1___ No

9. A budget is the financial statement of a plan, so if budgets are prepared from plans that utilize human resources personnel projections, there should be full coordination between the budget and the plan. If you do not provide such plans to the Organization, give yourself 5 points for this question.

___9___ Yes ___1___ No

10. A management succession chart is a device that indicates the backup available within the Organization for management positions, any training that the identified employees may require to move into a position, and positions for which replacements must be obtained from outside the Organization. If a management succession chart is not used, some type of device to accomplish the same objective should be used.

_____8_____ Yes _____2_____ No

11. Generally, management succession charts, like tactical plans and personnel projections, are developed or updated annually. If you do not have management succession charts or similar devices, give yourself 3 points for this question.

_____7_____ Every six months

_____8_____ Every year

_____6_____ Every one to two years

_____4_____ Every three or more years

_____6_____ When requested

_____1_____ Never

12. Your answer to this question depends on the purpose for which your Organization uses a management succession chart or similar device. If the chart merely identifies vulnerable positions, it may not be used when a need to fill a management opening occurs. However, if the chart reflects what the Organization believes to be likely management successions, it should then be considered in making promotions. If your Organization uses such a chart only to identify vulnerability or you do not use such a chart, give yourself 4 points for this question.

_____8_____ Yes _____3_____ No

13. As with personnel projections, the information used for a management succession chart should come from all sources, particularly from the area in which a position is assigned. If you do not use management succession charts, give yourself 4 points for this question.

_____3_____ Individual department heads

_____2_____ Human resources

    __1__ External sources

    __2__ Senior Organization managers

    __1__ External consultants

    __0__ No one

14. Identifying replacements for key positions other than management is just as important as identifying management replacements.

    __7__ Yes   __2__ No

15. Replacements for management positions or key positions should not be limited to the functional areas of the positions.

    __7__ Yes   __2__ No

16. Employees identified as replacements for other positions always seem to learn of it, even when attempts are made to keep such information confidential. Since such identification is usually perceived positively by the employee, our Advisory Board feels the employee should be told.

    __6__ Yes   __2__ No

17. If a replacement employee requires specific training, consideration should be given to providing the training in advance. Then the employee can move into the position faster. If time is available for training when the opening occurs, it is usually better to wait until training is actually required.

    __7__ Yes   __1__ No

18. One of the best forms of training for a replacement is to have him actually perform the duties in advance. Rotational assignments can accomplish this.

    __7__ Yes   __1__ No

19. If employees are told they have been identified as replacements, it is relatively easy and productive to assign them appropriate development objectives.

    __7__ Yes   __1__ No

20. Replacements are usually identified based on the Organization's needs. However, equally important are the career objectives of the identified employees. If employee career objectives are not considered, the employees may decline to accept the position.

_____7_____ Yes _____1_____ No

21. It is difficult to accurately predict job success in major assignment changes. For example, there is little in a nonmanagement job that can be used to predict management success. However, an individual's performance in a first-level management position is generally quite predictive of performance in a second-level management position. Assessment centers or other standardized and validated devices can be used when appropriate.

_____7_____ Yes _____2_____ No

22 through 27. Earlier questions asked about the use of human resources personnel projections with the Organization's plans. The inclusion of human resources tactical and strategic plans in the Organization's tactical and strategic plans is equally important, as is the involvement of the human resources senior manager in the development of those plans.

22. _____8_____ Yes _____1_____ No

23. _____8_____ Yes _____1_____ No

24. _____8_____ Yes _____2_____ No

25. _____8_____ Yes _____1_____ No

26. _____8_____ Yes _____1_____ No

27. _____8_____ Yes _____1_____ No

28 and 29. Another aid to planning is the identification of logical job families. These provide an identified path for employee development and promotion. Also, if communicated to employees, job families provide individual guidance for development because they show the employee what promotional opportunities are available. If your answer to Question 28 was no, give yourself 3 points for Question 29.

28. ___6___ Yes ___2___ No

29. ___6___ Yes ___1___ No

30. As a part of the planning process, as well as part of employee training and development, human resources needs to provide assistance to employees in developing their career objectives.

___7___ Yes ___2___ No

31. It is crucial to consider employees in any merger or acquisition. They represent a significant cost and often a unique set of skills and abilities. An evaluation of and recommendations for employee programs in a merger or acquisition requires involvement of a human resources representative.

___9___ Yes ___1___ No ___7___ Not applicable

32, 33, and 34. Whatever number you used to answer each of these questions is the rating for that question.

ORGANIZATION DEVELOPMENT—EVALUATION

If this category is not one for which your human resources department is accountable, go directly to the next category beginning on page 247.

1. Again, this is a significant category of human resources activities requiring someone within the human resources department to assume full accountability for its implementation.

_____9_____ Yes _____1_____ No

2. Organization development is one of the more recent additions to human resources. Many of its techniques are being refined and expanded. Organizations are increasingly identifying the need for the type of assistance the Organization development specialist can provide, so not only should an individual be accountable for the activity, someone needs to be actively involved with developments in the field.

_____8_____ Yes _____2_____ No

3. Most Organizations have a culture—a combination of beliefs, operating style, and customer base. For many Organizations, their culture just evolved. Others have identified a specific type of culture to support their mission. whether this identification occurred with the creation of the Organization or late in its life.

_____9_____ Yes _____2_____ No

4 and 5. If a desired Organization culture has been identified, a written description allows it to be communicated to employees, so they can understand what is wanted. If you do not have an identified culture, give yourself 3 points for each of these two questions.

4. _____7_____ Yes _____2_____ No

5. _____7_____ Yes _____1_____ No

6. Generally, an Organization benefits from a consistent culture designed to support its mission. Employees can then easily move from one location or department to another and continue to function successfully.

_____9_____ Yes _____2_____ No

7. The organizational development function of the human resources department should be the area that ensures the desired culture is obtained. This function has the expertise to assess current culture and recommend any needed steps to modify it.

_____8_____ Yes _____1_____ No

8. If the Organization has not obtained its desired culture, steps to achieve that culture should be planned and implemented. If your answer to the previous question was yes, give yourself 7 points for this question.

_____7_____ Yes _____3_____ No

9. There are various types of Organization structures. The one employed by an Organization should support its mission and desired culture. As with culture, it is far better for an Organization to have an identified desired Organization structure than to just allow one to develop.

_____7_____ Yes _____2_____ No

10 and 11. As with the Organization's culture, if a desired Organization structure has been identified, a written description allows it to be communicated to employees, so they can understand what is wanted. If you do not have an identified Organization structure, give yourself 4 points for each of these two questions.

10. _____6_____ Yes _____3_____ No

11. _____6_____ Yes _____3_____ No

12. Just as an Organization benefits from a consistent culture, it will benefit from a consistent Organization structure. Employees can easily move from one location or department to another and continue to function successfully.

_____7_____ Yes _____2_____ No

13. The organizational development function of human resources should be the easiest and ensure the desired Organization structure is obtained. The function has the expertise to assess the current structure and recommend any steps necessary to modify it.

_____6_____ Yes _____2_____ No

14. If the Organization has not obtained its desired Organization structure, steps to achieve that should be planned and implemented. If your answer to the previous question was yes, give yourself 6 points for this question.

_____6_____ Yes   _____2_____ No

15. An Organization's strategic plan should reflect the Organization's desired culture and Organization structure along with plans for dealing successfully with projected changes. These are all part of Organization development. If your Organization does not have a strategic plan, give yourself 5 points for this question.

_____7_____ Yes   _____2_____ No

16. Although not as crucial to a tactical plan, consideration should be given to the overall direction of Organization activities. If your Organization does not have a tactical plan, give yourself 5 points for this question.

_____6_____ Yes   _____2_____ No

17. Planned Organization changes and nonanticipated changes that affect an Organization should always be dealt with in a manner that considers Organization structure and desired culture.

_____6_____ Yes   _____2_____ No

18. The only way to determine whether or not an Organization structure is functioning as desired is to obtain information on its effectiveness. There are several way to accomplish this. One effective way is to survey employees.

_____6_____ Yes   _____2_____ No

19. Whenever a significant change or an identified problem affects the Organization, an investigation or survey should be conducted. However, even without such an event regular surveys should be conducted. If you do not conduct surveys, give yourself 4 points for this question.

_____2_____ Every six months

_____4_____ Every year

_____4_____ Every one to two years

_____3_____ Every three or more years

_____2_____ When requested

_____4_____ When there is a significant change impacting the Organization

_____4_____ When an Organization structure or culture problem is identified

_____2_____ Never

20. The only way to determine whether or not the Organization's culture is functioning as desired is to obtain information on its effectiveness. There are several ways to accomplish this. An effective way is to survey employees.

_____8_____ Yes _____2_____ No

21. Again, when there is a significant change affecting the Organization or an identified problem, an investigation or survey should be conducted. However, even without such an event regular surveys should be conducted. If you do not conduct surveys, give yourself 4 points for this question.

_____2_____ Every six months

_____4_____ Every year

_____4_____ Every one to two years

_____3_____ Every three or more years

_____2_____ When requested

_____3_____ When there is a significant change impacting the Organization

_____4_____ When a culture problem is identified

_____2_____ Never

22. Managers and supervisors are primarily accountable for making the Organization structure and culture effective realities. They can be most successful if they are provided assistance and training in appropriate techniques.

_____8_____ Yes _____2_____ No

23. No one activity is more important to a successful Organization than proper communication. Not only is what is communicated important, so is how, when, and where the communication occurs. Employee opinion surveys regularly identify an Organization's communications as the activity most in need of improvement.

<u>   7   </u> Yes   <u>   1   </u> No

24. Communications to employees should be of major concern to the Organization. Organization development professionals are usually the individuals most skilled in such activities. They should review all communications prior to their distribution to employees.

<u>   8   </u> Yes   <u>   1   </u> No

25. From time to time Organization conflicts between departments, units and even employees will occur. Organization development professionals are knowledgeable and skilled in dealing with such problems. They can be used both to establish procedures to reduce conflicts and to assist in resolving conflicts.

<u>   8   </u> Yes   <u>   1   </u> No

26. Meetings are a way of life in most Organizations and can easily consume unneeded amounts of time. Training managers in how to plan, conduct, and control a meeting can lead to more effective results as well as fewer unnecessary meetings.

<u>   8   </u> Yes   <u>   1   </u> No

27. Along with training in meetings management, an analysis of the frequency and quality of meetings can be very helpful. One Organization conducted an analysis and discovered meetings were consuming more than 70 percent of a typical manager's normal workday. Another found that with a few changes meetings could be shortened by more than 25 percent.

<u>   3   </u> Frequency   <u>   3   </u> Quality

<u>   6   </u> Both   <u>   1   </u> Neither

28. Voice mail and e-mail are becoming an increasingly significant tool for Organizations. Used properly they can improve efficiency. Unfortunately, they can also reduce efficiency when improperly used.

<u>   8   </u> Yes   <u>   1   </u> No

29. Often the methods in which e-mail and voice mail are used do not support the Organization's mission and culture. Some Organizations, priding themselves on quality customer service, make it almost impossible for an external caller to speak with a human being. The caller can only leave a voice mail. With e-mail, many people, not knowing what to do with a message, forward it to everyone they can think of, apparently hoping someone will deal with it.

_____8_____ Yes _____2_____ No

30. Some Organizations allow personal use of e-mail and the Internet. Others do not. The correct answer depends on your Organization's culture and approach to its employees. The key point is that you can answer this question.

_____8_____ Yes _____1_____ No _____2_____ Do not know

31 and 32. If there is a policy, it should be in writing and should have been communicated to all employees. If you do not have a policy, give yourself 2 points for each of these two questions.

31. _____7_____ Yes _____2_____ No

32. _____8_____ Yes _____1_____ No

33. Lunchrooms, parking spaces, and office assignments should support the desired culture. Unfortunately, that is not always the case. Some Organizations that state equality of treatment for all employees have lunchrooms for different levels of management. Whenever such assignments are provided, they should be reviewed to ensure they support the desired culture. Actions speak louder than words.

_____8_____ Yes _____2_____ No

34. For the reasons stated in the explanations for the previous questions, any changes to conditions of employment should be reviewed to make sure they support the desired culture.

_____8_____ Yes _____1_____ No

35. Communication and employee identification with the Organization are greatly assisted by department and Organization meetings. They provide a way to

ensure the correct information is provided in a timely fashion and build employee feelings of involvement and identification, as well as promoting teamwork.

_____8_____ Yes _____1_____ No

36 and 37. Almost every function or department within an Organization has customers. Only—some have external customers (the ones we typically think of when the word "customer" is used) but almost all departments have internal customers (other employees and departments of the Organization to whom services and/or products are provided). An Organization's effectiveness generally is improved when employees are encouraged to identify both types of customers and to ensure all are provided quality service.

36. _____8_____ Yes _____1_____ No

37. _____8_____ Yes _____1_____ No

38. Customer service generally can be improved by raising the consciousness of employees as to what constitutes quality and by providing the methods to deliver it. Quality customer service training is the best approach.

_____8_____ Yes _____2_____ No

39. There is probably no correct answer to this question. Some parking situations require space identification and others do not. The key point is that you know the answer.

_____6_____ Yes _____6_____ No

40, 41, and 42. These three questions are getting at one condition of employment as it relates to your Organization's mission and desired culture. Our Advisory Board has based their preferred answers on the theory that all employees should be assigned spaces or none should be. The only exception would be for someone similar to an employee of the month or employees who are arriving and departing on a frequent basis, such as messengers. Otherwise, the Board believes parking assignments should be for visitors and customers, and those assignments should be in the best locations. If you do not assign parking spaces, give yourself 8 points for each of these questions.

40. _____2_____ All employees

_____1_____ Senior managers of the Organization

_____1_____ All managers of the Organization

_____3_____ Employee of the month

_____4_____ Visitors

_____3_____ Employees frequently visiting the facility during the day such as messengers

_____4_____ Employees with disadvantages such as impaired mobility

_____2_____ Other

41. _____0_____ Senior managers of the Organization

_____0_____ All managers of the Organization

_____3_____ Employee of the month

_____3_____ Visitors

_____3_____ Employees frequently visiting the facility during the day such as messengers

_____4_____ Employees with disadvantages such as impaired mobility

_____2_____ Other

42. _____0_____ Senior managers of the Organization

_____0_____ All managers of the Organization

_____2_____ Employee of the month

_____3_____ Visitors

_____3_____ Employees frequently visiting the facility during the day such as messengers

_____4_____ Employees with disadvantages such as impaired mobility

_____2_____ Other

43. A code of business conduct is a statement of the behaviors employees are expected to exhibit as a citizen of the Organization. Such a code also generally describes behavior that, while not actually prohibited, might be perceived as being prohibited. A code of business conduct should be a natural extension of the Organization's mission and culture. The development of such a code is in itself a worthwhile activity for the Organization.

<u>   9   </u> Yes   <u>   1   </u> No

44. Typically, senior managers are required to sign a code of business conduct. Their signatures indicate they have read the code and are in agreement. Codes of business conduct that describe specific types of behavior on the Organization's premises can be used with nonemployees who work on the premises, such as consultants. If you do not have a code of business conduct, give yourself 4 points for this question.

<u>   2   </u> All employees

<u>   2   </u> All managers

<u>   3   </u> Senior managers of the Organization

<u>   2   </u> Nonemployees doing business with the Organization who work on its premises

<u>   2   </u> Other

45. Those required to sign a code of business conduct should do so at the time they begin whatever position or work meets the code's criteria, such as at the time of hire, at the time of promotion, or accepting an appropriate assignment. For nonemployees the code should be signed when they begin an assignment with the Organization. If your answer reflects this, give yourself 6 points. If you do not have a code of business conduct or you had any other answer to this question, give yourself 4 points.

46. Some Organizations require the code of business conduct to be resigned. They feel this reminds the signers of the code's requirements. Generally, such re-signing is on an annual basis.

<u>   6   </u> Yes   <u>   2   </u> No

47. At several points in this audit, the reality of constant change and its impact on the Organization has been mentioned. For many employees change is

threatening. Training in the positive acceptance and adjustment to change can help ensure change becomes less a threat and more of an opportunity for continued individual and Organization improvement.

____8____ Yes ____2____ No

48. Organizations are increasingly using work teams, sometimes for temporary projects and other times as an Organization unit. Teams can produce effective work groups, but often in their initial formation, problems can develop. Organization development professionals should be available to assist in analyzing team structure and operating procedures.

____8____ Yes ____1____ No

49. Organization development professionals have the skills and techniques to provide the type of assistance and training required to improve team performance.

____8____ Yes ____1____ No

50, 51, and 52. Whatever number you used to answer each of these questions is the rating for that question.

DIVERSITY AND EQUAL EMPLOYMENT OPPORTUNITY—EVALUATION

If this category is not one for which your human resources department is account-able, go directly to the next category beginning on page 253.

1. The significance of having someone accountable for one of these impor-tant human resources activities as been covered a number of times.

<u> 9 </u> Yes   <u> 1 </u> No

2. In today's society, where the workforce is more diverse than ever, and with the laws in this area, having an equal employment opportunity policy describing the Organization's commitment to the fair and equal treatment of all employees is an absolute must.

<u> 9 </u> Yes   <u> 1 </u> No

3 and 4. As with all other important Organization policies, this one needs to be in writing and communicated to all employees. If you have no such policy, give yourself 1 point for each of these two questions.

3. <u> 9 </u> Yes   <u> 1 </u> No

4. <u> 9 </u> Yes   <u> 1 </u> No

5. Having an equal employment opportunity policy is just the first step in ensuring the fair and equal treatment of all employees. To make that policy an operating reality of the Organization, the supervisors and managers must be trained in its execution.

<u> 8 </u> Yes   <u> 1 </u> No

6. No matter how well the policy is stated and how well the supervisors and managers are trained, eventually an employee will perceive that he has been treated unfairly. To ensure the policy is correctly implemented and to deal posi-tively with an employee's perception of unfair treatment, there needs to be a pro-cedure to handle grievances.

<u> 8 </u> Yes   <u> 1 </u> No

247

7 and 8. While our Advisory Board has continually stressed the need for written policies and procedures to avoid misunderstandings and for ease of communication to all employees, the grievance area is the area about which the Board feels the strongest need to have the policy and procedures in writing. If you have no such procedure, give yourself 2 points for each of these questions.

7. ____8____ Yes ____1____ No

8. ____8____ Yes ____1____ No

9. Training in the equal employment opportunity grievance procedure should be a part of a supervisor's and manager's training. In addition, these individuals should each have some type of manual or other instructions in exactly how to deal with grievances and their specific role in resolving them. If you have no procedure, give yourself 2 points for this question.

____7____ Yes ____2____ No

10. As indicated in a previous answer, an employee's equal employment opportunity grievance may be based on reality or on a false perception. It is important to determine which, and to obtain all the facts in order to resolve the grievance.

____8____ Yes ____1____ No

11. Whatever the results of an investigation of an employee's grievance, the facts obtained should be the basis for a communication to the grieving employee. If you do not have such a grievance procedure, give yourself 2 points for your answer to this question.

____7____ Yes ____2____ No

12. The grievance procedure should include a description of how an employee's grievance will be handled, and what the employee can do if he disagrees with the proposed resolution. The employee should have a method to appeal an initial resolution. If you do not have such a grievance procedure, give yourself 2 points for your answer to this question.

____8____ Yes ____1____ No

13. An important element of grievance procedures is that they ensure the grieving employee there will be no retribution for her filing a grievance. If you do

not have such a grievance procedure, give yourself 2 points for your answer to this question.

    8   Yes   1   No

14 through 25. These questions are identical to those for equal employment opportunity but cover sexual harassment. The Advisory Board's explanations are similar to those given for equal employment opportunity, but sexual harassment has been separated because it is a separate issue, and some Organizations that have successfully met equal employment opportunity requirements seem to be slower in dealing with sexual harassment.

14. ____9____ Yes ____1____ No

15. ____8____ Yes ____1____ No

16. ____8____ Yes ____1____ No

17. ____8____ Yes ____1____ No

18. ____8____ Yes ____1____ No

19. ____8____ Yes ____1____ No

20. ____8____ Yes ____1____ No

21. ____8____ Yes ____1____ No

22. ____8____ Yes ____1____ No

23. ____8____ Yes ____1____ No

24. ____8____ Yes ____1____ No

25. ____8____ Yes ____1____ No

26 and 27. Equal employment opportunity has to do with the relationship of an employee to his Organization as demonstrated by the Organization's conditions of employment and the supervision and management the employee receives. On the other hand, sexual harassment can, and often does, result from an employee's relationship with her peers—other employees. Therefore, supervisors and managers need to understand exactly what sexual harassment is and how to both

identify and eliminate it in the workplace. All Organization employees should be trained in the sexual harassment policy, grievance procedures, and what constitutes sexual harassment.

26. ___8___ Yes ___1___ No

27. ___8___ Yes ___1___ No

28. Surprisingly, some Organizations miss the significance of this. Advertisements without it clearly stand out, and many possible candidates perceive its omission as an effort to indicate preferential treatment, so they do not apply.

___7___ Yes ___2___ No

29. If your Organization uses search firms or employment agencies on a regular basis, you should notify them of your equal employment opportunity policy, preferably in writing, since in effect they are acting as your agents.

___7___ Yes ___2___ No

30 and 31. All required posters in these two areas should be displayed. This means that you need to be aware of state and local requirements as well as federal ones.

30. ___9___ Yes ___1___ No

31. ___9___ Yes ___1___ No

32. Here either answer is acceptable although our Advisory Board feels such information is more effectively gathered as a part of a survey of all conditions of employment. If you are not surveying or otherwise independently gathering such information, you may not have an accurate feel for how the employees perceive the Organization's actions in these two areas.

___7___ Yes ___2___ No ___2___ Do not survey such information

33. Such information should be gathered whenever there is any indication of a problem or a change in opinions. Otherwise, every year or two is probably adequate. If you do not gather this information, give yourself 3 points.

___2___ Every six months

___4___ Every year

____3____ Every one to two years

____2____ Every three or more years

____1____ When requested

34. Even when all appropriate policies and procedures are in place and all appropriate training of management has occurred, there may be disparate treatment of employees. Like actual discrimination, this type of disparity can lead to problems for the Organization. Collecting and analyzing appropriate information on a regular basis is one method to identify possible problems.

____8____ Yes ____1____ No

35. Selection devices, such as tests, can be of assistance in identifying some competencies and measuring knowledge. However, to ensure equal and fair treatment, they need to be based on actual job requirements and be valid for the job. Even then, the results have to be reviewed to ensure equal treatment.

____8____ Yes ____1____ No ____7____ Not applicable

36. The employment application must meet the same requirements as all other devices and procedures used in making a selection decision, so it should be reviewed to ensure it is consistent with appropriate laws and the Organization's policy of equal and fair treatment.

____8____ Yes ____1____ No

37. As with the continual review of employee statistics, all transfers, assignments, demotions, and promotions should be reviewed to ensure equal employment opportunity compliance.

____7____ Yes ____2____ No

38. Human resources should be the function continually reviewing and monitoring Organization performance with respect to equal employment opportunity and sexual harassment. Discoveries should be reported to senior management regularly.

____7____ Yes ____2____ No

39. Disadvantaged and/or disabled people can provide valuable services to Organizations. Studies indicate that, as a class, these people tend to be excellent

employees. Many times small revisions to facilities and equipment can allow some-one with a disability to be employed successfully.

_____9_____ Yes   _____1_____ No

40. Accessible workplaces contribute to the employment of disadvantaged people. Another reason to make the workplace accessible is the existence of local, state, and federal laws regarding access to an Organization's facilities.

_____9_____ Yes   _____1_____ No

41 and 42. Sexual harassment and equal employment opportunity complaints and grievances can also be filed with external agencies. In these situations, an Organization needs professional advice, so it should have a relationship with or have identified appropriate legal counsel. The legal counsel used, whether internal or external, should be qualified and experienced in these areas.

41. _____8_____ External legal counsel   _____7_____ Internal legal counsel

_____9_____ Both   _____2_____ Neither

42. _____8_____ Yes _____2_____ No

43, 44, and 45. Whatever number you used to answer each of these questions is the rating for that question.

SAFETY AND ENVIRONMENT—EVALUATION

If this category is not one for which your human resources department is accountable, go directly to the next category beginning on page 261.

1. Here again is an area that requires specific accountability.

       8   Yes   1   No

2. The Organization should have a safety and environment policy.

       8   Yes   2   No

3 and 4. Like other important policies, the safety and environmental policy should be both written and communicated to all employees. If you do not have a safety and environment policy, give yourself 3 points for each of these questions.

3.   8   Yes   2   No

4.   7   Yes   2   No

5. Accident records are necessary. They are needed for possible as well as current Workers Compensation claims. They assist in identifying problem areas within the Organization, and they can identify trends that may be related to other factors such as external conditions or overtime.

       8   Yes   1   No

6. Accident frequency (the number of accidents per time worked or number of employees) and severity (the average lost time per accident) are standard calculations that provide a further basis for identifying problems and trends. These figures that can be used for comparisons.

       7   Yes   1   No

7. Accident reports need to be reviewed by senior management and operating management of areas in which accidents are occurring. Any other distribution

depends on your Organization's operations and policies. If you do not produce safety reports, give yourself 2 points for your answer to this question.

_____3_____ Individual department heads

_____2_____ Human resources

_____1_____ External sources

_____2_____ Senior Organization managers

_____1_____ External consultants

_____0_____ No one

8. There are local, state, and federal requirements regarding notices to be posted. You need to know what they are and that they are properly displayed.

_____9_____ Yes   _____1_____ No

9. A safety committee provides additional input for maintaining a safe work environment, as well as involving employees who are working in various parts of the Organization. The committee's existence increases the perception that safety is the job of everyone in the Organization.

_____9_____ Yes   _____1_____ No

10. The greater the variety of employees involved in a safety committee, the better. In addition to the advantages mentioned in the previous answer, membership contributes to individual safety education. If you do not have a safety committee, give yourself 3 points for your answer to this question.

_____2_____ Individual department employees

_____2_____ Individual department supervisors and managers

_____2_____ Human resources employees

_____1_____ External sources such as insurance carrier representatives

_____1_____ Senior Organization managers

_____1_____ External consultants

_____1_____ Other

11. Inspections can be an important contributor to the prevention of accidents by the early identification of hazardous conditions. Production facilities require more inspections than offices, but office situations also present numerous possibilities for accidents.

_____8_____ Yes   _____2_____ No

12. Whenever there are changes to the physical operation of an area, inspections should be conducted. In addition, they should be conducted regularly. Their frequency is somewhat determined by your operation, current accident experience, and the results of previous inspections. If you do not conduct such inspections, give yourself 3 points for this question.

_____2_____ Every month

_____2_____ Every six months

_____1_____ At least once a year

_____1_____ Every year or more

_____1_____ When requested

_____2_____ Whenever an accident occurs

_____1_____ Whenever required by the government

13. Whoever is accountable for safety in the human resources department should be on any inspection team. Someone from operating management also should be included. External consultants and insurance carrier representatives can be of assistance. If you do not conduct safety inspections, give yourself 4 points for your answer to this question.

_____1_____ Individual department employees

_____2_____ Individual department heads

_____2_____ Human resources

_____1_____ External sources such as insurance carrier representatives

_____1_____ Senior Organization managers

_____1_____ External consultants

14 and 15. The information gained from safety inspections needs to be communicated. Those who can correct situations need to receive it, but so should those who manage the Organization. Many Organizations make inspection results available to department employees, so they can assist in improving working conditions. If you do not conduct such inspections, give yourself 3 points for your answer to each of these two questions.

14. _____7_____ Yes _____2_____ No

15. _____1_____ Department employees

_____2_____ Department heads

_____2_____ Human resources

_____1_____ External sources such as insurance companies

_____1_____ Senior Organization managers

_____1_____ External consultants

_____0_____ No one

16. Safety and environmental training should be provided to all supervisors and managers. These individuals need to know the legal requirements, the Organization's policy, how to identify potential problem areas, and what to do in case of an accident.

_____8_____ Yes _____1_____ No

17 and 18. Some people within the Organization should be trained in first aid procedures and, ideally, someone so trained should be available whenever there are employees working—certainly when are there any employees working in a production area with equipment or hazardous chemicals.

17. ___8___ Yes ___2___ No

18. If your answer to the previous question was no, give yourself 3 points for this question.

___8___ Whenever employees are working

___8___ During normal business hours including scheduled overtime

___6___ During normal business hours excluding scheduled overtime

___5___ At specified times during the day or week

___3___ At nonscheduled times

19. Whether there is a person trained in first aid available or not, there should always be an appropriate supply of first aid materials available.

___9___ Yes ___1___ No

20. All employees need to know the locations of first aid materials. Materials should be available in all work areas. If you do not have first aid supplies, give yourself 2 points for this question.

___8___ Yes ___1___ No

21. A competent professional should have determined what first aid supplies should be available by areas of the Organization. If you do not have first aid supplies, give yourself 2 points for your answer to this question.

___8___ Yes ___2___ No

22. First aid supplies need to be regularly checked to ensure they are all present and in good condition. If you do not have first aid supplies, give yourself 2 points for your answer to this question.

___8___ Yes ___2___ No

23. Managers and supervisors all need to know exactly what to do in case of an accident.

___9___ Yes ___1___ No

24. A hospital should be identified for injured employees. The time of an accident is not the time to try and identify where to take an injured employee.

_____9_____ Yes _____1_____ No

25. The telephone number and location of the hospital need to be prominently posted in all work areas.

_____9_____ Yes _____1_____ No

26. An ambulance service needs to have been identified and arrangements made for its use in case of an accident requiring transportation to a hospital or doctor.

_____9_____ Yes _____1_____ No

27 and 28. The Organization should have identified a physician to deal with any accidents, and her telephone number and location should be displayed prominently.

27. _____8_____ Yes _____1_____ No

28. _____8_____ Yes _____1_____ No

29. The Organization's Workers Compensation insurance information (carrier, policy number, address, and telephone number) needs to be available, either posted or with all managers and supervisors.

_____8_____ Yes _____1_____ No

30 through 33. These questions have to do with ensuring that all new, revised, and repaired facilities and equipment are safe. This is best accomplished by having safety consideration be a part of the design and planning phases, and then requiring a safety inspection of the finished facility or equipment before it goes into service.

30. _____8_____ Yes _____1_____ No

31. _____9_____ Yes _____1_____ No

32. _____8_____ Yes _____1_____ No

33. _____9_____ Yes _____1_____ No

34. Accidents should be investigated immediately to determine what happened, identify any witness and take their statements, and correct any unsafe condition.

_____9_____ Yes _____1_____ No

35. This type of analysis can contribute to the identification of both dangerous work areas and safety procedures, as well as being used for safety training.

_____8_____ Yes _____1_____ No

36. By calculating such standard accident statistics as frequency and severity, comparisons can be made with statistics from similar industries. This procedure can assist in identifying areas of concern that require attention.

_____7_____ Yes _____2_____ No

37. As important as safety is, a healthy work environment is equally important. Unhealthy work environments generally do not produce immediate problems, but their potential for causing harm is as great as accidents. Work environments need to be checked and checked regularly, ideally by a trained industrial hygienist or similar professional.

_____8_____ Yes _____1_____ No

38. Whenever there are changes to the physical operation of an area or in the materials being used, inspections should be conducted. They also should be conducted on some type of regular schedule. Their frequency is somewhat determined by your operation, current accident experience, and the results of previous inspections. If you do not conduct such inspections, give yourself 3 points for this question.

_____3_____ Every month

_____4_____ Every six months

_____3_____ At least once a year

_____5_____ Whenever there are changes to the operations

39. It is important for all employees to know what to do in case of an accident—where the first aid person and/or first aid kit is located, who to call for transportation to a hospital or doctor, what the Organization's insurance information is, and what transportation can be used.

_____7_____ Yes _____2_____ No

40. Safety and environmental rules and regulations as well as other environmental and safety related information are always changing. Someone needs to be

monitoring this information consistently to ensure the Organization is in full legal compliance and is providing maximum protection for its employees.

<u>   8   </u> Yes   <u>   1   </u> No

41. The Organization's Workers Compensation insurance carrier will usually provide a full range of services for improving safety. These services include posters, newsletters, training, videos, and inspections. Making use of them provides expert services at little or no additional cost.

<u>   7   </u> Yes   <u>   2   </u> No

42. Employees with the proper individual safety equipment can assist in preventing serious and costly accidents. Our Advisory Board believes support of individual safety equipment offers many benefits to the Organization and the employees.

<u>   8   </u> Provides   <u>   7   </u> Partial payment

<u>   5   </u> Discounts   <u>   1   </u> None

43. The number of employees working at home is increasing. However, a recent Department of Labor bulletin suggested Organizations may be responsible for the safety of the home work area. This is a relatively new development, but one that requires consideration.

<u>   8   </u> Yes   <u>   4   </u> No

44, 45, and 46. Whatever number you used to answer each of these questions is the rating for that question.

Security—Evaluation

If this category is not one for which your human resources department is accountable, go directly to the next category beginning on page 269.

1. Here again is the need for an individual to be assigned accountability for an important human resources activity.

_____8_____ Yes _____1_____ No

2. The first step in security is the control of who is allowed to enter the Organization's facilities.

_____9_____ Yes _____1_____ No

3. A record of any nonemployee entering the facility should be made. It should include date, time, purpose, and who was visited.

_____8_____ Yes _____1_____ No

4. Depending on the size of the Organization, identification badges may be required. However, even smaller Organizations have found badges help in maintaining security.

_____9_____ Yes _____1_____ No

5. Include photographs of the employees on identifications. This is a relatively simple and inexpensive procedure and it helps to eliminate employee switching of IDs. If you do not have employee IDs, give yourself 3 points for this question.

_____7_____ Yes _____2_____ No

6. Different Organizations have different rules, but increasingly identifications are required for employees to be on the Organization's premises. Employees who lose their IDs or leave them at home are required to obtain replacement temporary IDs before being allowed on the premises. If you do not have employee IDs, give yourself 3 points for this question.

_____7_____ Yes _____4_____ No

7. Employee IDs should be collected and access ability terminated when employees leave the Organization. Otherwise, a nonauthorized person has access to your facilities. If you do not have employee IDs, give yourself 3 points for this question.

___9___ Yes ___1___ No

8. Visitors should be issued temporary identifications, such as visitors' badges, and be required to wear or display them while on the Organization's premises. This makes it easy to identify nonauthorized people quickly.

___9___ Yes ___1___ No

9. If there is control over who can be on the premises, it's easier to develop a procedure covering what to do in the event there is an unauthorized individual there.

___9___ Yes ___2___ No

10. Any procedure should be communicated to all employees. Managers and supervisors should be trained in exactly what actions to take. If you have no procedure, give yourself 3 points for this question.

___8___ Yes ___1___ No

11. Having a visit by the local police can provide additional insight into your security arrangements. Establish a direct contact with police and develop procedures that include them in the event of a security problem.

___7___ Yes ___2___ No

12. A visit by the local fire department can make similar contributions to fire security. In addition, the local fire department may provide specialized training, posters, and videos.

___8___ Yes ___1___ No

13. Evacuation can only be conducted safely if proper plans have been developed. Such plans must include evacuation routes, exits, and accountabilities.

___9___ Yes ___1___ No

14. The Organization's managers must have training in what actions to take in case of an emergency—whom to call, how to evacuate, whom to notify.

_____9_____ Yes _____1_____ No

15. One type of evacuation that should be practiced is a fire drill that requires everyone to leave the facilities.

_____8_____ Yes _____2_____ No

16. Many fire protection and fire-fighting devices have a limited active life, so they need to be regularly inspected to ensure they are functional.

_____9_____ Yes _____1_____ No

17. As with other types of emergencies, appropriate personnel such as managers, switchboard operators, and receptionists need to be trained in what to do in case of a bomb scare or other threat. Their training should include whom to call, how to evacuate, and other important information.

_____9_____ Yes _____1_____ No

18. The local fire department needs to know what type of materials are employed and/or stored at your facility, what type of fire protection devices exist, and who is in charge.

_____8_____ Yes _____2_____ No

19. Some type of security system or personnel needs to be in place when the facilities are closed.

_____9_____ Yes _____1_____ No

20. There should be a list in declining order of notification of what managers to notify in case of an emergency. The list should include telephone numbers (home and business) and beeper and cell phone numbers if appropriate.

_____8_____ Yes _____2_____ No

21. Those numbers should in the possession of two individuals present during business hours. Other employees should be made aware of how to obtain the

numbers quickly. However, since the lists include personal telephone numbers, their distribution should be somewhat restricted.

_____8_____ Yes   _____2_____ No

22. Another form of important security is the protection of all employee records. Security is required to preserve the Organization's records and also to ensure their confidentiality.

_____9_____ Yes   _____1_____ No

23. All employee records should be in locked files with controlled access.

_____8_____ Yes   _____2_____ No

24. Only those authorized to view an employee's records should be allowed to see them.

_____9_____ Yes   _____1_____ No

25. As a general rule, employee records should be maintained on the premises by human resources. At times, individual documents may be allowed out with proper signing procedures in place to ensure the individual understands the ethical and legal responsibilities of maintaining confidentiality.

_____8_____ Yes   _____4_____ No

26. Generally there are two types of information an Organization has for each employee: information on the employee's work history, knowledge, and experience that can be used for making employment decisions; and personal information obtained through reference checks, testing, and other means normally not required to make employment decisions. These two types of information should be maintained in separate files with different controlled access procedures.

_____9_____ Yes   _____1_____ No

27. Security systems should be reviewed regularly to ensure they are functioning properly. In addition, passwords should be changed regularly.

_____8_____ Yes   _____1_____ No

28. As a general rule, frequent review of security systems is desirable, but, to some extent, confidentiality of your information and processes should govern the

review frequency. If you do not review your security systems, give yourself 3 points for this question.

_____2_____ Every month

_____3_____ Every six months

_____1_____ At least once a year

_____1_____ Every year or more

_____2_____ When requested

_____3_____ Whenever there is a security breach

_____1_____ Whenever required by the government

29. Even if the Organization has no special proprietary information, it still should have a confidentiality agreement limiting what can be said about the Organization and its operations.

_____9_____ Yes   _____1_____ No

30. As a general rule all employees should sign a confidentiality agreement, but the following indicates how important each group is. If you have no confidentiality agreement, give yourself 3 points for this question.

_____1_____ All nonmanagement employees

_____2_____ All managers other than senior managers

_____3_____ Senior managers of the Organization

_____3_____ All employees who have access to confidential information

_____3_____ External people doing business with the Organization who have access to confidential information

_____2_____ Other

31. The proper time to sign a confidentiality agreement is before the confidential information is seen. If that is your answer, give yourself 7 points. If you

answered anything else or have no confidentiality agreement, give yourself 3 points for this question.

32. While it is probably no more legally binding to have employees regularly sign the same confidentiality agreement, many Organizations prefer to do so since it is a reminder of the terms. Generally, this is done annually. If you have no confidentiality agreement, give yourself 4 points for this question.

___6___ Yes   ___3___ No

33. Many security activities have been outsourced, most typically security personnel such as guard and parking lot attendants. Although there is no one correct answer, this is an area you should have considered for an informed decision.

___8___ Yes   ___3___ No

34 and 35. The Organization should have a policy on who can give reference check information and what information can be given. That policy should be communicated to all managers.

34. ___8___ Yes   ___1___ No

35. ___8___ Yes   ___1___ No   ___3___ Not applicable

36. References checks should be given only by someone trained in how to handle such inquiries. Generally, the best employee for this purpose is a human resources department employee.

___2___ Former employee's supervisor

___2___ Manager of the former employee's supervisor

___8___ Someone in human resources

___5___ No one

37. There should be a procedure requiring proper authorization for the removal and return of the Organization's property. This should include equipment for use in business trips and for at home work.

___8___ Yes   ___2___ No

38. There should be protection of the Organization's information and equipment when removed from the premises.

_____8_____ Yes _____2_____ No

39, 40, and 41. Whatever number you used to answer each of these questions is the rating for that question.

EQUIPMENT AND FACILITIES—EVALUATION

If this category is not one for which your human resources department is accountable, go directly to the next category beginning on page 273.

1. Human resources, like any other area in which work is performed, can function most efficiently when its facilities have been designed for that work and for the number of employees in the department.

_____8_____ Yes _____1_____ No

2. Human resources often works with confidential information of employees and candidates. Private areas in which such work can be performed are necessary.

_____9_____ Yes _____1_____ No

3. The human resources department serves all employees of the Organization, so it should be conveniently located.

_____7_____ Yes _____3_____ No

4. Selecting a new employee should be viewed somewhat as a selling situation. You want to present the best possible initial impression of the Organization to candidates, so careful thought should be given to supplying a reception area.

_____8_____ Yes _____1_____ No

5. A reception area for candidates should include tables and desks for completing applications and other documents.

_____6_____ Yes _____3_____ No _____5_____ Not applicable

6. The required local, state, and federal notices to be posted for candidates should be identified and displayed in the reception or similar area.

_____9_____ Yes _____1_____ No

7. In addition to good work design for office space, environmental conditions such as heat, light, and sound should support the work and provide a healthy atmosphere.

_____8_____ Yes   _____2_____ No

8. Generally, human resources requires a number of forms and other office supplies to accomplish its work. These should be stored in an area that is convenient and offers easy access for the employees who use them.

_____6_____ Yes   _____3_____ No

9. Someone needs to have the accountability for maintaining the desired levels of inventory to ensure the needed supplies are always on hand.

_____7_____ Yes   _____2_____ No

10. In addition to providing training, human resources often needs to hold meetings with employees, employees and their supervisors, and the department's staff.

_____7_____ Yes   _____2_____ No

11. A modern office whose occupants deal with both employees and visitors to the building requires certain specific equipment. Although the actual equipment needs may differ by human resources departments, the following should have been considered and/or made available.

Considered	Available	
2	2	Fax
2	2	Photocopier
2	2	Individual desk PCs
2	1	Individual laptop PCs
2	2	Telephone voice mail
2	3	Central department telephone number

___2___   ___1___   Employee beepers

___2___   ___1___   Cellular or digital telephones

12. Human resources often sends and receives personal information by fax, so it is best to have a dedicated fax machine within the department.

___8___ Yes ___1___ No

13. The printer for computer-generated documents also should be within the human resources department.

___8___ Yes ___1___ No

14. Some Organizations have all mail, regardless of how addressed, opened in a central mail-receiving area, time stamped, and then distributed. Since so much of human resources correspondence is of a personal nature, human resources should receive its mail unopened.

___1___ Yes ___8___ No

15. Concerns for privacy require outgoing human resources mail leave the department sealed.

___8___ Yes ___1___ No

16. All human resources department employees should have a telephone with a separate number or extension, with the exception of any employees who are never contacted by telephone and never have to make calls.

___8___ Yes ___2___ No

17. People calling a human resources department often are experiencing a problem that requires an immediate answer. In such situations, being put through to voice mail can be very frustrating and irritating. It also is counterproductive. Human resources telephones should be answered by a person. Voice mail should be used only when absolutely necessary. If you do not have voice mail, give yourself 7 points for this question.

___9___ Yes ___1___ No

18. Whenever a caller is routed to a voice mail system in human resources, the caller should have the option to reach a real person immediately. If you do not have voice mail, give yourself 7 points for this question.

_____8_____ Yes   _____1_____ No

19. Working at home is more common because of technological developments. If this is a possibility for any of your employees or it is already a reality, you need a policy regarding any equipment they may require to perform their assignments.

_____7_____ Yes   _____3_____ No   _____6_____ Not applicable

20. Once you have a policy regarding equipment for employees who work at home, it needs to be written as a procedure covering how the equipment is furnished, maintained, and returned.

_____6_____ Yes   _____2_____ No   _____5_____ Not applicable

21, 22, and 23. Whatever number you used to answer each of these questions is the rating for that question.

Documentation and Information Systems—Evaluation

If this category is not one for which your human resources department is accountable, go directly to the next step beginning on page 279.

1. Again, here is an important area that requires an accountability assignment.

<u>   9   </u> Yes <u>   1   </u> No

2. There are both ethical and legal requirements regarding the confidentiality of employee personal information. You should know these and ensure the human resources systems comply.

<u>   9   </u> Yes <u>   1   </u> No

3. Here there are ethical, operational, and legal requirements. In addition, as a rule there should be nothing in an employee's records that he cannot see.

<u>   9   </u> Yes <u>   1   </u> No <u>   2   </u> Not applicable

4. If an employee cannot see her complete record, there should be a specific reason for any information withheld, and that reason should meet the Organization's operational procedures, ethical standards, and legal requirements.

<u>   7   </u> Yes <u>   2   </u> No

5. In the Security section, the importance of maintaining two separate files for an employee was described. One file should contain general information regarding work history, education, and experience—the basis for making employment decisions. The other file should contain any personal and confidential information that is not used for making employment decisions. Poor performance notification is one piece of information not used in initial hiring decisions. Some Organizations maintain current employee performance data in the general file and past performance data in the restricted file.

<u>   3   </u> Current <u>   5   </u> Past <u>   2   </u> Neither

6 and 7. Employee reference check information, test results, and medical records are some examples of information to be kept in a separate (restricted) file.

6. ___8___ Yes ___1___ No ___5___ Not applicable

7. ___8___ Yes ___1___ No ___6___ Not applicable

8. There are many types of employee statistics. Those in this list are the more common, but human resources should calculate as many types of statistics as will provide information to improve human resources activities.

___3___ Employee turnover

___2___ Employee absences

___1___ Employee lateness

___2___ Employee first aid visits

___2___ Training costs

___3___ Employee accident frequency

___3___ Employee accident severity

___3___ Employee accident lost time

___3___ Employee benefit costs

___2___ Employee productivity

___3___ Average compensation increases

___2___ Recruiting cost per employee hired

___3___ Average benefit cost per employee

___2___ Other

9. The frequency of calculating reports will vary by the Organization and the report. However, the following is a general guideline. If you do not calculate any of these reports, give yourself 3 points for this question.

___4___ Every month

___3___ Every three months

___2___ Every six months

___2___ At least once a year

___1___ Every year or more

___1___ When requested

___1___ Whenever required by the government

___0___ Never

10. Such reports should be used by human resources and appropriate individual department heads and should be shared with senior management.

___2___ Individual department heads

___2___ Human resources

___1___ External sources such as insurance companies

___2___ Senior company managers

___1___ Consultants

___0___ No one

11. The mere calculation and preparation of such statistics and reports only creates the information. An analysis of what the information means is crucial.

___8___ Yes   ___2___ No

12 and 13. So much information regarding employees is required these days for analysis, such as identification of individual abilities, government require-

ments, and benefits administration, that a computerized system provides the most logical method of collecting and storing the information. In addition, most systems offer the added advantage of being able to manipulate the data for future needs or requirements.

12. ___9___ Yes ___1___ No

13. ___6___ Yes ___2___ No

14. Just as access to individual employee records and files is controlled, access to the human resources information system also should be controlled.

___9___ Yes ___1___ No

15. This is particularly important with respect to computerized systems for which employees are assigned passwords. As soon as an employee leaves the human resources department, that employee's password should be invalidated.

___9___ Yes ___1___ No

16. This will, to some extent, depend on your Organization's information-processing equipment configuration. Our Advisory Board believes the best approach is for the system to be a human resources dedicated system, running on human resources computers. However, if it is necessary to run on the Organization's mainframe or client server, it is important that access be restricted even for the systems people who install and maintain the information system. If your answer to the previous question was no, give yourself 6 points for Question 16.

16. ___7___ Department PC

___4___ Mainframe, network, or server located outside the human resources department

17. If your answer to Question 16 was Department PC, give yourself 8 points for this question.

___9___ Yes ___1___ No

18. If your human resources information is not computerized, you should have at least considered that possibility. If your answer to Question 13 was yes, give yourself 7 points for this question.

___8___ Yes ___2___ No

19. Personal information changes rapidly as employees acquire additional experiences and education or other changes in their personal lives. To ensure currency of such information, some type of regular review and updating is required.

_____7_____ Yes _____1_____ No

20. Updates of human resources information should be on a scheduled basis. If you do not update such information, give yourself 3 points for this question.

_____2_____ Every month

_____6_____ Every six months

_____8_____ At least once a year

_____4_____ Every year or more

_____0_____ Never

21 and 22. One of the benefits of calculating standard employee statistics is that it allows for comparisons to other Organizations to help identify areas that may require attention. An analysis of differences can help to improve human resources activities in your own Organization.

21. _____7_____ Yes _____2_____ No

21. _____8_____ Yes _____1_____ No _____4_____ Not applicable

23. Outsourcing of human resources information is an approach some Organizations use to eliminate the need to purchase, operate, and update a human resources information system. If you do this, you must be sure you can access the information and maintain its confidentiality.

_____8_____ Yes _____2_____ No

24, 25, and 26. Whatever number you used to answer each of these questions is the rating for that question.

STEP THREE—
ANALYSIS

You have now completed Step Two—Evaluation. Each of the questions you answered in Step One—Information Gathering should now have a numerical rating on the short line in front of it. If you disagreed with any ratings or the basis for them, you should have made a note next to those questions.

This step analyzes what those evaluation ratings mean. You will first analyze each category. Then you will examine other factors to assist you in understanding how well each category is being performed within your Organization. Finally, you will do the same type of analysis for the entire department.

In the process, you will use both the Advisory Board's weightings of the categories and your own. This will provide you with an evaluation of your department's performance compared with a group of external human resources professionals and an additional evaluation based on a customization of the categories to your situation.

At the conclusion of this step, you will have identified your department's strengths and areas that may require improvement. You also will have made adjustments for your unique situation, and you will have identified additional information you need to provide a more detailed evaluation of the categories.

So, go through each page of a category in Step One—Information Gathering and total the numbers you have written on the short lines preceding each question. You can enter the totals for each category on the lines in the table on the next page.

TOTAL CATEGORY RATINGS

Category	Total
Department Mission	_____
Department Organization	_____
Department Employees	_____
Labor Relations	_____
Recruitment and Selection	_____
Education, Training, and Development	_____
Employee Relations	_____
Benefits	_____
Compensation	_____
Human Resources Planning	_____
Organization Development	_____
Diversity and Equal Employment Opportunity	_____
Safety and Environment	_____
Security	_____
Equipment and Facilities	_____
Documentation and Information Systems	_____

You can refer to the above totals as you review the following Step Three—Analysis pages.

Department Mission—Analysis

The overall objective or purpose of the human resources department within the Organization and its relationship to the Organization's overall mission.

If this is one of the areas not applicable to your human resources department and/or Organization and you did not answer questions in it, go on to page 285.

To analyze this category, you first need to total the ratings for all its questions. Those are the rating numbers you have written on the short lines preceding each question. Total those numbers for the 26 questions in the Department Mission category (pages 3 through 8) and write that total on the following line.

———

As a first part of your analysis, you need to discover how your total points compared with the total points developed by the Advisory Board. The ratings provided for the answers to the questions in this category were based on the category's definition and what our Advisory Board members felt was the best answer for a well-run, successful human resources department. However, although the Board provided ratings to be used for all human resources functions, and they comprise a wide variety of education and experience, each rating must be considered in terms of the unique needs of your Organization.

If your total points were 183 or more for Department Mission, our Advisory Board believes your human resources department is functioning very well in this area. Your actions appear to be fulfilling the category's definition and providing the human resources department and Organization with a solid base for an effective human resources function. Your major need in this category will be to continually ensure that the department's mission is used as a guide and reflects the philosophy of the Organization.

If your total points were at least 149 but no more than 182 for Department Mission, our Advisory Board believes your human resources department is functioning better than a typical human resources department, but you may need to give this area some attention. Even though it is currently better than typical, the rapid changes in technology, laws, and society may have a performance impact. At a minimum, you should review the questions in which you received the lowest points and determine whether or not these are areas that require attention.

If your total points were at least 103 but no more than 148 for Department Mission, our Advisory Board believes your human resources department is functioning at a level that requires improvement in this area. Very possibly, the total rating is impacted by questions concerning one or two activities. If this is the case, it is only those areas of the category that require additional attention, so a first step here is to review the ratings, answers, and basis for the answers to those questions.

If your total points were below 103 for Department Mission, our Advisory Board believes your human resources department may be in real trouble in this category. If most of your questions received relatively low ratings, the entire category may require attention. If this is the case, you want to be sure activities in this area are designed to meet the Organization's requirements.

Each category ended with the same three questions. They asked for your perceptions of how the human resources department is performing in the category and your perceptions of how the employees and clients of the department would rate how well the department is performing.

Although these questions request three different ratings, the answers all reflect your perceptions. Even so, if there are differences, you should determine why you would rate the category differently from one or both of the other groups.

Department Organization—Analysis

The department's internal relationships; relationships with other functions, departments, and employees of the Organization; and the structuring of resources within the department.

If this is one of the areas not applicable to your human resources department and/or Organization and you did not answer questions in it, go on to page 287.

To analyze this category, you first need to total the ratings for all its questions. Those are the rating numbers you have written on the short lines preceding each question. Total those numbers for the 56 questions in the Department Organization category (pages 9 through 20) and write that total on the following line.

As a first part of your analysis, you need to discover how your total points compared with the total points developed by the Advisory Board. The ratings provided for the answers to the questions in this category were based on the category's definition, and what our Advisory Board members felt was the best answer for a well-run, successful human resources department. However, although the Board provided ratings to be used for all human resources functions and they comprise a wide variety of education and experience, each rating must be considered in terms of the unique needs of your Organization.

If your total points were 363 or more for Department Organization, our Advisory Board believes your human resources department is functioning very well in this area. Your actions appear to be fulfilling the category's definition and providing the human resources department and Organization with a solid base for an effective human resources function. Your major need in this category will be to continually ensure that the department's mission is used as a guide and reflects the philosophy of the Organization.

If your total points were at least 295 but no more than 362 for Department Organization, our Advisory Board believes your human resources department is functioning better than a typical human resources department, but you may need to give this area some attention. Even though it is currently better than typical, the rapid changes in technology, laws, and society may have a performance impact. At a minimum, you should review the questions in which you received the lowest points and determine whether or not these are areas that require attention.

If your total points were at least 204 but no more than 294 for Department Organization, our Advisory Board believes your human resources department is functioning at a level that requires improvement in this area. Very possibly, the total rating is impacted by questions concerning one or two activities. If this is the case, it is only those areas of the category that require additional attention, so a first step here is to review the ratings, answers, and basis for the answers to those questions.

If your total points were below 204 for Department Organization, our Advisory Board believes your human resources department may be in real trouble in this category. If most of your questions received relatively low ratings, the entire category may require attention. If this is the case, you want to be sure activities in this area are designed to meet the Organization's requirements and the mission of the human resources department.

Each category ended with the same three questions. They asked for your perceptions of how the human resources department is performing in this category and your perceptions of how the employees and clients of the department would rate how well the department is performing.

Although these questions request three different ratings, the answers all reflect your perceptions. Even so, if there are differences, you should determine why you would rate the category differently from one or both of the other groups.

DEPARTMENT EMPLOYEES—ANALYSIS

The selection, training, motivation, development, and retention of a qualified human resources team.

If this is one of the areas not applicable to your human resources department and/or Organization and you did not answer questions in it, go on to page 289.

To analyze this category, you first need to total the ratings for all its questions. Those are the rating numbers you have written on the short lines preceding each question. Total those numbers for the 41 questions in the Department Employees category (pages 21 through 27) and write that total on the following line.

_____

As a first part of your analysis, you need to discover how your total points compared with the total points developed by the Advisory Board. The ratings provided for the answers to the questions in this category were based on the category's definition, and what our Advisory Board members believe was the best answer for a well-run, successful human resources department. However, although the Board provided ratings to be used for all human resources functions and they comprise a wide variety of education and experience, each rating must be considered in terms of the unique needs of your Organization.

If your total points were 250 or more for Department Employees, our Advisory Board believes your human resources department is functioning very well in this area. Your actions appear to be fulfilling the category's definition and providing the human resources department and Organization with a solid base for an effective human resources function. Your major need in this category will be to continually ensure that the department's mission is used as a guide and reflects the philosophy of the Organization.

If your total points were at least 204 but no more than 249 for Department Employees, our Advisory Board believes your human resources department is functioning better than a typical human resources department, but you may need to give this area some attention. Even though it is currently better than typical, the rapid changes in technology, laws, and society may have a performance impact. At a minimum, you should review the questions in which you received the lowest points and determine whether or not these are areas that require attention.

If your total points were at least 141 but no more than 203 for Department Employees, our Advisory Board believes your human resources department is functioning at a level that requires improvement in this area. Very possibly, the total rating is impacted by questions concerning one or two activities. If this is the case, it is only those areas of the category that require additional attention, so a first step here is to review the ratings, answers, and basis for the answers to those questions.

If your total points were below 141 for Department Employees, our Advisory Board believes your human resources department may be in real trouble in this category. If most of your questions received relatively low ratings, the entire category may require attention. If this is the case, you want to be sure activities in this area are designed to meet the Organization's requirements and the mission of the human resources department.

Each category ended with the same three questions. They asked for your perceptions of how the human resources department is performing and your perceptions of how the employees and clients of the department would rate how well the department is performing.

Although these questions request three different ratings, the answers all reflect your perceptions. Even so, if there are differences, you should determine why you would rate the category differently from one or both of the other groups.

LABOR RELATIONS—ANALYSIS

*The human resources role in the relationship between the Orga-
nization and any bargaining unit of an employee-organized labor
group, including labor-organizing campaigns.*

If this is one of the areas not applicable to your human resources department and/or Organization and you did not answer questions in it, go on to page 291.

To analyze this category, you first need to total the ratings for all its questions. Those are the rating numbers you have written on the short lines preceding each question. Total those numbers for the 38 questions in the Labor Relations category (pages 29 through 37) and write that total on the following line.

———————

As a first part of your analysis, you need to discover how your total points compared with the total points developed by the Advisory Board. The ratings provided for the answers to the questions in this category were based on the category's definition, and what our Advisory Board members believe was the best answer for a well-run, successful human resources department. However, although the Board provided ratings to be used for all human resources functions and they comprise a wide variety of education and experience, each rating must be considered in terms of the unique needs of your Organization.

If your total points were 249 or more for Labor Relations, our Advisory Board believes your human resources department is functioning very well in this area. Your actions appear to be fulfilling the category's definition and providing the human resources department and Organization with a solid base for an effective human resources function. Your major need in this category will be to continually ensure that the department's mission is used as a guide and reflects the philosophy of the Organization.

If your total points were at least 203 but no more than 248 for Labor Relations, our Advisory Board believes your human resources department is functioning better than a typical human resources department, but you may need to give this area some attention. Even though it is currently better than typical, the rapid changes in technology, laws, and society may have a performance impact. At a minimum, you should review the questions in which you received the lowest points and determine whether or not these are areas that require attention.

If your total points were at least 140 but no more than 202 for Labor Relations, our Advisory Board believes your human resources department is functioning at a level that requires improvement in this area. Very possibly, the total rating is impacted by questions concerning one or two activities. If this is the case, it is

only those areas of the category that require additional attention, so a first step here is to review the ratings, answers, and basis for the answers to those questions.

If your total points were below 140 for Labor Relations, our Advisory Board believes your human resources department may be in real trouble in this category. If most of your questions received relatively low ratings, the entire category may require attention. If this is the case, you want to be sure activities in this area are designed to meet the Organization's requirements and the mission of the human resources department.

Each category ended with the same three questions. They asked for your perceptions of how the human resources department is performing in the category and your perceptions of how the employees and clients of the department would rate how well the department is performing.

Although these questions request three different ratings, the answers all reflect your perceptions. Even so, if there are differences, you should determine why you would rate the category differently from one or both of the other groups.

RECRUITMENT AND SELECTION—ANALYSIS

Obtaining and evaluating qualified candidates from internal and external sources for positions throughout the Organization.

If this is one of the areas not applicable to your human resources department and/or Organization and you did not answer questions in it, go on to page 293.

To analyze this category, you first need to total the ratings for all its questions. Those are the rating numbers you have written on the short lines preceding each question. Total those numbers for the 62 questions in the Recruitment and Selection category (pages 39 through 51) and write that total on the following line.

_____

As a first part of your analysis, you need to discover how your total points compared with the total points developed by the Advisory Board. The ratings provided for the answers to the questions in this category were based on the category's definition, and what our Advisory Board members believe was the best answer for a well-run, successful human resources department. However, although the Board provided ratings to be used for all human resources functions and they comprise a wide variety of education and experience, each rating must be considered in terms of the unique needs of your Organization.

Before reviewing your total points a word needs to be said regarding the Advisory Board's answers to questions for this category. Several members noted that they would respond differently for different categories of employees (professionals, managers, technicians, production workers, salespeople, etc.). Their ratings, reflected here, are based on how they believed the overall function should be handled. Keep this in mind as you analyze your answers, and if your Organization's recruitment and selection are mainly in a single area or you answered for a single area, that needs to be considered and possible adjustments made to your ratings.

If your total points were 407 or more for Recruitment and Selection, our Advisory Board believes your human resources department is functioning very well in this area. Your actions appear to be fulfilling the category's definition and providing the human resources department and Organization with a solid base for an effective human resources function. Your major need in this category will be to continually ensure that the department's mission is used as a guide and reflects the philosophy of the Organization.

If your total points were at least 331 but no more than 406 for Recruitment and Selection, our Advisory Board believes your human resources department is functioning better than a typical human resources department, but you may need to give this area some attention. Even though it is currently better than typical, the rapid changes in technology, laws, and society may have a performance impact. At a minimum, you should review the questions in which you received the lowest points and determine whether or not these are areas that require attention.

If your total points were at least 229 but no more than 330 for Recruitment and Selection, our Advisory Board believes your human resources department is functioning at a level that requires improvement in this area. Very possibly, the total rating is impacted by questions concerning one or two activities. If this is the case, it is only those areas of the category that require additional attention, so a first step here is to review the ratings, answers, and basis for the answers to those questions.

If your total points were below 229 for Recruitment and Selection, our Advisory Board believes your human resources department may be in real trouble in this category. If most of your questions received relatively low ratings, the entire category may require attention. If this is the case, you want to be sure activities in this area are designed to meet the Organization's requirements and the mission of the human resources department.

Each category ended with the same three questions. They asked for your perceptions of how the human resources department is performing and your perceptions of how the employees and clients of the department would rate how well the department is performing.

Although these questions request three different ratings, the answers all reflect your perceptions. Even so, if there are differences, you should determine why you would rate the category differently from one or both of the other groups.

EDUCATION, TRAINING, AND DEVELOPMENT—ANALYSIS

Providing performance skills training and career development to employees, utilizing both internal and external resources, including providing expertise in assessing education, training, and development needs and identification of high-potential employees.

If this is one of the areas not applicable to your human resources department and/or Organization and you did not answer questions in it, go on to page 295.

To analyze this category, you first need to total the ratings for all its questions. Those are the rating numbers you have written on the short lines preceding each question. Total those numbers for the 51 questions in the Education, Training, and Development category (pages 53 through 61) and write that total on the following line.

_____

As a first part of your analysis, you need to discover how your total points compared with the total points developed by the Advisory Board. The ratings provided for the answers in this category were based on the category definition, and what our Advisory Board members believe is the best answer for a well-run, successful human resources department. However, although the Board provided ratings to be used for all human resources functions and they comprise a wide variety of education and experience, each rating must be considered in terms of the unique needs of your Organization.

If your total points were 334 or more for Education, Training, and Development, our Advisory Board believes your human resources department is functioning very well in this area. Your actions appear to be fulfilling the category's definition and providing the human resources department and Organization with a solid base for an effective human resources function. Your major need in this category will be to continually ensure that the department's mission is used as a guide and reflects the philosophy of the Organization.

If your total points were at least 271 but no more than 333 for Education, Training, and Development, our Advisory Board believes your human resources department is functioning better than a typical human resources department, but you may need to give this area some attention. Even though it is currently better than typical, the rapid changes in technology, laws, and society may have a performance impact. At a minimum, you should review the questions in which you received the lowest points and determine whether or not these are areas that require attention.

If your total points were at least 188 but no more than 270 for Education, Training, and Development, our Advisory Board believes your human resources department is functioning at a level that requires improvement in this area. Very possibly, the total rating is impacted by questions concerning one or two activities. If this is the case, it is only those areas of the category that require additional attention, so a first step here is to review the ratings, answers, and basis for the answers to those questions.

If your total points were below 188 for Education, Training, and Development, our Advisory Board believes your human resources department may be in real trouble in this category. If most of your questions received relatively low ratings, the entire category may require attention. If this is the case, you want to be sure activities in this area are designed to meet the Organization's requirements and the mission of the human resources department.

Each category ended with the same three questions. They asked for your perceptions of how the human resources department is performing and your perceptions of how the employees and clients of the department would rate how well the department is performing.

Although these questions request three different ratings, the answers all reflect your perceptions. Even so, if there are differences, you should determine why you would rate the category differently from one or both of the other groups.

EMPLOYEE RELATIONS—ANALYSIS

The formal policies and procedures governing all conditions of employment, including specific human resources activities not otherwise categorized.

If this is one of the areas not applicable to your human resources department and/or Organization and you did not answer questions in it, go on to page 297.

To analyze this category, you first need to total the ratings for all its questions. Those are the rating numbers you have written on the short lines preceding each question. Total those numbers for the 58 questions in the Employee Relations category (pages 63 through 72) and write that total on the following line.

_____

As a first part of your analysis, you need to discover how your total points compared with the total points developed by the Advisory Board. The ratings provided for the answers to the questions in this category were based on the category definition, and what our Advisory Board members believe is the best answer for a well-run, successful human resources department. However, although the Board provided ratings to be used for all human resources functions and they comprise a wide variety of education and experience, each rating must be considered in terms of the unique needs of your Organization.

If your total points were 384 or more for Employee Relations, our Advisory Board believes your human resources department is functioning very well in this area. Your actions appear to be fulfilling the category's definition and providing the human resources department and Organization with a solid base for an effective human resources function. Your major need in this category will be to continually ensure that the department's mission is used as a guide and reflects the philosophy of the Organization.

If your total points were at least 312 but no more than 383 for Employee Relations, our Advisory Board believes your human resources department is functioning better than a typical human resources department, but you may need to give this area some attention. Even though it is currently better than typical, the rapid changes in technology, laws, and society may have a performance impact. At a minimum, you should review the questions in which you received the lowest points and determine whether or not these are areas that require attention.

If your total points were at least 216 but no more than 311 for Employee Relations, our Advisory Board believes your human resources department is functioning at a level that requires improvement in this area. Very possibly, the total rating is impacted by questions concerning one or two activities. If this is the case, it is only those areas of the category that require additional attention, so a first step here is to review the ratings, answers, and basis for the answers to those questions.

If your total points were below 216 for Employee Relations, our Advisory Board believes your human resources department may be in real trouble in this category. If most of your questions received relatively low ratings, the entire category may require attention. If this is the case, you want to be sure activities in this area are designed to meet the Organization's requirements and the mission of the human resources department.

Each category ended with the same three questions. They asked for your perceptions of how the human resources department is performing and your perceptions of how the employees and clients of the department would rate how well the department is performing.

Although these questions request three different ratings, the answers all reflect your perceptions. Even so, if there are differences, you should determine why you would rate the category differently from one or both of the other groups.

BENEFITS—ANALYSIS

The noncash compensation provided to employees of the Organization including, but not limited to, such components as insurances, retirement saving plans, and paid time off, and the systems and support services and communications to successfully deliver the benefits.

If this is one of the areas not applicable to your human resources department and/or Organization and you did not answer questions in it, go on to page 299.

To analyze this category, you first need to total the ratings for all its questions. Those are the rating numbers you have written on the short lines preceding each question. Total those numbers for the 24 questions in the Benefits category (pages 73 through 78) and write that total on the following line.

———————

As a first part of your analysis, you need to discover how your total points compared with the total points developed by the Advisory Board. The ratings provided for the answers to the questions in this category were based on the above definition, and what our Advisory Board members believe is the best answer for a well-run, successful human resources department. However, although the Board provided ratings to be used for all human resources functions and they comprise a wide variety of education and experience, each rating must be considered in terms of the unique needs of your Organization.

If your total points were 190 or more for Benefits, our Advisory Board believes your human resources department is functioning very well in this area. Your actions appear to be fulfilling the category's definition and providing the human resources department and Organization with a solid base for an effective human resources function. Your major need in this category will be to continually ensure that the department's mission is used as a guide and reflects the philosophy of the Organization.

If your total points were at least 154 but no more than 189 for Benefits, our Advisory Board believes your human resources department is functioning better than a typical human resources department, but you may need to give this area some attention. Even though it is currently better than typical, the rapid changes in technology, laws, and society may have a performance impact. At a minimum, you should review the questions in which you received the lowest points and determine whether or not these are areas that require attention.

If your total points were at least 107 but no more than 153 for Benefits, our Advisory Board believes your human resources department is functioning at a level that requires improvement in this area. Very possibly, the total rating is impacted by questions concerning one or two activities. If this is the case, it is only those areas of the category that require additional attention, so a first step here is to review the ratings, answers, and basis for the answers to those questions.

If your total points were below 107 for Benefits, our Advisory Board believes your human resources department may be in real trouble in this category. If most of your questions received relatively low ratings, the entire category may require attention. If this is the case, you want to be sure activities in this area are designed to meet the Organization's requirements and the mission of the human resources department.

Each category ended with the same three questions. They asked for your perceptions of how the human resources department is performing and your perceptions of how the employees and clients of the human resources department would rate how well the department is performing.

Although these questions request three different ratings, the answers all reflect your perceptions. Even so, if there are differences, you should determine why you would rate the category differently from one or both of the other groups.

COMPENSATION—ANALYSIS

All cash payments to employees and also the systems by which positions are evaluated, salary and wage ranges and bands are determined, and adjustments are made, including commissions, lump sum payments, incentive payments, and bonuses.

If this is one of the areas not applicable to your human resources department and/or Organization and you did not answer questions in it, go on to page 301.

To analyze this category, you first need to total the ratings for all its questions. Those are the rating numbers you have written on the short lines preceding each question. Total those numbers for the 37 questions in the Compensation category (pages 79 through 86) and write that total on the following line.

————————

As a first part of your analysis, you need to discover how your total points compared with the total points developed by the Advisory Board. The ratings provided for the answers to the questions in this category were based on the above definition, and what our Advisory Board members believe is the best answer for a well-run, successful human resources department. However, although the Board provided ratings to be used for all human resources functions and they comprise a wide variety of education and experience, each rating must be considered in terms of the unique needs of your Organization.

If your total points were 261 or more for Compensation, our Advisory Board believes your human resources department is functioning very well in this area. Your actions appear to be fulfilling the category's definition and providing the human resources department and Organization with a solid base for an effective human resources function. Your major need in this category will be to continually ensure that the department's mission is used as a guide and reflects the philosophy of the Organization.

If your total points were at least 212 but no more than 260 for Compensation, our Advisory Board believes your human resources department is functioning better than a typical human resources department, but you may need to give this area some attention. Even though it is currently better than typical, the rapid changes in technology, laws, and society may have a performance impact. At a minimum, you should review the questions in which you received the lowest points and determine whether or not these are areas that require attention.

If your total points were at least 147 but no more than 211 for Compensation, our Advisory Board believes your human resources department is functioning at a level that requires improvement in this area. Very possibly, the total rating is impacted by questions concerning one or two activities. If this is the case, it is

299

only those areas of the category that require additional attention, so a first step here is to review the ratings, answers, and basis for the answers to those questions.

If your total points were below 147 for Compensation, our Advisory Board believes your human resources department may be in real trouble in this category. If most of your questions received relatively low ratings, the entire category may require attention. If this is the case, you want to be sure activities in this area are designed to meet the Organization's requirements and the mission of the human resources department.

Each category ended with the same three questions. They asked for your perceptions of how the human resources department is performing and your perceptions of how the employees and clients of the department would rate how well the department is performing.

Although these questions request three different ratings, the answers all reflect your perceptions. Even so, if there are differences, you should determine why you would rate the category differently from one or both of the other groups.

HUMAN RESOURCES PLANNING—ANALYSIS

The collection and analysis of data providing long-term (strategic) and short-term (tactical) plans and forecasts to meet the department's and Organization's missions, including such activities as succession planning, leadership development, and recruiting schedules.

If this is one of the areas not applicable to your human resources department and/or Organization and you did not answer questions in it, go on to page 303.

To analyze this category, you first need to total the ratings for all its questions. Those are the rating numbers you have written on the short lines preceding each question. Total those numbers for the 34 questions in the Human Resources Planning category (pages 87 through 92) and write that total on the following line.

_____

As a first part of your analysis, you need to discover how your total points compared with the total points developed by the Advisory Board. The ratings provided for the answers to the questions in this category were based on the category's definition, and what our Advisory Board members believe is the best answer for a well-run, successful human resources department. However, although the Board provided ratings to be used for all human resources functions and they comprise a wide variety of education and experience, each rating must be considered in terms of the unique needs of your Organization.

If your total points were 209 or more for Human Resources Planning, our Advisory Board believes your human resources department is functioning very well in this area. Your actions appear to be fulfilling the category's definition and providing the human resources department and Organization with a solid base for an effective human resources function. Your major need in this category will be to continually ensure that the department's mission is used as a guide and reflects the philosophy of the Organization.

If your total points were at least 170 but no more than 208 for Human Resources Planning, our Advisory Board believes your human resources department is functioning better than a typical human resources department, but you may need to give this area some attention. Even though it is currently better than typical, the rapid changes in technology, laws, and society may have a performance impact. At a minimum, you should review the questions in which you received the lowest points and determine whether or not these are areas that require attention.

If your total points were at least 117 but no more than 169 for Human Resources Planning, our Advisory Board believes your human resources department is functioning at a level that requires improvement in this area. Very possibly, the total rating is impacted by questions concerning one or two activities. If this is the case, it is only those areas of the category that require additional attention, so a first step here is to review the ratings, answers, and basis for the answers to those questions.

If your total points were below 117 for Human Resources Planning, our Advisory Board believes your human resources department may be in real trouble in this category. If most of your questions received relatively low ratings, the entire category may require attention. If this is the case, you want to be sure activities in this area are designed to meet the Organization's requirements and the mission of the human resources department.

Each category ended with the same three questions. They asked for your perceptions of how the human resources department is performing and your perceptions of how the employees and clients of the department would rate how well the department is performing.

Although these questions request three different ratings, the answers all reflect your perceptions. Even so, if there are differences, you should determine why you would rate the category differently from one or both of the other groups.

ORGANIZATION DEVELOPMENT—ANALYSIS

Improving communication and understanding in the Organization in order to produce effective, functioning management and employee teams; establishing or changing to a desired culture; responding to changing conditions; and analyzing and influencing Organization personnel, systems, structures, policies, and rewards to ensure synergy and maximize internal consistency.

If this is one of the areas not applicable to your human resources department and/or Organization and you did not answer questions in it, go on to page 305.

To analyze this category, you first need to total the ratings for all its questions. Those are the rating numbers you have written on the short lines preceding each question. Total those numbers for the 52 questions in the Organizational Development category (pages 93 through 101) and write that total on the following line.

_____

As a first part of your analysis, you need to discover how your total points compared with the total points developed by the Advisory Board. The ratings provided for the answers to the questions in this category were based on the category's definition, and what our Advisory Board members believe is the best answer for a well-run, successful human resources department. However, although the Board provided ratings to be used for all human resources functions and they comprise a wide variety of education and experience, each rating must be considered in terms of the unique needs of your Organization.

If your total points were 337 or more for Organization Development, our Advisory Board believes your human resources department is functioning very well in this area. Your actions appear to be fulfilling the category's definition and providing the human resources department and Organization with a solid base for an effective human resources function. Your major need in this category will be to continually ensure that the department's mission is used as a guide and reflects the philosophy of the Organization.

If your total points were at least 274 but no more than 336 for Organization Development, our Advisory Board believes your human resources department is functioning better than a typical human resources department, but you may need to give this area some attention. Even though it is currently better than typical, the rapid changes in technology, laws, and society may have a performance impact. At a minimum, you should review the questions in which you received the lowest points and determine whether or not these are areas that require attention.

If your total points were at least 190 but no more than 273 for Organization Development, our Advisory Board believes your human resources department is functioning at a level that requires improvement in this area. Very possibly, the total rating is impacted by questions concerning one or two activities. If this is the case, it is only those areas of the category that require additional attention, so a first step here is to review the ratings, answers, and basis for the answers to those questions.

If your total points were below 190 for Organization Development, our Advisory Board believes your human resources department may be in real trouble in this category. If most of your questions received relatively low ratings, the entire category may require attention. If this is the case, you want to be sure activities in this area are designed to meet the Organization's requirements and the mission of the human resources department.

Each category ended with the same three questions. They asked for your perceptions of how the human resources department is performing and your perceptions of how the employees and clients of the department would rate how well the department is performing.

Although these questions request three different ratings, the answers all reflect your perceptions. Even so, if there are differences, you should determine why you would rate the category differently from one or both of the other groups.

DIVERSITY AND EQUAL EMPLOYMENT OPPORTUNITY—ANALYSIS

Developing and implementing workforce programs to maximize employment of productive people with different characteristics, qualifications, and talents while recognizing the legal requirements and social responsibilities of equal treatment for all employees and the actions necessary to ensure those requirements are met.

If this is one of the areas not applicable to your human resources department and/or Organization and you did not answer questions in it, go on to page 307.

To analyze this category, you first need to total the ratings for all its questions. Those are the rating numbers you have written on the short lines preceding each question. Total those numbers for the 45 questions in the Diversity and Equal Employment Opportunity category (pages 103 through 109) and write that total on the following line.

_____

As a first part of your analysis, you need to discover how your total points compared with the total points developed by the Advisory Board. The ratings provided for the answers to the questions in this category were based on the category's definition, and what our Advisory Board members believe is the best answer for a well-run, successful human resources department. However, although the Board provided ratings to be used for all human resources functions and they comprise a wide variety of education and experience, each rating must be considered in terms of the unique needs of your Organization.

If your total points were 292 or more for Diversity and Equal Employment Opportunity, our Advisory Board believes your human resources department is functioning very well in this area. Your actions appear to be fulfilling the category's definition and providing the human resources department and Organization with a solid base for an effective human resources function. Your major need in this category will be to continually ensure that the department's mission is used as a guide and reflects the philosophy of the Organization.

If your total points were at least 237 but no more than 291 for Diversity and Equal Employment Opportunity, our Advisory Board believes your human resources department is functioning better than a typical human resources department, but you may need to give this area some attention. Even though it is currently better than typical, the rapid changes in technology, laws, and society may have a performance impact. At a minimum, you should review the questions in which you received the lowest points and determine whether or not these are areas that require attention.

If your total points were at least 164 but no more than 236 for Diversity and Equal Employment Opportunity, our Advisory Board believes your human resources department is functioning at a level that requires improvement in this area. Very possibly, the total rating is impacted by questions concerning one or two activities. If this is the case, it is only those areas of the category that require additional attention, so a first step here is to review the ratings, answers, and basis for the answers to those questions.

If your total points were below 164 for Diversity and Equal Employment Opportunity, our Advisory Board believes your human resources department may be in real trouble in this category. If most of your questions received relatively low ratings, the entire category may require attention. If this is the case, you want to be sure activities in this area are designed to meet the Organization's requirements and the mission of the human resources department.

Each category ended with the same three questions. They asked for your perceptions of how the human resources department is performing and your perceptions of how the employees and clients of the department would rate how well the department is performing.

Although these questions request three different ratings, the answers all reflect your perceptions. Even so, if there are differences, you should determine why you would rate the category differently from one or both of the other groups.

SAFETY AND ENVIRONMENT—ANALYSIS

The training, communication, and leadership required to provide a safe working environment; to provide an appropriate level of employee involvement and responsibility for implementing safe practices, using safety equipment, and complying with Organization safety rules and practices; and to ensure that federal, state, and local safety and environmental requirements are met.

If this is one of the areas not applicable to your human resources department and/or Organization and you did not answer questions in it, go on to page 309.

To analyze this category, you first need to total the ratings for all its questions. Those are the rating numbers you have written on the short lines preceding each question. Total those numbers for the 46 questions in the Safety and Environment category (pages 111 through 118) and write that total on the following line.

_____

As a first part of your analysis, you need to discover how your total points compared with the total points developed by the Advisory Board. The ratings provided for the answers to the questions in this category were based on the category's definition, and what our Advisory Board members believe is the best answer for a well-run, successful human resources department. However, although the Board provided ratings to be used for all human resources functions and they comprise a wide variety of education and experience, each rating must be considered in terms of the unique needs of your Organization.

If your total points were 305 or more for Safety and Environment, our Advisory Board believes your human resources department is functioning very well in this area. Your actions appear to be fulfilling the category's definition and providing the human resources department and Organization with a solid base for an effective human resources function. Your major need in this category will be to continually ensure that the department's mission is used as a guide and reflects the philosophy of the Organization.

If your total points were at least 248 but no more than 304 for Safety and Environment, our Advisory Board believes your human resources department is functioning better than a typical human resources department, but you may need to give this area some attention. Even though it is currently better than typical, the rapid changes in technology, laws, and society may have a performance impact. At a minimum, you should review the questions in which you received the lowest points and determine whether or not these are areas that require attention.

If your total points were at least 172 but no more than 247 for Safety and Environment, our Advisory Board believes your human resources department is functioning at a level that requires improvement in this area. Very possibly, the total rating is impacted by questions concerning one or two activities. If this is the case, it is only those areas of the category that require additional attention, so a first step here is to review the ratings, answers, and basis for the answers to those questions.

If your total points were below 172 for Safety and Environment, our Advisory Board believes your human resources department may be in real trouble in this category. If most of your questions received relatively low ratings, the entire category may require attention. If this is the case, you want to be sure activities in this area are designed to meet the Organization's requirements and the mission of the human resources department.

Each category ended with the same three questions. They asked for your perceptions of how the human resources department is performing and your perceptions of how the employees and clients of the department would rate how well the department is performing.

Although these questions request three different ratings, the answers all reflect your perceptions. Even so, if there are differences, you should determine why you would rate the category differently from one or both of the other groups.

SECURITY—ANALYSIS

Maintaining and protecting the Organization's employees, assets, and human resources documents, information, and facilities.

If this is one of the areas not applicable to your human resources department and/or Organization and you did not answer questions in it, go on to page 311.

To analyze this category, you first need to total the ratings for all its questions. Those are the rating numbers you have written on the short lines preceding each question. Total those numbers for the 42 questions in the Security category (pages 119 through 124) and write that total on the following line.

_____

As a first part of your analysis, you need to discover how your total points compared with the total points developed by the Advisory Board. The ratings provided for the answers to the questions in this category were based on the category definition, and what our Advisory Board members believe is the best answer for a well-run, successful human resources department. However, although the Board provided ratings to be used for all human resources functions and they comprise a wide variety of education and experience, each rating must be considered in terms of the unique needs of your Organization.

If your total points were 282 or more for Security, our Advisory Board believes your human resources department is functioning very well in this area. Your actions appear to be fulfilling the category's definition and providing the human resources department and Organization with a solid base for an effective human resources function. Your major need in this category will be to continually ensure that the department's mission is used as a guide and reflects the philosophy of the Organization.

If your total points were at least 229 but no more than 281 for Security, our Advisory Board believes your human resources department is functioning better than a typical human resources department, but you may need to give this area some attention. Even though it is currently better than typical, the rapid changes in technology, laws, and society may have a performance impact. At a minimum, you should review the questions in which you received the lowest points and determine whether or not these are areas that require attention.

If your total points were at least 159 but no more than 228 for Security, our Advisory Board believes your human resources department is functioning at a level that requires improvement in this area. Very possibly, the total rating is impacted by questions concerning one or two activities. If this is the case, it is

only those areas of the category that require additional attention, so a first step here is to review the ratings, answers, and basis for the answers to those questions.

If your total points were below 159 for Security, our Advisory Board believes your human resources department may be in real trouble in this category. If most of your questions received relatively low ratings, the entire category may require attention. If this is the case, you want to be sure activities in this area are designed to meet the Organization's requirements and the mission of the human resources department.

Each category ended with the same three questions. They asked for your perceptions of how the human resources department is performing and your perceptions of how the employees and clients of the department would rate how well the department is performing.

Although these questions request three different ratings, the answers all reflect your perceptions. Even so, if there are differences, you should determine why you would rate the category differently from one or both of the other groups.

EQUIPMENT AND FACILITIES—ANALYSIS

Providing the necessary equipment and facilities to fulfill the human resources mission and provide optimum service to the Organization.

If this is one of the areas not applicable to your human resources department and/or Organization and you did not answer questions in it, go on to page 313.

To analyze this category, you first need to total the ratings for all its questions. Those are the rating numbers you have written on the short lines preceding each question. Total those numbers for the 23 questions in the Equipment and Facilities category (pages 125 through 128) and write that total on the following line.

_____

As a first part of your analysis, you need to discover how your total points compared with the total points developed by the Advisory Board. The ratings provided for the answers to the questions in this category were based on the above definition, and what our Advisory Board members believe is the best answer for a well-run, successful human resources department. However, although the Board provided ratings to be used for all human resources functions and they comprise a wide variety of education and experience, each rating must be considered in terms of the unique needs of your Organization.

If your total points were 147 or more for Equipment and Facilities, our Advisory Board believes your human resources department is functioning very well in this area. Your actions appear to be fulfilling the category's definition and providing the human resources department and Organization with a solid base for an effective human resources function. Your major need in this category will be to continually ensure that the department's mission is used as a guide and reflects the philosophy of the Organization.

If your total points were at least 120 but no more than 146 for Equipment and Facilities, our Advisory Board believes your human resources department is functioning better than a typical human resources department, but you may need to give this area some attention. Even though it is currently better than typical, the rapid changes in technology, laws, and society may have a performance impact. At a minimum, you should review the questions in which you received the lowest points and determine whether or not these are areas that require attention.

If your total points were at least 83 but no more than 119 for Equipment and Facilities, our Advisory Board believes your human resources department is functioning at a level that requires improvement in this area. Very possibly, the total rating is impacted by questions concerning one or two activities. If this is the case, it is only those areas of the category that require additional attention, so a first step here is to review the ratings, answers, and basis for the answers to those questions.

If your total points were below 83 for Equipment and Facilities, our Advisory Board believes your human resources department may be in real trouble in this category. If most of your questions received relatively low ratings, the entire category may require attention. If this is the case, you want to be sure activities in this area are designed to meet the Organization's requirements and the mission of the human resources department.

Each category ended with the same three questions. They asked for your perceptions of how the human resources department is performing and your perceptions of how the employees and clients of the department would rate how well the department is performing.

Although these questions request three different ratings, the answers all reflect your perceptions. Even so, if there are differences, you should determine why you would rate the category differently from one or both of the other groups.

DOCUMENTATION AND INFORMATION SYSTEMS—ANALYSIS

Preparing, storing, and maintaining employee records and information, including computerized human resources information systems, and meeting federal, state, and local requirements.

If this is one of the areas not applicable to your human resources department and/or Organization and you did not answer questions in it, go on to page 315.

To analyze this category, you first need to total the ratings for all its questions. Those are the rating numbers you have written on the short lines preceding each question. Total those numbers for the 26 questions in the Documentation and Information Systems category (pages 129 through 133) and write that total on the following line.

———————

As a first part of your analysis, you need to discover how your total points compared with the total points developed by the Advisory Board. The ratings provided for the answers to the questions in this category were based on the category definition, and what our Advisory Board members believe is the best answer for a well-run, successful human resources department. However, although the Board provided ratings to be used for all human resources functions and they comprise a wide variety of education and experience, each rating must be considered in terms of the unique needs of your Organization.

If your total points were 186 or more for Documentation and Information Systems, our Advisory Board believes your human resources department is functioning very well in this area. Your actions appear to be fulfilling the category's definition and providing the human resources department and Organization with a solid base for an effective human resources function. Your major need in this category will be to continually ensure that the department's mission is used as a guide and reflects the philosophy of the Organization.

If your total points were at least 152 but no more than 185 for Documentation and Information Systems, our Advisory Board believes your human resources department is functioning better than a typical human resources department, but you may need to give this area some attention. Even though it is currently better than typical, the rapid changes in technology, laws, and society may have a performance impact. At a minimum, you should review the questions in which you received the lowest points and determine whether or not these are areas that require attention.

If your total points were at least 105 but no more than 151 for Documentation and Information Systems, our Advisory Board believes your human resources department is functioning at a level that requires improvement in this area. Very possibly, the total rating is impacted by questions concerning one or two activities. If this is the case, it is only those areas of the category that require additional attention, so a first step here is to review the ratings, answers, and basis for the answers to those questions.

If your total points were below 105 for Documentation and Information Systems, our Advisory Board feels that your human resources department may be in real trouble in this category. If most of your questions received relatively low ratings, the entire category may require attention. If this is the case, you want to be sure activities in this area are designed to meet the Organization's requirements and the mission of the human resources department.

Each category ended with the same three questions. They asked for your perceptions of how the human resources department is performing and your perceptions of how the employees and clients of the department would rate how well the department is performing.

Although these questions request three different ratings, the answers all reflect your perceptions. Even so, if there are differences, you should determine why you would rate the category differently from one or both of the other groups.

FUNCTIONAL CATEGORY GROUPING ANALYSIS

Still another approach to analyzing the human resources department is to group the categories into three basic functions: Department Management, Strategic Activities, and Operational Activities. This audit was not designed to specifically evaluate or examine these functions, but it is possible to obtain some insight by combining totals from selected categories.

Department Management

The two categories from this audit that can be used for insight into Department Management are Department Organization and Department Employees. Enter the total ratings for each on the appropriate lines and then total them.

Department Organization   _____

Department Employees   _____

Total Department Management   _____

If your total points were 608 or more for Department Management, your human resources department appears to be managing very well. If your total points were at least 494 but no more than 607, your human resources department is managing better than a typical human resources department. If your total points were at least 342 but no more than 493, your human resources department may require improvement in this area, and if your total points were below 342, you may have significant problems in the management of the department.

Strategic Activities

The three categories from this audit that can be used for insight into Strategic Activities are Department Mission, Human Resources Planning, and Organizational Development. Enter the total ratings for each on the appropriate lines and then total them.

Department Mission   _____

Human Resources Planning   _____

Organization Development   _____

Total Strategic Activities   _____

If your total points were 736 or more for Strategic Activities, your human resources department appears to be doing very well. If your total points were at least 598 but no more than 735, your human resources department is doing better than a typical human resources department. If your total points were at least 414 but no more than 597, your human resources department may require improvement in this area, and if your total points were below 414, you may have significant problems in providing strategic activities.

Operational Activities

All of the other categories from this audit can be used for insight into Operational Activities. Enter the total ratings for each on the appropriate lines and then total them. Place an "X" on any line for a category not applicable to your human resources department.

Labor Relations   _____

Recruitment and Selection   _____

Education, Training, and Development   _____

Employee Relations   _____

Benefits   _____

Compensation   _____

Diversity and Equal Employment Opportunity   _____

Safety and Environment   _____

Security   _____

Equipment and Facilities   _____

Documentation and Information Systems   _____

Total Operational Activities   _____

If your total points were 2,997 or more for Operational Activities, your human resources department appears to be doing very well in providing the Organization with human resources services. If your total points were at least 2,434 but no more than 2,996, your human resources department is doing better than a typical human resources department. If your total points were at least 1,685 but no more than 2,433, your human resources department may require improvement in this area, and if your total points were below 1,695, you may have significant problems in providing operational activities to the Organization.

Analysis

One of our Advisory Board members suggested the proper weightings for the contributions of these three functions to the success of a human resources department are:

Department Management   25%

Strategic Activities   50%

Operational Activities   25%

SUMMARY—ANALYSIS

Each category ended with the same three questions that asked for your perceptions of how the human resources department is performing, how well the employees of the department think the human resources department is performing, and how well the clients of the department think the department is performing.

The summary questions asked for similar perceptions for the entire human resources department's performance, so you have your perceptions regarding each category and the performance of the entire department. However, these are your perceptions, and although your own perception is accurate, your ideas about how the other two groups might rate may not be as accurate.

One way to discover their real perceptions is to ask them. On pages 321, 322, and 323 is a sample form that can be used. You will note it requests ratings for all 16 categories of human resources. In that format, it should only be used with people who have knowledge of the department's performance in all categories. If you wish to use it with people who know only performance in some of the categories, you need to revise the form to indicate only those categories. You still will probably want to include a request for an overall rating of the department's performance.

The form does not request any identification of the individual completing it. With these types of questions, you will receive more useful answers by not requesting identification. You are only going to solicit information from two groups: employees of the human resources department and clients of human resources within the Organization, so just use a different colored paper for each group. You then will be able to correctly classify the responses.

When you receive the completed forms, average the responses from each group and enter them along with your own ratings on the form on pages 325 and 326.

HUMAN RESOURCES SURVEY

TO:_____

The human resources department is currently conducting an audit of its performance. As one of our (clients/department employees), your perceptions will be of considerable assistance with this project, so it will be appreciated if you take a few moments to complete this form and return it. You do not have to provide your name.

Thank you for your assistance in our efforts to provide the best possible human resources services to our organization.

(Name and address of sending party)

_____

The following are the categories of human resources and the definitions we are using. Read each one and then rate how you feel our human resources department is performing in that category. The questions ask for your perceptions and not necessarily information based on an evaluation of factual performance criteria.

For your ratings, use a nine-point scale (one being low, five being typical, and nine being high). Select a single number from that scale for each rating. Write the number on the line in front of the category.

If you do not have any idea as to how well human resources is performing in a category, place an "X" on the line for that category.

_____ Department Mission—The overall objective or purpose of the human resources department within the Organization and its relationship to the Organization's overall mission.

_____ Department Organization—The department's internal relationships; relationships with other functions, departments, and employees of the Organization; and the structuring of resources within the department.

_____ Department Employees—The selection, training, motivation, development, and retention of a qualified human resources team.

_____ Labor Relations—The human resources role in the relationship between the Organization and any bargaining unit of an employee-organized labor group, including labor-organizing campaigns.

_____ Recruitment and Selection—Obtaining and evaluating qualified candidates from internal and external sources for positions throughout the Organization.

_____ Education, Training, and Development—Providing performance skills training and career development to employees, utilizing both internal and external resources, including providing expertise in assessing education, training, and development needs and identification of high-potential employees.

_____ Employee Relations—The formal policies and procedures governing all conditions of employment, including specific human resources activities not otherwise categorized.

_____ Benefits—The noncash compensation provided to employees of the Organization including, but not limited to, such components as insurances, retirement saving plans, and paid time off, and the systems, support services, and communications to successfully deliver the benefits.

_____ Compensation—All cash payments to employees and also the systems by which positions are evaluated, salary and wage ranges and bands are determined, and adjustments are made including commissions, lump sum payments, incentive payments, and bonuses.

_____ Human Resources Planning—The collection and analysis of data providing long-term (strategic) and short-term (tactical) plans and forecasts to meet the department's and Organization's missions, including such activities as succession planning, leadership development, and recruiting schedules.

_____ Organization Development—Improving communication and understanding in the Organization in order to produce effective, functioning management and employee teams; establishing or changing to a desired culture; responding to changing conditions; and analyzing and influencing Organization personnel, systems, structures, policies, and rewards to ensure synergy and maximize internal consistency.

_____ Diversity and Equal Employment Opportunity—Developing and implementing workforce programs to maximize employment of productive people with different characteristics, qualifications, and talents while recognizing the legal requirements and social responsibilities of equal treatment for all employees and the actions necessary to ensure those requirements are met.

_____ Safety and Environment—The training, communication, and leadership required to provide a safe working environment; to provide an appropriate level of employee involvement and responsibility for implementing safe practices, using safety equipment, and complying with Organization safety rules and practices; and to ensure that federal, state, and local safety and environmental requirements are met.

_____ Security—Maintaining and protecting the Organization's employees, assets, and human resources documents, information, and facilities.

_____ Equipment and Facilities—Providing the necessary equipment and facilities to fulfill the human resources mission and provide optimum service to the Organization.

_____ Documentation and Information Systems—Preparing, storing, and maintaining employee records and information, including computerized human resources information systems, and meeting federal, state, and local requirements.

Now that you have rated each of the categories, please answer the following question. All things considered, how well is the human resources department performing and fulfilling its mission? Again use the nine-point scale and write your rating on the following line.

CATEGORY AND DEPARTMENT PERCEPTIONS ANALYSIS SUMMARY

When you have received all the completed Human Resources Survey forms, total the ratings for each group in each category and divide that number by the number of ratings received for the category. (You are calculating an average rating for each category.) Enter the average ratings on the appropriate lines of this form. Be sure to also enter your own ratings.

Category	Your Ratings	Client Ratings	Department Employee Ratings
Department Mission	_____	_____	_____
Department Organization	_____	_____	_____
Department Employees	_____	_____	_____
Labor Relations	_____	_____	_____
Recruitment and Selection	_____	_____	_____
Education, Training, and Development	_____	_____	_____
Employee Relations	_____	_____	_____
Benefits	_____	_____	_____
Compensation	_____	_____	_____
Human Resources Planning	_____	_____	_____
Organization Development	_____	_____	_____
Diversity and Equal Employment Opportunity	_____	_____	_____
Safety and Environment	_____	_____	_____

Security   —————   —————   —————

Equipment and Facilities   —————   —————   —————

Documentation and Information
Systems   —————   —————   —————

The Entire Human Resources
Department   —————   —————   —————

The next step is to identify those areas of agreement and disagreement. If all the ratings for a category or the department are the same, that is a positive result. Where there are differences of more than 2 full points, you need to perform some additional investigation. You need to learn why those ratings differ.

HUMAN RESOURCES DEPARTMENT ANALYSIS

Now that you have analyzed your ratings in each of the human resources categories and have compared perceptions on performance, it is time to combine the individual category ratings for an analysis of the entire function. You are going to do this in two ways. You will compare your overall department evaluation with that of the Advisory Board. Then you will do a second comparison using the earlier weightings you gave each category.

First you must convert your total rating for each category to an Adjusted Rating. These are the total ratings for the categories you recorded on the second page of the analysis (page 281). You accomplish this by entering those ratings on the appropriate lines (Rating column) in the following table. Enter a zero for the categories you did not use. Then multiply each rating by the number following it, and enter the result in the Adjusted Rating column. You will probably require a calculator. (Be sure to note the number of decimal places. After multiplying, you may round off to the nearest whole number.)

Category	Rating			Adjusted Rating
Department Mission	_____	× 2.1	=	_____
Department Organization	_____	× 1.1	=	_____
Department Employees	_____	× 1.6	=	_____
Labor Relations	_____	× 1.6	=	_____
Recruitment and Selection	_____	× 1	=	_____
Education, Training, and Development	_____	× 1.2	=	_____
Employee Relations	_____	× 1.1	=	_____
Benefits	_____	× 2.4	=	_____
Compensation	_____	× 1.5	=	_____
Human Resources Planning	_____	× 1.9	=	_____
Organizational Development	_____	× 1.2	=	_____
Diversity and Equal Employment Opportunity	_____	× 1.4	=	_____
Safety and Environment	_____	× 1.3	=	_____
Security	_____	× 1.5	=	_____
Equipment and Facilities	_____	× 2.8	=	_____
Documentation and Information Systems	_____	× 2.1	=	_____

For the comparison with how our Advisory Board sees the function, use the form on the next page.

1. First, enter your Adjusted Rating for each category from your above calculations on the appropriate lines in the Rating column. Enter a zero on the lines for categories that do not apply.

2. Multiply each number in the Rating column by the number following it, and enter the result in the Evaluation column. (Be sure to note the number of decimal places. After multiplying, you may round off to the nearest whole number.)

3. Total the resulting numbers in the Evaluation column.

4. Draw a line through the number in the Basis column for each category that does not apply—categories to which you assigned a zero.

5. Total the numbers in the Basis column that do not have lines through them. If you used all categories, the total for the Basis column is 5,010.

6. Divide the total for the Evaluation column (Step 3) by the total for the Basis column (Step 5), and multiply the result by 100 to obtain a percentage.

When you have completed that, go on to page 330.

HUMAN RESOURCES DEPARTMENT ANALYSIS
COMPARISON WITH ADVISORY BOARD WEIGHTINGS

Basis	Category	Rating	Evaluation
450	Department Mission	_____	× .9 = _____
400	Department Organization	_____	× .8 = _____
400	Department Employees	_____	× .8 = _____
350	Labor Relations	_____	× .7 = _____
400	Recruitment and Selection	_____	× .8 = _____
400	Education, Training, and Development	_____	× .8 = _____
360	Employee Relations	_____	× .7 = _____
350	Benefits	_____	× .7 = _____
350	Compensation	_____	× .7 = _____
350	Human Resources Planning	_____	× .7 = _____
400	Organizational Development	_____	× .8 = _____
200	Diversity and Equal Employment Opportunity	_____	× .4 = _____
200	Safety and Environment	_____	× .4 = _____
100	Security	_____	× .2 = _____
100	Equipment and Facilities	_____	× .2 = _____
200	Documentation and Information Systems	_____	× .4 = _____
_____	*Totals		_____

*If all categories apply, the total for the Basis column is 5,010.

If the Comparison Percentage is 80 or more, your human resources department is functioning very well in comparison to the weightings you gave the various categories. Your actions in the categories appear to be fulfilling your human resources department mission and role, and providing the Organization with an effective human resources function. Your major need here will be to continually ensure that the department maintains this position.

If the Comparison Percentage is at least 65 but no more than 79, your human resources department is functioning better than a typical human resources department based on your weightings of the categories, but you may need to give the function some attention. Even though it is currently better than typical, the rapid changes in technology, laws, and society may have a performance impact on your department. If this were to occur, there might be a reduction in the points your answers would receive. At the least, you should review the categories in which you received the lowest points, and determine whether or not these are areas that require attention.

If the Comparison Percentage is at least 45 but no more than 64, your human resources department is functioning at a level that requires improvement in comparison to a typical human resources department based on your weightings of the categories. Very possibly, the total rating is affected by one or two categories. If that is the case, it is those areas that require attention, so a first step here is to review the appropriate answers and basis for the ratings in those categories.

If the Comparison Percentage is below 45, your human resources department may be in real trouble in comparison to a typical human resources department based on your weightings of the categories. If most of your categories received relatively low ratings, the entire function may require attention. If that is the case, you want to be sure your department's mission and activities are designed to meet the Organization's requirements and mission.

Now that you have compared your total human resources department weighted rating from the audit with the ratings of the Advisory Board, you are going to complete a second comparison. This one uses the weightings you earlier gave the 16 categories, so it will reflect your view of the importance of the various categories to your human resources department.

For this comparison, use the form on the page 333.

The final step in order to make this comparison is to calculate what percentage of a possible total your total ratings are. For this calculation, use the following instructions:

1. Enter in the Weighting column of the form the weighting you gave each category on pages xxii and xxiii.

2. Enter zeros on the lines for any categories that do not apply.

3. Multiply each number in the Weighting column by 500, and enter the result in the Possible column.

4. Enter your Adjusted Rating for each category from your calculations on page 327.

5. Multiply each number in the Adjusted Rating column by the number in the Weighting column, and enter the result in the Evaluation column.

6. Total the numbers in the Possible and Evaluation columns.

7. Divide the total for the Evaluation column by the total for the Possible column, and enter the result on the Result line below.

8. Multiply the number on the Result line by 100, and enter it on the Comparison Percentage line.

Result   _____

$$\times\ 100$$

Comparison Percentage   _____

Now go to page 335.

Human Resources Department Analysis Using Your Weightings

Category	Weighting	Possible	Adjusted Rating	Evaluation
Department Mission	____	____	____	____
Department Organization	____	____	____	____
Department Employees	____	____	____	____
Labor Relations	____	____	____	____
Recruitment and Selection	____	____	____	____
Education, Training, and Development	____	____	____	____
Employee Relations	____	____	____	____
Benefits	____	____	____	____
Compensation	____	____	____	____
Human Resources Planning	____	____	____	____
Organizational Development	____	____	____	____
Diversity and EEO	____	____	____	____
Safety and Environment	____	____	____	____
Security	____	____	____	____
Equipment and Facilities	____	____	____	____
Documentation and Information Systems	____	____	____	____
Totals			____	____

If you score 80 percent or more, your human resources department is functioning very well in comparison to the weightings you gave the various categories. Your actions in the categories appear to be fulfilling your human resources department mission and role, and providing the Organization with an effective human resources function. Your major need here will be to continually ensure that the department maintains this position.

If you score at least 65 percent but no more than 79 percent, your human resources department is functioning better than your weightings indicate a typical human resources department does, but you may need to give the function some attention. Even though it is currently better than typical, the rapid changes in technology, laws, and society may have a performance impact. You should review the categories in which you received the lowest points and determine whether or not these are areas that require attention.

If you score from 45 percent to 64 percent, your human resources department is functioning at a level that requires improvement in comparison to the weightings you gave the various categories. Very possibly, the total rating is impacted by one or two categories. If this is the case, it is those areas that require attention, so a first step here is to review the appropriate answers and basis for the ratings in those categories.

If you score below 45 percent, your human resources department may be in real trouble in comparison to the weightings you gave the various categories. If most of your categories received relatively low ratings, the entire function may require attention. If this is the case, you want to be sure the department's mission and activities are designed to meet the Organization's requirements and mission.

COST COMPARISON ANALYSIS

If you wish to further pursue the audit of your human resources department, there are a number of standard calculations and measures that can be of assistance. Some of these were mentioned in the text: internal and external employee turnover, training cost per employee, productivity per employee, accident frequency, and accident severity were a few. (These are listed on page 130 , Question 8 of the Documentation and Information Systems category.)

Some other measures that can be of assistance can be obtained by answering the following questions:

1. What is the annual cost of operating the human resources department?
    $_____

2. What percentage of the Organization's total income or sales does the cost of operating the human resources department represent? _____%

3. What percentage of the Organization's total operating costs does the cost of operating the human resources department represent? _____%

4. What is the value of the Organization's assets assigned to the human resources department? $_____

5. What percentage of the Organization's total capital investment do the human resources assets represent? _____%

6. What percentage of the Organization's total employees are in the human resources department? _____%

7. What percentage of human resources department employees are management, what percentage are professionals, and what percentage are administrative?
    Management _____% Professionals _____% Administrative _____%

8. What is the ratio of human resources employees to the total employees of the Organization (number of human resources employees divided by total Organization employees)? _____

ASSET COMPARISON MATRIX

Insight also can be gained by using a matrix to identify how human resources department assets are assigned. The following form is provided for that purpose. For this analysis your assets are considered to be employees, budget dollars, equipment, and time.

If a function/activity does not apply, place an "X" on the appropriate line. If some employees, budget dollars, equipment, or time is assigned to more than one function/activity, use partial numbers. For example, an employee assigned to both Labor Relations and Benefits could be entered as .5 in each. For time entries you may want to enter the time actually consumed by the activity rather than the time assigned.

Function/Activity	Employees	Budget Dollars	Equipment	Time
Labor Relations	_____	_____	_____	_____
Recruitment and Selection	_____	_____	_____	_____
Education, Training, and Development	_____	_____	_____	_____
Employee Relations	_____	_____	_____	_____
Benefits	_____	_____	_____	_____
Compensation	_____	_____	_____	_____
Human Resources Planning	_____	_____	_____	_____
Organization Development	_____	_____	_____	_____
Safety and Environment	_____	_____	_____	_____
Security	_____	_____	_____	_____
Equipment and Facilities	_____	_____	_____	_____
Documentation and Information Systems	_____	_____	_____	_____

The advantage of creating such a matrix is that it allows you to see how your assets are being used. Are you putting them where they are needed? Are some areas overstaffed and some understaffed? Does the budget money assigned to an activity reflect its relative contribution to the success of the Organization? How do the categories of needed improvement (if any) from the audit relate to the assets assigned to them?

FINAL ANALYSIS

You now have acquired a number of pieces of information regarding your human resources department performance, and you have identified additional information for further investigation. You have:

- An analysis of each category's rating as compared to the Advisory Board's rating of that category
- A comparison of your category and department performance perceptions with those of human resources department employees and department clients within the Organization
- A comparison of performance by basic human resources functions
- An identification of standard calculations for comparison purposes
- A completed asset comparison matrix
- Overall evaluations of the department compared with the Advisory Board and your own weightings

You have acquired a great deal of information. Now you need to further analyze it by identifying areas of agreement and differences, discovering why those differences are occurring, and examining the specific reasons for any low ratings. All this should be accomplished with the Organization's objectives and mission as a guide. You want to be able to answer questions such as:

- Is the human resources department providing the Organization the services it desires?
- How well is the human resources department performing?
- How well is the human resources department perceived by its Organization clients to be providing services?
- How is human resources utilizing the assets provided it?
- How does the human resources department compare with similar departments in other Organizations?
- What should be done to improve the performance of human resources?

With the last question in mind, it is time to move to the final step of this audit—Action Planning.

Step Four—Action Planning

Step Four—Action Planning is the final step in this audit. Here you take the results of your analysis and prepare appropriate action plans, plans to capitalize on your human resources department's strengths and correct any areas of needed improvement.

James Hayes, former president of the American Management Association, once commented, "Three areas requiring significant improvement are about all that can be handled successfully at one time." He was speaking of employees, but the same is probably true for a function such as human resources, so for your action planning let's identify what those three areas are.

Go back over all the information you have and identify which three categories most demand your immediate attention. If you are in the position of not having three categories greatly in need of improvement, then select the three categories you want to develop further.

When you have identified those categories, select the appropriate three forms from the following pages. A separate form is provided for each category. Then complete a form for each identified category by:

1. First, developing an overall objective to describe what you wish to accomplish. Make it a specific objective, one with completion times and measures. The objective should focus on the identified areas of needed improvement within the category.

   Here you may not have all the details you need. You should find suggestions from employees in the human resources department who work in that area or with clients of that area helpful.

2. Next identifying three areas within the category that most need improvement and identify what is required to improve these areas.

3. The final step is developing specific actions. They should include completion times and measures. Each of these actions can then be assigned a due date to someone within the department.

When you have completed your action plans, you have completed the first step of good management—planning. The next steps are implementation delegating the assignments—and controlling the results. As with any management undertaking, you must be flexible and willing to adjust to changing conditions.

You have now completed the four steps of this audit, so turn to page 344.

DEPARTMENT MISSION

Priority _____

The overall objective or purpose of the human resources department within the Organization and its relationship to the Organization's overall mission.

Improvement Objective

_____

_____

_____

Areas of Needed Improvement   Requirements

1. _____   _____

                                         _____

2. _____   _____

                                         _____

3. _____   _____

                                         _____

Actions   Assigned to   Due Date

_____   _____   _____

_____   _____   _____

_____

_____   _____   _____

_____

345

DEPARTMENT ORGANIZATION

Priority _____

The department's internal relationships; relationships with other functions, departments and employees of the Organization; and the structuring of resources within the department.

Improvement Objective

_____

_____

_____

Areas of Needed Improvement   Requirements

1. _____   _____

                                           _____

2. _____   _____

                                           _____

3. _____   _____

                                           _____

Actions   Assigned to   Due Date

_____   _____   _____

_____

_____   _____   _____

_____

_____   _____   _____

_____

Department Employees

Priority _____

The selection, training, motivation, development, and retention of a qualified human resources team.

Improvement Objective

_____

_____

_____

Areas of Needed Improvement   Requirements

1. _____   _____

                                      _____

2. _____   _____

                                      _____

3. _____   _____

                                      _____

Actions   Assigned to   Due Date

_____   _____   _____

_____

_____   _____   _____

_____

_____   _____   _____

_____

349

LABOR RELATIONS

Priority _____

The human resources role in the relationship between the Organization and any bargaining unit of an employee-organized labor group, including labor-organizing campaigns.

Improvement Objective

_____

_____

_____

Areas of Needed Improvement | Requirements

1. _____ | _____

_____

2. _____ | _____

_____

3. _____ | _____

_____

Actions | Assigned to | Due Date

_____ | _____ | _____

_____

_____ | _____ | _____

_____

_____

RECRUITMENT AND SELECTION

Priority _____

Obtaining and evaluating qualified candidates from internal and external sources for positions throughout the Organization.

Improvement Objective

_____

_____

_____

Areas of Needed Improvement   Requirements

1. _____   _____

                                      _____

2. _____   _____

                                      _____

3. _____   _____

                                      _____

Actions   Assigned to   Due Date

_____   _____   _____

_____

_____   _____   _____

_____

_____   _____   _____

_____

EDUCATION, TRAINING, AND DEVELOPMENT

Priority _____

Providing performance skills training and career development to employees, utilizing both internal and external resources, including providing expertise in assessing education, training, and development needs and identification of high-potential employees.

Improvement Objective

_____

_____

_____

Areas of Needed Improvement	Requirements
1. _____	_____
	_____
2. _____	_____
	_____
3. _____	_____
	_____

Actions	Assigned to	Due Date
_____	_____	_____
_____		
_____	_____	_____
_____		
_____	_____	_____
_____		

EMPLOYEE RELATIONS

Priority _____

The formal policies and procedures governing all conditions of employment, including specific human resources activities not otherwise categorized.

Improvement Objective

_____

_____

_____

Areas of Needed Improvement   Requirements

1. _____   _____

                                      _____

2. _____   _____

                                      _____

3. _____   _____

                                      _____

Actions   Assigned to   Due Date

_____   _____   _____

_____

_____   _____   _____

_____

_____   _____   _____

_____

BENEFITS

Priority _____

The noncash compensation provided to employees of the Organization including, but not limited to, such components as insurances, retirement saving plans, and paid time off, and the systems, support services, and communications to successfully deliver the benefits.

Improvement Objective

_____

_____

_____

Areas of Needed Improvement   Requirements

1. _____   _____

                                    _____

2. _____   _____

                                    _____

3. _____   _____

                                    _____

Actions   Assigned to   Due Date

_____   _____   _____

_____

_____   _____   _____

_____

_____

COMPENSATION

All cash payments to employees and also the systems by which positions are evaluated, salary and wage ranges and bands are determined, and adjustments are made, including commissions, lump sum payments, incentive payments, and bonuses.

Improvement Objective

_____

_____

_____

Areas of Needed Improvement	Requirements
1. _____	_____
	_____
2. _____	_____
	_____
3. _____	_____
	_____

Actions	Assigned to	Due Date
_____	_____	_____
_____		
_____	_____	_____
_____		
_____	_____	_____
_____		

Human Resources Planning

Priority _____

The collection and analysis of data providing long-term (strategic) and short-term (tactical) plans and forecasts to meet the department's and Organization's missions, including such activities as succession planning, leadership development, and recruiting schedules.

Improvement Objective

_____

_____

_____

Areas of Needed Improvement   Requirements

1. _____   _____

                                                            _____

2. _____   _____

                                                            _____

3. _____   _____

                                                            _____

Actions   Assigned to   Due Date

_____   _____   _____

_____   _____   _____

_____

_____

ORGANIZATION DEVELOPMENT

Priority _____

Improving communication and understanding in the Organization in order to produce effective, functioning management and employee teams; establishing or changing to a desired culture; responding to changing conditions; and analyzing and influencing Organization personnel, systems, structures, policies, and rewards to ensure synergy and maximize internal consistency.

Improvement Objective

_____

_____

_____

Areas of Needed Improvement	Requirements
1. _____	_____
	_____
2. _____	_____
	_____
3. _____	_____
	_____

Actions	Assigned to	Due Date
_____	_____	_____
_____		
_____	_____	_____
_____		
_____	_____	_____
_____		

DIVERSITY AND EQUAL EMPLOYMENT OPPORTUNITY

Priority _____

Developing and implementing workforce programs to maximize employment of productive people with different characteristics, qualifications, and talents while recognizing the legal requirements and social responsibilities of equal treatment for all employees and the actions necessary to ensure those requirements are met.

Improvement Objective

_____

_____

_____

Areas of Needed Improvement   Requirements

1. _____   _____

                                        _____

2. _____   _____

                                        _____

3. _____   _____

                                        _____

Actions   Assigned to   Due Date

_____   _____   _____

_____

_____   _____   _____

_____

_____   _____   _____

_____

367

SAFETY AND ENVIRONMENT

Priority _____

The training, communication, and leadership required to provide a safe working environment; to provide an appropriate level of employee involvement and responsibility for implementing safe practices, using safety equipment, and complying with Organization safety rules and practices; and to ensure that federal, state, and local safety and environmental requirements are met.

Improvement Objective

_____

_____

_____

Areas of Needed Improvement   Requirements

1. _____   _____

                                       _____

2. _____   _____

                                       _____

3. _____   _____

                                       _____

Actions   Assigned to   Due Date

_____   _____   _____

_____

_____   _____   _____

_____

_____   _____   _____

_____

SECURITY

Priority _____

Maintaining and protecting the Organization's employees, assets, and human resources documents, information, and facilities.

Improvement Objective

_____

_____

_____

Areas of Needed Improvement

Requirements

1. _____

_____

2. _____

_____

3. _____

_____

Actions

Assigned to

Due Date

_____

_____

_____   _____   _____

_____

_____   _____   _____

_____

EQUIPMENT AND FACILITIES

Priority _____

Providing the necessary equipment and facilities to fulfill the human resources mission and provide optimum service to the Organization.

Improvement Objective

_____

_____

_____

Areas of Needed Improvement	Requirements
1. _____	_____
	_____
2. _____	_____
	_____
3. _____	_____
	_____

Actions	Assigned to	Due Date
_____	_____	_____
_____		
_____	_____	_____
_____	_____	_____
_____		

DOCUMENTATION AND INFORMATION SYSTEMS

Priority _____

Preparing, storing, and maintaining employee records and information, including computerized human resources information systems, and meeting federal, state, and local requirements.

Improvement Objective

_____

_____

_____

Areas of Needed Improvement	Requirements
1. _____	_____
	_____
2. _____	_____
	_____
3. _____	_____
	_____

Actions	Assigned to	Due Date
_____		
_____		
_____	_____	_____
_____		
_____	_____	_____
_____		

Summary and Conclusion

Management is continually asking, "How are we doing?" Unfortunately, this is not always an easy question to answer.

Managers are active people, generally with dual accountabilities, first to the Organization as a whole and second to their assigned functions. Often the decisions they are required to make for each seem in conflict with the other. Increasing changes in society demand problem solving but simultaneously provide tremendous opportunities.

It is relatively difficult for a manager to step back and evaluate the results while continuing the management process. It is also difficult to obtain some type of measuring device to determine how well the function is performing. It becomes an activity most often performed for the manager by an external consultant.

This audit was developed to provide managers a tool for discovering objectively "how we are doing in human resources." It utilizes the manager's knowledge of the function and provides a format to express and evaluate that knowledge.

The audit's primary device is the question asked of the person who knows the answer—the manager who should be the most knowledgeable of the function. A method was provided to evaluate that information. In this audit an Advisory Board of experienced human resources professionals from a wide variety of Organizations provides perspective for those answers.

The audit provides a way to analyze the manager's evaluation in terms of the Organization's requirements, and finally to develop action plans for the specific situation.

You now know how you are doing and you have a plan to benefit from your department's strengths and address areas that need improvement. Probably the next step is to review your department's performance a year or so from now, using this same instrument, and again ask the question, "How are we doing?"

Index

About the Author

John H. McConnell is president of McConnell-Simmons and Company, Inc., a management consulting firm located in Morristown, New Jersey. The firm specializes in human resources products and services. Prior to establishing his current company in 1974, McConnell held a number of human resources executive positions with Capital Holding; M and M/Mars; Garan, Inc.; and Wolverine Tube Division of Calumet and Hecla. He has undergraduate and graduate degrees from Wayne State University in Detroit, Michigan. He has written more than two dozen books on management and human resources, many published by AMACOM, and has been a frequent speaker at AMA seminars, the AMA Management Course, and national and international human resources conventions.

Breinigsville, PA USA
16 February 2011
255675BV00001B/40/A